01 14

BEFORE
THEY
WERE
MEN

Essays on Manhood, Compassion, and
What Went Wrong

BEFORE THEY WERE MEN

Jacob Tobia

HARMONY
NEW YORK

Harmony Books
An imprint of Random House
A division of Penguin Random House LLC
1745 Broadway, New York, NY 10019
harmonybooks.com | randomhousebooks.com
penguinrandomhouse.com

Library of Congress Cataloging-in-Publication Data
Names: Tobia, Jacob, author
Title: Before they were men / by Jacob Tobia.
Description: First edition. | New York, NY: Harmony, [2025] | Includes bibliographical references.
Identifiers: LCCN 2025008047 (print) | LCCN 2025008048 (ebook) |
ISBN 9780593797945 hardcover | ISBN 9780593797952 ebook
Subjects: LCSH: Men—Social conditions | Patriarchy | Masculinity | Sex role | Misogyny
Classification: LCC HQ1090 .T6155 2025 (print) | LCC HQ1090 (ebook) |
DDC 305.31—dc23/eng/20250429
LC record available at https://lccn.loc.gov/2025008047
LC ebook record available at https://lccn.loc.gov/2025008048

Printed in the United States of America on acid-free paper

1st Printing

FIRST EDITION

BOOK TEAM: Production editor: Robert Siek • Managing editor: Allison Fox • Production manager: Sarah Feightner • Copy editor: Bonnie Thompson • Proofreaders: Alisa Garrison, Cameron Schoettle, and Christopher Ross

The authorized representative in the EU for product safety and compliance is Penguin Random House Ireland, Morrison Chambers, 32 Nassau Street, Dublin D02 YH68, Ireland. https://eu-contact.penguin.ie

For Josephine

Suppose someone has made you suffer a lot. You may believe that you are the only one who suffers and that the other person is thoughtless or vindictive and that's why they made you suffer. But if you have the time and patience to look deeply, you will recognize the suffering in the other person. Because that person does not know how to handle their own suffering, they remain the first and biggest victim of their suffering. You are only victim number two.

—*Thich Nhat Hanh*

There's a happy medium, between these poles to which the genders have been pushed, a warm equatorial belt of give and take where we should all meet.

—*Rebecca Solnit*

He who is truly a man keeps walking, dragging his guts behind.

—*Robert Bly*

CONTENTS

PRELUDE

First things first:

If you think that men are *okay,*
that power is the same thing as joy,
that controlling others is a path toward freedom,
that we live in a world that affords men and boys *kindness, love,* or
   empathy,

If you look at the men around you and think,
"These guys are doing well"

Or

If you believe that our approach to masculinity,
is one that is helping men to heal, find peace, or live less violent lives,

Please,
dunk your head in some cold water,
Eat a ghost pepper whole.
Something. Anything.
To shock your system,
To wake back up.

Then, for the sake of us all, keep reading.

Second things second:

I am not asking you to do this all in one go.
In fact, I'd recommend against it.

Take it as slowly as you can.
Read an essay, put it on your nightstand, wait a week.
Read an essay, decide it's all too much, too soon, place it lovingly back
  on the shelf.
Pick it up a year later if you need to.
This work is urgent,
but cannot be *urgently done.*

Lift with your knees, not your back.
It is heavy,
gargantuan.
Try not to carry it alone.

Take breaks.
Take a walk.
Rest.
And when you're ready, resume.

Third things third:

As we embark on this work together,
it is natural to shut down.
Empathy,
either for *yourself* as a man,
or for the men you've known,
is astonishingly difficult.

In this text, we are encountering the brutality of all human history.
War. Famine. Murder. Rape. Abuse. Death. Torture.
In addressing the lives of men,
we address the heart of human suffering itself.
Pulsating, raw,
blood pushing the ache around.

And so, before we leave port,
I am giving you a prayer.
A psalm.
An incantation.

If, in reading this, you find yourself out at sea.
Reeling in the roiling swell.
Drowning in sorrow and bloodlust and anguish.
Furious that, as a man, you must consider yourself differently.
Or furious that, as someone who has known men, you must consider
    them differently.
I want you to put down this book,
and repeat to yourself, as many times as you need:

Before they were men, they were children.

Before they were men, they were children.
Before they were men, they were children.

Men are made, not born.

Before I was a man, I was a child.

Before I was a man, I was a child.
Before I was a man, I was a child.

I was not born a man.
I was made one.

INTRODUCTION
TO THE BOYS IN THE BACK

They just sat there. Staring down at their desks, eyes blank, they barely seemed to move. It would've been easier if they'd lashed out, if they'd tried to spar with me, if they'd made some attempt to derail the class, but no.

Roll your eyes, I thought to myself. *Smack your lips in contempt. Suck your teeth. Laugh cruelly under your breath. Whisper something awful or pass a nasty little note. Ask an aggressive, insulting question, maybe. Something. Anything. I dare you.*

Nothing.

For almost an hour, they sat there—detached, deflecting, disengaged—and as they sat, I crumbled. They broke me, those two boys. Split me in half. Their silence and disconnection, the stoicism, the quietude in the face of trauma, the apparent lack of any feeling at all. It ripped me up, not because of my pain, but because of *theirs*. Frankly, they exuded the stuff. It was everywhere.

Bearing witness to it was grisly, but as I stood in front of the class in a cheap, glorious faux-flapper dress and sparkly Chucks, I tried not to show it. I had a job to do.

. . .

It was the fall, and at long last, after two years of virtually no outside speakers allowed on university campuses due to COVID restrictions, I was guest lecturing at Santa Monica College. I cannot emphasize enough just how much I love speaking at schools. Each time I take to the stage or the podium, I get to be the quirky, hot, fashionable professor I was born to be—the edgy gender studies department chair I probably would've become if my life's course had been altered by a millimeter or two. I put on a skimpy dress, a hyperpigmented lip, and a pair of chunky clip-ons and strut to the front of the room with the powerfemme authority of my dreams. And then, for an hour or so, I celebrate and entertain and mourn and cry and giggle about gender alongside young people who are the future of everything we know.

It's a mutual process, the secret being that I get every bit as much out of speaking to students as they get out of listening to me. If I'm being honest, I might get even more out of it than they do. Yes, they're afforded the chance to listen to a hairy nonbinary lady wax poetic about queerness and the state of the trans movement, but I receive something much greater in return: an abiding faith in the future of this world. As I share an hour with them, I learn what young people are thinking, hear what they're talking about, and leave knowing that this particular culture war is already being won. That, at least in terms of gender and sexuality, this world is headed somewhere amazing. The fact that I am often paid to do so is beyond me. Truth be told, I'd give keynotes for free, out of sheer bliss, if for no other reason than to give the sequins in my closet and the sequins in my heart more opportunities to shimmer for others.

This day was no different. I'd already given my keynote lecture in an auditorium across campus, and following a swig of coffee and a quick strut across the quad, I was now leading an undergrad queer studies class in a forty-five-minute workshop entitled Gender and Memoir.

I began the class as I always do, by reading excerpts from one of my books. Story time.

Being read to is highly underrated. You'd assume it'd be boring, but people love it. They feel like kindergartners again, and I transform into their trans Ms. Frizzle–esque kindergarten librarian, complete with a nineties geometric-print dress. When it comes to gender, a system of power and identity that's been instilled in most of us from before we were even born, I find that being read *to* gives rise to exactly the type of child mind required to see things with fresh eyes. It's my belief that if you learned something when you were three years old, you should return to your three-year-old mind in order to unlearn it.

For that day's readings, I focused on moments of gender challenge and gender joy. Instead of standing behind the podium like a respectable transvestite, I popped up onto a table at the front of the classroom and read from there.

I started by sharing a story about the time my brother and his friends found my Barbie, cut off all her hair, and hung her in effigy from the banister in my childhood home. It's not a light note to begin on; it's a heavy story that lands at a pivotal symbolic moment. Because, of course, my brother and his friends weren't really hanging *my Barbie in effigy;* they were hanging *my femininity.* They weren't symbolically killing *her;* they were symbolically killing *a part of me.* Understandably, most people in the room were quiet.

But then I moved along to a story all about the ways that, in contradiction to everything you might think, church was one of the only places I found gender safety as a child. At church, I was allowed to be a glorious little queen because my enthusiasm for performance and crafts and fagging out was always misconstrued as enthusiasm for my personal lord and savior, Jesus Christ. Singing in church, performing in musicals, excelling at art, and wearing flowy acolyte robes that were basically dresses didn't make me gay, darling: they made me a good lil' Christian boy.

That reading did the trick. By the time I got to the sentence "Yes, I may have been queening out in the church musical, but I was queening out *for Jesus,* so it was fine," the mood in the room had become one of jovial, blasphemous, sacred laughter.

It was then that I first noticed them, the boys in the back. They hadn't laughed once, let alone smiled. For the most part, they hadn't even been able to look at me. Eyes glued to the floor, they simply sat. I made a quick mental note of that, concerned by their emotional shutdown, but

I had to keep moving. It didn't feel appropriate to stop the whole lecture and say, "Hey, you two dudes who're clearly not listening and have decided not to participate, are you okay and can we get you a therapist?" in front of everyone.

I proceeded to give the class their first assignment: take five minutes to yourself and reflect on moments of gender challenge and joy from your own life, ones that you think would make for compelling memoiristic essays. "Try to think outside the box," I told them. "Find stories that transcend the normative ways we're taught to talk about gender. Stories that are unexpected or surprising, that take a small detail and spin it into a web of meaning. Don't hold yourself back or be afraid to really go there."

(It's an activity that you, dear reader, might want to consider doing yourself.)

I set a five-minute timer on my phone, and we were off: they dutifully journaled to themselves as I dutifully scrolled through memes on my phone. Two minutes and three pictures of silly cats in, I looked up. Most students were sitting quietly, scribbling down notes, lost in reflection.

But not the boys in the back. One was on his phone. The other was picking at his notebook. *That's okay,* I thought. *It doesn't mean they aren't engaged.* Thinking looks different for different people. Some people chew their nails or a pencil. Others tap their feet or doodle until inspiration strikes. I pull the hairs out of my eyebrows and gaze aimlessly around the room.

After five minutes were through, I told everyone to form small groups and share the memories that had come to mind. I set another timer, this one for seven minutes, and sat back, basking in the cacophony of voices that sprang forth the moment I said, "Go." Nothing makes for a happier teacher than a loud room of enthusiastic students. I scrolled through a few more memes on my phone, sent a quick email or two, then got up to check in with the professor and confirm that we were still on schedule.

I surveyed the classroom again. It was buzzing. You could track the

flow of individual conversations as each group oscillated between compassionate listening and raucous giggles. I drank it all in: a room full of
thirty young people thinking critically about their experience with gender, sharing with one another in the discoveries they were making,
dusting off memories until they sparkled again, and getting academic
credit for it? Pinch me. It was one of those apex moments in life when
you're able to see in real time the impact you're having, where you can
witness, firsthand, the effect of your life's work.

Then I glanced over at the boys in the back, and it all came crashing
down. As the rest of the room hummed with energy, they slouched in
their chairs, doing absolutely nothing. Although they were sitting directly next to each other, not a single word passed between them.

The contrast was unsettling: like looking at a photograph of a group
of smiling children only to realize, upon closer inspection, that one kid
in the back is just standing there, staring off. It'd be less alarming if the
kid were crying or seemed angry, because at least then there's a story: he
was having a bad day, he didn't want to be in the picture, he didn't feel
like smiling and let everyone know. He cried out or screamed or scowled
and made his displeasure known.

It's far more haunting when a child looks shut down. When they
aren't smiling in the photo but aren't frowning or crying, either. When
they're just standing there, compliant, dissociating, clearly displeased
with what's happening but feeling too scared to make their displeasure
known. The worst kind of pain is not pain that's expressed; it's pain
that's silenced. The scariest phase of abuse is when you stop crying out
upon being hurt. When you're so lost and crushed, have been so singularly dismissed and gaslit and fucked over that you no longer see a reason to express your sadness. When you're so damaged, you no longer
scream as you're cut. When you cease to feel at all.

Perhaps I was reading too much into it, but as I looked at those boys
in the back, my heart dropped. I stared. They were so detached that
they didn't notice my gaze. They didn't seem to be taking in anything
that was happening around them.

The timer on my phone went off, signaling that both the activity and the class were over. I sat back down on the table in the front and could manage only a few concluding words before students began pouring in for the next class. I said goodbye to the professor, hung back to chat with a few students outside, then hustled off to my car so I could get on the road before Los Angeles rush hour picked up.

I thought about saying something to those boys, about seeing if they were all right, but I couldn't muster the courage.

By the time I might've, they were long gone, melting back into the world, like so many other lost men.

• • •

In the weeks that followed, I couldn't stop thinking about them. I thought about them on the drive home. I thought about them that night as I fell asleep. I thought about them the next morning on my daily walk. I thought about them a week later on a hike. I thought about them a month later on a retreat at a Buddhist monastery. They became paired gashes, coupled glaring wounds, dual phantoms hanging their pallid shrouds over the memory of what had otherwise been a beautiful day in my life. I couldn't get them out of my mind.

I kept asking myself, on repeat: Why were they so shut down? Out of that entire room filled with trans folks and nonbinary kiddos and queer ladies and gay boys—all replete with gender trauma of their own—why were those boys the only two people who couldn't bring themselves to participate? Why did hearing a story about my brother brutalizing my Barbie short-circuit their minds? What traumas were they hiding? What wounds were they concealing? Could they see their own hurt? Could they acknowledge it? Were they just *bored*?

Teaching those two boys—those two young men—whatever you're supposed to call two struggling twenty-year-old guys—hurt. But not because they hurt me. They hadn't called me a faggot or asked aggressive questions or tried to take me down or embarrass me in front of the class. I almost wish they had. Between you and me, that would've been easier. I can handle a sassy, aggro male student. I'm good at dealing with those types of situations, because if you're sparring with me, at least it means you're listening. You're engaged. You heard what I said and had a real, human reaction. If you attack me while I'm in the middle of giving a lecture, I am perfectly capable of using the force of your blow to take you down instead. Punch me, and I know how to make meaning of it for the whole class. Scar me, and I'll turn it into a beautiful tattoo. Pierce me, and, babe, I'll just throw an earring in that hole.

Being ignored was worse.

In hindsight, it occurs to me that I cannot know for sure what was going through either of their heads in that moment.

They may have been ignoring me deliberately, performatively, hoping that I'd notice. In the context of a college class, ignoring me and disregarding the assignment could've been a form of protest, their way of fighting back against someone they'd grossly, albeit understandably, misinterpreted and perceived to be against them. Having spent their entire lives marinated in a popular queer/feminist discourse that has vilified them and treated them without compassion, they may have gotten defensive. They'd found a way to fight back against some neoliberal, "woke," nonbinary asshat telling them that identifying as a man made them abominable, without doing anything explicit enough to get them in trouble. Here I was, yet another feminist lecturer on campus declaring that men are inherently bad. They were going to stick it to me by turning up their noses.

Or they might've just been bored. Perhaps they didn't think that what I was sharing mattered for their lives. They couldn't see the application of it, couldn't understand how it had anything to do with them, and chose to stare off into space instead. They may have also been hungover. It's a college campus, after all.

But my *suspicion* is that they were shutting down. That when faced with the topic of gender trauma, so much came up they couldn't figure out where to begin.

I can't decide which response is the saddest:

- hearing about someone's gender trauma and shunning them,

- hearing about someone's gender trauma and shutting down, or

- hearing about someone's gender trauma and yawning.

Underneath each of those responses, the pain is visceral. None of those are how a healthy, whole person should react. Whatever the cause, witnessing it gave rise to the type of secondhand bystander injury for which I have few remedies. The raw, burning feeling of watching another human being falling apart and not being able to do anything about it. Of watching another soul broken, the Tower of Babel toppling, stone by stone, in front of your very eyes.

It haunts you.

I tried to let myself forget and give myself permission to move on. I wanted to let go of the itching, corrosive feeling that rose up from my stomach and into my chest each time I remembered those two boys.

I couldn't. Above all, what I felt was guilt. Though it goes counter to everything I've been told by the internet and social justice practice, though it grates my very nonbinary soul to acknowledge it, I don't feel I can afford to live in a world where I deny the truth any longer: those boys in the back needed me more than any other people in that classroom.

Men need me more than anyone else in the world right now.

And I need them, too.

We need each other.

Stay with me.

I have spent my entire life being told that, as a nonbinary person who was assigned male at birth and raised as a man, my voice is critical for the nonbinary and trans community. That the people who have the most to learn from me are young queer and trans kids who are in the process of figuring out who they are and need a role model.

And while, yes, serving other queer and trans folks in that way is an honor, I'm starting to realize that the people in my community aren't the ones who need me the most. Though we're struggling against political attacks—right-wing nutjobs trying to regulate our bodies and lives, "concerned" parents working to ban our books, transphobic legislators and judges attempting to write us out of existence—we're doing better than any other community of people on earth in one crucial, underdiscussed dimension: we have acknowledged, on a life-shattering level, the trauma that gender has wrought in our hearts. We are doing—

and have done—the work to heal from the gender-based trauma that has shaped our stories. We know that we have a problem, that gender has hurt us, and we are committed to spending the rest of our lives inventorying, healing, and transforming that pain into something constructive.

Yes, trans people and nonbinary people struggle. Structural discrimination and anti-trans legislation alike hurt us and make our lives more difficult. But spiritually speaking, we are leaps and bounds ahead of the rest. We see the truth of gender. We understand the power that gender self-determination brings us. We support one another as we grow into ourselves.

The queer and trans students in that classroom will face challenges in their lives, but current political reality notwithstanding, I believe they will be fine. They are strong beyond measure and have glorious community, rich cultural history, and map upon map to guide them toward healing. They were able to hear my stories about gender trauma and face them with courage, to hold them alongside me. They were able to acknowledge the parts of themselves they saw in me, to take the coordinates of my pain and gingerly trace them onto their own experience. They were able to turn the class into a site of healing, growth, and joy. It was beautiful to witness.

In a similar way, I have been told that gender nonconforming people like me have a lot to teach women. And yes, of course, on both sides that's true. As women and feminine-of-center people, we have much to teach one another. Together, we are expanding our understanding of what womanhood and femininity mean. We are building strategies for surviving, organizing, and ultimately transforming a patriarchal world. We are healing one another, healing ourselves, and learning to celebrate that womanhood and power, femininity and strength, are not mutually exclusive. We share solidarity and feminist visions alongside film recommendations and guidance on where to get the best lipstick.

In that frame, I have been told that nonbinary people are vital. With the exception of a few naysayers, women have embraced people like me and welcomed us into women's spaces and communities. Consequently,

I am in a sisterhood with so many astounding women. I wear that mantle with pride.

But I believe the women and femmes in that classroom will also be fine. Yes, the present right-wing backslide is mortifying and threatens the very foundations of feminist progress. And, of course, there is still a pay gap to navigate, discrimination to address, healthcare inadequacy (reproductive and otherwise) to fix, and a legacy of sexual violence and assault to contend with. There are deep wounds to heal from the struggle we wage against patriarchal domination. That struggle is far from over. But the women and femmes in that class have the requisite skills to continue (and win) the fight. They have a powerful, centuries-long tradition of resistance, empowerment, and community to rely upon. They, too, have acknowledged the pain that gender has ushered into their lives, the trauma that comes from embodying who they are.

Call me delusional, but I have confidence that, spiritually and existentially speaking, those young women are going to be okay. While there is still a long road ahead, I have every faith that they are powerful, self-actualized, and have the tools necessary to become whole again, if they aren't already. They were able to hear my stories about being tormented as a gender nonconforming child with compassionate ears, with kindness, and with an understanding that being brutalized by the men and boys in our lives has bonded us forever. They were able to hear what I shared, hold it in their hearts, participate actively, and leave class feeling, I hope, more at peace with who they are.

Not so with the boys in the back.

It is precisely because men do not acknowledge how much they need nonbinary and trans people that I know they need us the most. The alcoholic in greatest need is the one who vehemently dismisses the idea of attending a meeting. The trauma survivor who claims that PTSD is ridiculous and everyone needs to get over it is the one who's most in need of treatment. The person who contemptuously talks about how absurd they find anger management is the one who should sign up, like, tomorrow. Those in the greatest need of help, compassion, and love are mostly those who profess to need it least.

The truth that, of late, has been clawing at my ventricles, punching at my chambers, and burning along my aortic valve is this: the boys in the back of the class needed me more than anyone else in that room.

They probably *still* need someone like me. And the longer I sit with it, the more patently obvious it becomes: men and boys are now the ones suffering the most under the gender binary.

Yes, truly.

They are the least free among all of us, the least empowered, the least spiritually at peace, and have the fewest tools with which to cope. They're the ones who are incapable of hearing a story about gender trauma without fighting back, hurting others, or shutting down. They're the ones who are mostly incapable of digesting and processing the ways their gender has hurt them. They're the ones who consider themselves beyond or above help. And in today's environment, they're the ones whose gender-based suffering is most often belittled and erased.

I believe that men and boys need us right now. They need our help untangling and making sense of it all, because most of them still haven't learned how.

And it's precisely because I *lived as one of them* that I can do so effectively.

It's hard for me to talk about myself in this manner. I have spent the better part of twenty years trying to find my way out of being understood as a man, to escape the expectations of masculinity that were placed upon me as a child. I've worked hard to establish myself as someone who no longer identifies that way. It took every ounce of strength I had to find my way out.

So I have a great deal of fear talking about the fact that I was (nonconsensually) raised as a boy. I approach any conversations about my masculine past with trepidation, because I am afraid that by simply mentioning those times in my life, I will be drawn right back in. That if I admit I once was a boy, if I confess that I once briefly navigated life as a (failure of a) man, they will find me and force me to go back. That by acknowledging the past, my whole nonbinary identity will somehow be revoked. I'm afraid people will point at me vindictively and declare, "See! Jacob isn't who they say they are! *He's* really been *a man* all along!"

But for the good of the billions of men and boys around the world who are still suffering under the yoke of manhood, it's a risk I feel I must now take. I need to talk about my masculine past. About what it felt like to have manhood forced so aggressively down my throat that I had no choice but to let it in.

My history with manhood and masculinity feels less like an intellectual journey of self-discovery and more like a desperate flight from mandatory conscription. These days, I don't see myself as "neither a man nor a woman" so much as I see myself as a *gender defector.*

Manhood is an army. Its scale is global and imperial, colonizing communities everywhere it can, extracting their resources to fortify itself, committing unspeakable atrocities along its path, and threatening any people that resist with death, violence, poverty, and despair.

It's an army that you're predestined for. If you are born male, you're in, whether you like it or not. You are conscripted from birth. You're conscripted in utero, the moment a doctor divulges your sex to your parents. And from the earliest age, you begin your training. A child soldier by birthright, you are taught how to enact violence, how to endure violence, and how to hold violence in your mind. You are given a uniform, assigned strict standards of grooming, and told how to behave. You are instructed to prove your worth by developing your body's physical prowess, strength, and capacity to inflict pain. And when the moment's right, you are initiated into manhood, told that you are now an active-duty member whose job it is to do violence and follow orders blindly and hoard power and control the world under the harshest fist you can muster.

You're deployed. You're sent to war.

And you're told that this is both mandatory and inevitable. There is little room for dissent. There is no escape from your destiny. If you try to run off, you'll no longer be viewed as a human being. You will be neglected, punished, beaten, raped, and murdered, too. If you try to resist the army or change its structures, you will face its wrath more singularly than anyone.

Not everyone has an active-duty role. Many men manage to avoid the worst of it for their entire lives. They stay quietly in the reserves, take desk jobs, serve as metaphorical cooks or medics, or play in the allegorical military band. It is possible to survive the Army of Men without doing terrible violence *yourself.* And that can make it spiritually easier. But the truth is that—no matter your role, no matter how much you attempt to compartmentalize or deny it—as long as you're cooperating and obediently following orders, a large part of what you do is ultimately somehow in service of violence and domination.

If you want to understand the brutality of an army, you can't just ask those who are enlisted or in the reserves. They're still serving. If you want to understand the horrors of war, how it dehumanizes you and rips you up and fucks you over and destroys your soul, you can't just talk to veterans, either. At least, not those who are categorically proud of their service. Because they're often still clinging to their identity as soldiers, still trying to justify what they did, to reclaim the violence as somehow necessary or productive or virtuous rather than useless and cruel and horrid, to make meaning of the fact that they lost a leg or murdered civilians, to give their mutilated bodies and minds a sense of purpose.

If you want the whole truth, you have to talk to defectors. They're the only ones who can tell you what it's really like, because they occupy the unique position of having disowned and escaped the institution altogether. Us defectors are not proud of our service. We are not proud of what we did on the front lines. We aren't beholden to the mental gymnastics required to try to justify it. We can simply acknowledge the violence we perpetrated for what it was: violence. We can acknowledge the abuse we suffered for what it was: abuse. We can be honest with you about what it was like to involuntarily serve in the Army of Men.

Other than caring for my father as he died, defecting from masculinity is the single greatest accomplishment of my life.

As a child, I, too, was conscripted. By the tender age of four, I was already attempting to set my draft card alight. But they put a stop to that, punished me, and forced me to enlist anyway. For a while, I did my best to just be a terrible recruit. I skipped training, barely learned how to use my weapons, and didn't cultivate my body to be powerful or violent in any of the ways my regiment found useful.

Then, after a decade of methodical planning, when the time was just right, I made my escape. I ripped up my uniform, buried my dog tags, and fled. I ran until my legs were weak and my feet were bloody. I ran until the borders blurred and I wasn't even sure where I was anymore. I ran until I felt certain that they could no longer catch me, and only then, when I was finally safe in the company of women, did I rest.

I know that, to some, this metaphor may read as drastic or melodramatic. Not every person raised as a man experiences masculinity or manhood in terms so stark.

But I did. For me, this metaphor rings true.

I will never forget the cruelty of masculine conscription. I will never forget the brutality of being made into a man. I can't, because my body and psyche alike are riddled with the scars. They glare back at me each time I look at my reflection.

That's precisely why I need to speak up. Because in spite of the propaganda and the lies we are told, men are not okay. Men are not powerful or privileged in any uncomplicated sense. Men are suffering ruthlessly under the weight of the violence they have been forced to enact. They have been conscripted into a system of brutality and spiritual abuse that no person should ever be forced to endure. And most of them still feel trapped within that system, unable to safely escape, find their way out, or even speak of it.

In response to that system of patriarchal domination, feminist, queer, and trans movements have united around men as our common enemy. We have labeled men inherently violent, cruel, and despotic, because they often are. But also because it was easiest to oversimplify them as such; a palimpsestic shorthand, sloppily scrawled over the punishing realities we are too afraid to face en masse. In the pivotal words of bell hooks:

> The radical feminist labeling of all men as oppressors and all
> women as victims was a way to deflect attention away from the

reality of men and our ignorance about them. To simply label them as oppressors and dismiss them meant we never had to give voice to the gaps in our understanding or to talk about maleness in complex ways. We did not have to talk about the ways our fear of men distorted our perspectives and blocked our understanding. Hating men was just another way to not take men and masculinity seriously. It was simply easier for feminist women to talk about challenging and changing patriarchy than it was for us to talk about men—what we knew and did not know, about the ways we wanted men to change. Better to just express our desire to have men disappear, to see them dead and gone.

Each time we bemoan violent men, I fear we are not only avoiding the real conversation we need to be having, but also creating a self-fulfilling prophecy: treating cruelty not only as a *desirable* state of being, but as somehow inevitable or inherent to *who men are*. If someone is abused to the point that they become a monster, insisting that they are a monster and continually vilifying them as such accomplishes little. They have already become hydra-headed. The more heads you attempt to cut off, the more heads they will grow.

Yes, acknowledging the violence of men is imperative. Men *have* committed atrocities. Men *have* done unspeakable things. Men *have* hurt us.

But this acknowledgment is of limited use if we cannot *also* acknowledge that this violence has hurt *the men who've enacted it*. Men have created violence at their own expense. As difficult as it may be to face, the reality is that no man truly benefits from this system of patriarchal domination, either. All violence is senseless. The moment you murder someone else in order to eat, you've both lost. There is no winner. *Ça n'existe pas.*

In these pages, I'm wondering aloud. I'm imperfectly speculating. I may not have all of the answers, but, damnit, I've gotten the questions right:

What would change if we no longer envied the position of men and began *pitying* it?

What if we stopped naming men as beneficiaries of patriarchy and began boldly declaring them as *co-survivors* of it?

What if we stopped asking how we can *get back* at men and began asking, *What do men need right now?*

· · ·

Consider this book a challenge. I am demanding that we look at the problem from a different angle, commanding a new approach, imploring us all to dig deep, past our own trauma and pain, in order to find compassion.

When we watch others suffering, we're forced to make a choice: we can either cultivate empathy—that sacred part of ourselves that allows us to connect to others, to feel their pain as our pain, to experience their joy as our joy, to remain a part of humanity—or we can decide that empathy bears too high a cost and cut it at the root. We can determine that the flowers aren't worth the thorns they require and kill the whole plant. We can shut ourselves off from the suffering of others because we've determined that their suffering is too great to hold.

When we cut ourselves off from the suffering of others, we almost never acknowledge what we're doing. Which, in fact, makes the act of doing so all the more dangerous. Our entire economic system and way of life teaches us to rarely think of the suffering of others.

Take your morning coffee, for instance. When's the last time you took a moment to think about where it came from? When's the last time you tasted those bitter grounds and considered their bitter source? Have you ever sipped your morning cup and realized that brewed into it, laced into every molecule of that charred bean, is the suffering of people who were exploited, underpaid, and worked to the bone to procure it?

We live in a world where people work with all their capitalist might to erase the misery they create. We are raised in a world that, from our very birth, instructs us to glide past the suffering of others. Denial may be our greatest skill, but it comes at an excruciating spiritual cost.

As a feminist movement, are we willing to continue paying that? Are we willing to ignore the misery and brokenness of men? Are we willing to gloss over it, wholesale? To continue averting our eyes and denying the truth—that the ones who are inflicting the greatest pain may just be the ones who need our help the most? Are we able to move from asking how we might punish men to asking how we might help them *escape*? Can we, as feminist writer adrienne maree brown puts it, "intentionally decide to stay in relationship with humanity, to not count anyone out based on identity?"

The reality is this: men will either process their trauma as a vital, valued, and respected part of the feminist movement or they will process their trauma with insidious people like Andrew Tate. The choice is ours to make.

• • •

To the boys in the back of the class, this book is first and foremost for you. Because when I spoke of my brother and his friends hanging my Barbie in effigy, I fear what you heard was "Look how bad men and boys are. Look how inevitable your cruelty is. Watch as I now take delight in shaming you."

That could not be further from my meaning. What I meant was "Look at how much my brother was broken by masculinity and the expectations of manhood. Look at how trapped he was by the cycle of masculine abuse. Look at how abominably he took that abuse out on me in order to keep himself safe. Look at how he had to sell out his own sibling in order to prevent the bullying from turning his way. Look at how desperately in need of help and kindness and radical love he was, too. And look at how the boys and men around him reinforced not his need for healing, but his cruelty. Look how they, too, have been brutalized. Look how they, too, have been abused."

What I really meant was that I care for you more deeply than I know how to say. I know you to be gentle and kind and filled with joy, because above what it means to be a man, this is what it means to be human. I, too, had gentleness and joy stomped out of me by the crushing weight of masculine expectation. I was brutalized alongside you. I also found myself in an impossible labyrinth of pressure and fire and violence whereby I had to choose between my dignity as a person and my survival in this world.

I know, in part, what you have been through. But I want to know more. I want you to share your moments of gender joy with me. I want you to share your moments of gender challenge with us all. And as you do so, I will do my damnedest to ensure that we listen with the compassion and love that you deserve.

What I really meant was that men like you are not *toxic* or *fragile;* you are merely breakable.

And in many cases, you are already broken. Everywhere we look across culture, we find broken men. In most positions of power, we find broken men. Almost every president, tyrant, and CEO is spiritually in pieces on the floor. And their insistence to the contrary, their insistence that they are big, powerful, and strong, only places their fractures in starker relief.

You are breakable as I am breakable. You have been broken as I have been broken. Instead of being enemies, what would it mean for me to pick up a broom alongside you? To help you lovingly sweep the pieces of your shattered hearts into a pile, delicately pick through them one by one, and piece them back together, *kintsugi*-like, with gold?

That's the purpose of this book: to take a fresh look at masculinity and manhood, to examine the plentiful shards of the broken men around us and figure out what we might be able to do as a culture, a society, and a world to heal and put them all back together. With profound love, radical compassion, and a bit of grout, we can use those pieces to cover the world in shimmering mosaic.

Men, this book is also a promise. You are not beyond redemption. You are deserving of kindness and compassion. There is nothing inevitable or predestined about the cruelty and violence you've endured. You didn't need the abuse to become who you are.

But more than a promise, it's an invitation: the rest of us have worked hard to identify and bandage the wounds that gender inflicted upon our hearts.

Are you finally ready to join us?

BEFORE
THEY
WERE
MEN

Men are
four times
more likely to
die by suicide
than women.

CATCALLS

New York City was contrary to everything I'd been told.

As a queer person, you're supposed to move to New York and finally feel *free*. It's sold as an epicenter—arguably *the* epicenter—of liberation for queer and trans folks.

But there's a reason Stonewall happened in New York. There's a reason why New York City was one of the first places where the trannies and faggots and dykes and whores finally said "ENOUGH" and began punching back.

It's because New York City is the single cruelest place I've ever lived. Because, when you're weird and different and have to rely on public transportation because you *don't* happen to be a multimillionaire with car service, daily life can feel something like a war zone. Or, perhaps, a post-conflict region.

Navigating New York City as a gender nonconforming person isn't necessarily a battlefield. It's not organized warfare, with clearly delineated fronts, places where fighting occurs contrasted against places that are safe. There are no stable boundaries of armistice or conflict. Trans women and gender nonconforming people have been murdered in the West Village and Harlem and Bed-Stuy and the Financial District alike.

It's a region that, after war, was left littered with land mines. The anger and brutality are buried, thinly veiled by a shallow layer of dirt, a lush field waiting to explode at any moment. As a trans person, you are just as likely to be accosted leaving your apartment as you are leaving a queer club as you are leaving a museum as you are leaving a deli as you are leaving your job. Everywhere is dangerous. Nowhere is safe. There isn't a single place outdoors where you can truly let your guard down. Violence, slander, and cruelty are every bit as likely to explode at three P.M., in broad daylight, as they are at three A.M., deep underground, in the subterranean bowels of the city.

The moment you set foot outside your apartment, you simply pray that you won't step on it. That it won't be *your* foot that trips the wire. That your weight won't trigger the switch.

That you won't be blown to bits.

• • •

If there's one thing I must give New York City credit for, it's that she was up front about it.

It was a perfect, crisp, early-fall day. I'd just graduated college a few months earlier, moved to New York City with nothing lined up, and, by the grace of God, landed a big-girl job doing diversity consulting for capitalists, telling the likes of Bank of America and Goldman Sachs how to ensure they're being trans inclusive as they foreclose on your house and plunder the earth.

It was far from a dream job. But it was a spark, an economic lifeline, a foothold in one of the most antagonistic metropolises in the world. With this start, maybe I could become somebody after all.

It would be dishonest to say that I was thinking this acerbically at the time. At the time, I was *thrilled*. Overnight, I'd become the most glamorous creature on planet Earth: a young, single lady in the Big Apple. The Archetypical New York Young Professional: Genderqueer Edition. Promise and passion and potential oozing from every pore, I woke up that morning in the confidence that this was my future. That *I* was the future. As I got dressed and did my makeup, I had "Welcome to New York" blaring on repeat. I was the cheesiest flavor of girl imaginable. A country gal who turned pop the moment she discovered a bold red lip. Delusion personified.

I was still trying to figure out what dressing professionally as a gender nonconforming person even looked like. I'd had a little bit of practice interning in Washington, D.C., the previous summer and at the United Nations a year or so before that. But my professional best was still a work in progress.

For my first day of work, I put on a chocolate brown, faux-silk sleeveless top, a maroon, calf-length pencil skirt, a brown leather suitcase, pearls, a corresponding matte maroon lip, and supple, navy-blue leather pumps. I looked impeccable. Main-character energy. *Sex and the City. Emily in Paris.* Jacob in New York.

I gave my eyeliner a final check in the mirror, sashayed down the stairs, and set out into the world. Golden early-autumn rays lapped at my feet as they click-clacked down the sidewalk. An oblivious trans gentrifier, blissfully unaware of the crushing economic realities confronting the New Yorkers whose neighborhood I was sauntering through, I whisked along Franklin Avenue and crossed over Atlantic, headed toward Fulton and the C train. My life was a storybook.

Here's what I can accept: by its very nature, New York City must wreck you. You cannot move to Brooklyn and remain unscathed. You must be broken. The Metropolis commands it. You must be shaken to your very core by *something.* You must grapple and claw in order to earn the privilege of calling yourself a New Yorker.

What I struggle to accept is the immediacy with which it occurred. I would've at least liked to *make it to my first day of work* before being shattered. It would've been nice to get one day of full-time, salaried, adult employment under my twenty-two-year-old belt before being cut to the bone.

New York had different plans for me. More specifically, men did.

I vividly remember the location where it occurred. For someone who can barely remember what they ate for breakfast, this is no small feat. A common trait of PTSD is precise, meticulous memory.

Trauma commands it. It's an evolutionary response. In the Paleolithic era, if you were almost eaten by a lion and narrowly escaped with your life, it was important for you to record the exact place so that you could avoid encountering that lion again. Give your brain enough cortisol, and it starts jotting down geographic coordinates on autopilot.

It was at the northeast corner of Fulton and Franklin in Bed-Stuy. On that corner, there's a grungy Popeyes smooshed up against an equally grungy Dunkin' Donuts smooshed up directly against the entrance to the subway, which is along Franklin about twenty feet north of the crosswalk. Across the street, a pedestrian bridge looms over Fulton. It has a sheet metal roof and tall, windowed sides that look out over the street, leading down to the S train shuttle to Prospect Park. In the mid-morning, sun radiates down Fulton from the east.

As I approached the subway stairs, a man was resurfacing from underground. He looked at me as I approached, considered me for a split second, then hatefully made up his mind.

"Hey, *FUCK* you," he declared, loudly enough for everyone to hear. He didn't even need to say faggot. The faggot was implied.

Then he spit on me.

My brain lit up, neurons firing throughout my body as I braced myself for whatever was coming next. I attempted the Herculean task of continuing to walk while simultaneously preparing myself for the fist or the knife that, statistically speaking, could be coming next. Fire ants in my blood, my body crawled with anxiety.

I descended the stairs, not hesitating, not pausing. With each step downward, I waited for the feeling of brute force against my back, for the wind to be knocked out of me, for the stairs to be suddenly rushing forward as I plummeted.

I was Orpheus and Eurydice both. If I wanted to save the burgeoning feminine spirit inside me, I couldn't look back.

I had to walk forward in absolute faith. If I turned around and made eye contact with the man who'd spit on me, if I so much as acknowledged his existence, he could cast my brittle, fledgling womanhood into the underworld. If I let him *know* that I'd heard him, if I had the audacity to double back and face him, he would take it as a challenge. It would cement the fact that, yes, I was vulnerable. Yes, I was paying attention. Yes, he'd gotten to me.

When swimming with sharks, you can't shed blood.

I left the spit on my skirt. Pausing to remove it was out of the question. I walked all the way down the stairs, through the turnstile, onto the platform, and into the train before I summoned the courage to wipe it off.

•   •   •

From then on, I lived in fear.

At night, as I drifted off to sleep, I'd imagine it. I'd imagine what the knife might feel like as it slid between my ribs. I'd imagine what it would feel like for my skull to crack open as it was bashed against the trash-strewn curb or the metal trimmings of the subway stairs. I'd imagine the cool metal barrel against my temple, the flash, the *pop*, what it would be like to bleed out, late at night, on the frozen sidewalk. I'd imagine what it'd feel like to be thrown into a trunk or be hurled, bound and almost dead, into the Hudson, filthy water rushing into defeated lungs. I imagined it all. I couldn't help it, couldn't seem to stop myself.

It's what they wanted me to do. Each man who catcalled me in the street, each man who labeled me a *faggot* or a *tranny* or a *fucking freak* or a *fucking bitch* or a *disgusting animal* or a *fucked-up motherfucker* loudly enough for anyone within a hundred feet to hear, each man who shoved me or glared at me or spit at me or followed me wanted me to be reminded: I was asking for it. If I continued expressing my femininity and my womanhood on this unruly, masculine body, I would be next.

They wanted me to understand: We can kill you. We can rape you. We can do so with impunity. And it is coming. The desecration of your body is inevitable. If you insist on flying so close to the sun, we will melt down your wings, crash you back to earth, and shatter you onto the pavement. You have it coming, and soon.

They also wanted me to understand that I was alone. They'd loudly proclaim on the subway that I was a degenerate and someone should set me on fire. They'd say it loudly enough for the entire subway car or sidewalk or bus stop or park or CVS to hear: first, because they wanted to be sure that I'd heard them over my headphones (I always pretended I couldn't) and, second, because they wanted to be sure I knew that everyone *else* had heard it, too. They wanted me to hear both the hideous words they said *and* the collective silence that came after. Because trust me: no one ever took those men to task. They'd yell, "FUCK YOU, FAGGOT," as loudly as they could, snarling and hurling trash at me, and the rest of the world would turn away in shame.

Hundreds of people would watch it happen and avert their eyes.

No one ever stepped in. No one boldly intervened or asked, "The fuck did you just say to them?" No Wonder Woman swooped in with lycra and a cape, grabbed them by the collar, shoved them against the wall, and demanded that they apologize. Spider-Man never showed.

No one offered me comfort, either. They never walked over after witnessing my degradation. No one had the courage to break the unspoken fourth wall of New York public observation to ask, "Are you okay?" or to say, "I'm sorry. You didn't deserve that." Everyone was a bystander. No one intervened. Not once.

And don't get me started on the NYPD. As if they'd ever do *anything* to protect me. If given the chance, they were more likely to join in than help.

It became an accepted fact in my mind that unless I renounced my femininity, buried my high heels, and burned my dresses, I was going to have the living shit beaten out of me. I was going to be assaulted. I was going to be raped. I was going to be murdered. And as it was happening, no one was going to stop it. They were going to flee, terrified that the unchecked brutality of men would turn against them next.

Honestly, I look back on this part of my life with astonishment. Why did no one ever gift me pepper spray? Why did no one ever encourage me to buy a knife? Sometimes I wonder if I should've carried a gun.

Daily, I walked out into the world, into the threat of violence and death, with my head held high, like a fool. Convinced that *martyr* was the best I'd ever be.

Eventually, my head began to stoop. With enough pressure and heat, even a diamond will melt.

For my safety, I learned meekness. I learned to hide. I learned to conform on the train and bring what I *really* wanted to wear in a book bag. I commuted exclusively in sneakers, putting on my heels only when I was safely in a lobby. I learned to keep my hands in my pockets in order to conceal the nail polish. I wore long coats to cover up my skirts and dresses. Even in the brutal swamp heat of New York City summers, I often wore long coats. May through September, I would pour sweat and arrive home drenched.

But at least I *arrived home.*

· · ·

After only ten months of living in New York City, I found myself lying in bed, contemplating how I was going to end my own life.

My death wish felt autonomic, closer to a flinch than a choice. Pavlovian, even. If you scare a dog every time they leave the house, the door itself will eventually become a source of fear. It felt like my gender was being trained by an invisible fence. Each time I attempted to step outside the unseen social boundaries of acceptable masculinity, I got a rough shock. The invisible line was always somewhere, lying in wait, binding up my existence in its ever-constricting radius. Eventually, I learned to just stay in the apartment.

The men who catcalled me knew that if they were consistent enough in their harassment, they could eventually succeed in changing my behavior. And they did. Expressing myself stopped being fun. Dresses were no longer tools of self-empowerment; they were sites of struggle. I couldn't put on lipstick with joy or a sense of whimsy. I could only put it on in fear.

There'd be periods when the harassment wasn't so bad, of course. I'd go a month or two without an incident, start to let my guard down and feel better. But then, inevitably, something horrific would happen and it'd start all over again.

Eventually, I decided that it would be better to take matters into my own hands. These men were going to kill me anyway. I was going to die because of who I was and how I dressed. I accepted that my gender itself was lethal, that existing in the world as a nonbinary person meant embracing death.

Murder was only a matter of time, and I didn't want to give them the satisfaction.

I didn't want some horrible man's hateful gaze to be the last thing I ever saw.

So I'd do it myself.

There was comfort in the fantasy. Control, even. *It's so pathetic to be murdered in a hate crime,* I'd tell myself. *Why bleed out on the sidewalk by someone else's hand when you can elegantly throw yourself off a building?* I'd lie in bed for hours, dreaming about it. I did extensive research on the best methods. The studies are out there if you know where to look. Pills are ineffective most of the time. Though razors are what you see most often in movies, the odds that you'll actually bleed out aren't as high as you'd think. Most people who try that way are discovered passed out in the tub and promptly committed to the psych ward. The internet is a terrifying place.

I am not sharing this with you for dramatic effect or to be grim. I do not enjoy talking about how authentically I wanted to die. Trans people wanting to die is a trope I'm exhausted by.

I am sharing this with you as a matter of fact. It was a fact that the violence I encountered from men on the street while living in New York City was so terrifying and psychologically destructive, it made me want to die. It was so pervasive and spiritually brutal, I sought to take matters into my own hands. It's important for you to know this because it colors what comes next. It's important for you to know how dark things got, lest you feel that what comes next is just me being pollyannaish, lest you think that what comes next was easy for me because I didn't really have it that bad.

I had it that bad. After a year of living in New York City, men had taken all of my power. *Men* were in control of my happiness, not me. My life was no longer really my own.

The psychological terror was so intense, I prayed for someone to do it. Stop snarling at me and just *bite*. Stop screaming at me and just shove me onto the tracks. Get it over with. Brutalize my femininity. End this. End *me*. *Just do it*.

Please.

. . .

If I were to survive, I would have to find another way.

The turning point for me was, strangely enough, reality television. In 2015, I was featured on an episode of MTV's documentary series *True Life*, a show I'd grown up watching. At a dark time in my life, it was a gargantuan opportunity. And to my knowledge, it was the first documentary to profile genderqueer or nonbinary people on national television. It felt thrilling to be even a fractional part of trans history. For the show, a crew followed me from New York back to North Carolina, where I was going to spend some time with my family and give the keynote speech for North Carolina Trans Pride.

As part of the project, the crew shot extensive interviews with my parents, including my dad who, at that point in our relationship, was still struggling to wrap his head around my gender. He still said nasty things to me about it sometimes and expressed in no uncertain terms that he wished I could just be "normal." At that point in our relationship, he refused to be seen with me in public when I was wearing lipstick or a dress.

And then a television crew came knocking and he had to make a choice. One way or another, he was going to be portrayed—how did he want to be seen by the world and by the hundreds of thousands of people who still watched MTV in the mid-2010s? Did he want to be portrayed as the rejecting father, unwilling to try, abandoning his child because they happened to be different? Or did he want to be seen in a more complicated light? As a father who was trying? Failing, but trying nonetheless?

Miraculously, he chose the latter. He decided to participate. He sat down for extensive interviews with the documentary crew. He spoke openly and honestly. At one point, he crawled on all fours through the attic of our house to turn off a fan that was causing audio problems for the crew. He even came to hear my speech at NC Trans Pride—willingly, if reluctantly, interacting with me in a dress for the first time in public.

Him agreeing to be seen in public with me in a dress was a significant breakthrough in our relationship. And after doing it on national television, he got a lot better at doing it in real life. But what I remember most is something he said during an interview with the crew.

If you've never had a documentary crew plumb the depths of your life, you may not know this, but reality television can actually be a beautiful process. When done correctly, participating in a documentary can be just the thing you need to synthesize how you're feeling. Nothing gets people talking quite like a giant camera, an eager producer, and an assumed audience of millions.

At one point in the episode, my father told the producers something he'd never said to me in my entire life. He told them that *he was scared for me.* He understood that having a child with a male body who wears dresses makes them a target. He shared that he lost sleep worrying about whether I'd be hurt. He just wanted me to be safe. He just wanted his child, whom he loved more than anything in the world, to be okay.

I was shocked. All he'd ever expressed *to me* was anger, frustration, and resentment. He'd only ever told me that he wished I wouldn't be so eccentric, that he hated how I dressed, that he wished this whole "trans phase" would end, that I'd knock it off with "that San Francisco faggot shit." He'd expressed hatred of and loathing for my femininity, but he'd never told me *why*.

The "why" landed deep. At his core, in his heart of hearts, he didn't hate his son's femininity because he thought it was inherently disgusting so much as he hated it because it *terrified him*. Because he was horrified about what might happen to me. Because he, too, had nightmares about my mangled body in an alley, sequined skirt caked in blood.

After all those years, I realized that my father was not really bigoted. He was simply afraid.

That's when something clicked. If my father was afraid, and his fear had caused him to lash out at me for who I am, might that be true for other men? Might that be true for the men whose catcalls and harassment were making my life in New York a living hell?

The realization crashed on me like a wave, rolling through my mind. All of a sudden, the path to freedom was clear.

The path to freedom was empathy.

Let me take a moment to pause and say that I know how neoliberal and annoying that sounds. *Empathy* is a watered-down buzzword these days. As a concept, it's been hollowed out, cheapened, and mass-produced. It doesn't pack the punch it used to. But it's the only word I can come up with to describe what I know to be true.

When a dog aggressively barks at us, it's scary because we think that barking signifies malice, aggression, and a desire to harm. Through empathy, we can see that most dogs bark at us simply because they're afraid. They're nervous. They don't know us. We're bigger than they are, and they feel a need to signify a boundary. They bark at us precisely because they see *us* as the ones with power and control. They bark at us because we are, in fact, more powerful than they are. No matter how scary or large the dog is, it is a fallible creature, a vulnerable being scared of the myriad ways the world can hurt it.

I couldn't find my way back to a joyful, empowered life by hating the men who terrorized me. But I realized I didn't have to. Through the vulnerability of my father and years of contemplation, I found another way. If I wanted my life to be *mine* again, all I needed to do was *love* these men. *Care* for them. *Empathize* with them, instead.

I pursue such empathy not because it is the *right* thing to do so much as because it is the *only* thing to do. I don't empathize with the men who hurt me because I owe it to *them*; I empathize with the men who hurt me because I owe it to *myself.* Because I understand that it is only through empathy that I can set myself free.

Before I discovered empathy for the men who catcalled me, some man would scream, "FUCK YOU, TRANNY-ASS BITCH!" at me from across the street and it would send me reeling. I'd be ruined for days or weeks. My inner monologue would go something like this:

He hates me because of who I am, and I hate him. He hates me from the core of his being. He's a monster who wants to kill me because he hates me so much.

So many men hate me. So many men want to kill me because they hate me. Most men are monsters. The world is filled to the brim with monsters like him.

How will I ever be happy? How will I ever feel safe? I am doomed to have hatred like that hurled at me for the rest of my life. *There is no escape.*

It was paralyzing. It was ruinous. It made me want to die.

But when I learned a new approach, one that focused on empathizing with the men who catcalled me, something real changed. Possibilities opened up. Prospects bloomed. Expectations shifted.

Now when a man screams, "THE FUCK IS THAT FAGGOT SHIT?" at me from across the street (something that, thankfully, happens a lot less now that I live in L.A. and *drive*), I work to fill my internal monologue with compassion, possibility, and a sense of futurity. Instead of spiraling dark, I push myself to be curious: probative, even. I steer my thoughts toward understanding that man not as a terrifying monster but as a fractured human being. And in the process, I get to save my own soul.

It goes something like:

Okay, first things first: Am I safe? Is he pursuing me? Am I being followed? Do I need to seek help? No? Okay. Good. *Phew.*

You poor man. You must be so broken to say something like that to me. How much pain must you be in in order to yell at a complete stranger like that? How much suffering must you endure each day, navigating the world with all that anger and sadness?

I wonder what happened to you? I wonder what your childhood was like? Did you ever feel loved by your father? Did your brother discover you with a Barbie once and beat you so badly, you couldn't go to school the next day? Maybe it was your father who discovered you, wearing one of your mother's dresses. Maybe he screamed at you until his voice went hoarse. Maybe your mother caught you coloring a picture of a fairy and refused to look you in the eye for days afterward. Maybe your friends at school dragged you out by the dumpster and broke your nose because they caught you looking at one of their dicks in the locker room.

You poor man.

Maybe none of it happened directly to you; maybe you just witnessed it. Did you watch your father beat your brother when he explored gender differently? Did you watch your father beat your mother? Did he relent, or did he refuse to stop? Does me breaking the rules of *my gender* remind you of your mother breaking the rules that your father set *for hers*? Is that why you're acting like this?

Or perhaps you were the bully. Perhaps you're inundated with guilt. Your best friend tried to kiss you once and you smashed his head into a tree. You saw your little brother wearing a tutu and you threw him into a lake. And now you see someone like me breaking the rules of gender and have to contend with a culpability so powerful you cannot breathe. Are you crushed by the sight of me?

Or maybe it's jealousy. Maybe you want freedom from the gender binary so badly, it makes your blood boil. Do you want to wear bright colors, exciting patterns, and flowing fabric, too? Do you want your internal femininity to be recognized, loved, and adored? Is seeing me a cruel reminder of all of the parts of yourself that you were forced to kill off in the name of creating your masculinity? Do you want to forget about the beautiful, gentle, feminine parts of your soul that were murdered long ago? Do you hate me for reminding you of them?

Or is it that you're turned on and you hate yourself for it? Is that it? Do you want to fuck me? Am I your shameful kink? I wonder what would happen in a world where you could acknowledge your desire for me. Perhaps we could be lovers. Maybe then you could mess up my lipstick in the good way.

I wonder.

Whatever the case may be, I refuse to shut down. I refuse to harden. I refuse to make my heart icy in return or sever our connection as human beings.

I want to help you more badly than I know how to say. I understand your pain intimately, because your pain and mine are one and the same. It's a pain that I've healed from, too. It's a pain I know *how* to heal from. A pain that you *also* deserve to heal from. I could teach you the way, if only you'd let me. If only the world hadn't pushed us so far apart.

I wonder what it would be like for us to be friends? What TV shows do you like? What music do you listen to? What would it be like for us to meet under different circumstances, as colleagues or as in-laws or at a Christmas party? What gift would you get me for Secret Santa? I would get you a cactus. It would be an apt metaphor.

I wish I could talk to you right now, in this moment. It would help me to know more about your struggles, to see you in 3D. Are you worried that you won't be able to pay your rent this month? Are your parents healthy? When's the last time you called them? Do you have children? What are their names? Are you miserable at your job? Are you looking for a new one? Are you barely scraping by? Are you okay?

I know I can't actually talk to you right now. It isn't safe, and that breaks my heart. Our separation, this cleft between us, rips me in two.

I look at you and all I see is a scared little boy in desperate need of a hug. I wish you would let me give you that hug.

I will settle for what I can do. At this moment, what's within my power is how I frame this interaction and make meaning of it. Though I could view this moment as a degradation of my personhood, I will choose to see it, more accurately, as you *learning.* I will work to understand your words not as slander but as a begrudging embrace of the world I am dreaming into existence. A positive, albeit contradictory, sign pointing toward a better existence for trans people and men alike.

Because the fact that you lashed out at me means that you *saw* me. It means that you perceived me enough for it to mean something. It means that I entered your heart and unearthed pain you didn't remember was there. It means that simply by wearing a piece of clothing and walking past you, I changed how you see gender by a millimeter or two. A smidge. An iota.

What power: to change hearts simply by existing. For a mere garment to serve as source and site of healing? For a mere outfit to alter someone's perception of reality? Being catcalled by you does not mean that I am weak; it means that I am strong. It is not an affirmation of my vulnerability so much as it is a confirmation of my power.

For now, I will continue walking down this sidewalk, I will get where I'm going, and I will carry on with my life.

But one day, when I've been able to rest and heal a bit, I will write a book. In it, there will be a chapter about you. About how scared men like you made me feel, about how hard I worked to overcome that fear, and about how I learned to wish the best for you in spite of it all.

A message in a bottle, I will drop it into the proverbial ocean and pray that it makes its way to—

Ding! The subway doors open. It's my stop. I've been on the train for thirty minutes, lost in empathic exploration, turning harassment into something more.

These days, street harassment no longer has the same effect on me. When a man catcalls me, I no longer internalize the slurs or the things he says. I no longer take it home with me. His words don't ring in my mind with the same voracity, because I no longer see him as an enemy or as someone I hate.

Instead, I see him as a friend who is struggling. A friend who isn't acting right because he's scared, traumatized, and lonely.

I have yet to rid myself of the devastation entirely, but the texture has changed meaningfully enough. These days, I'm merely devastated *differently:* devastated that, in the moment of being catcalled, it is not safe for me to show this broken man the love he so clearly needs.

Men commit
eighty-one percent
of violent crime.

DON'T YOU KNOW THAT YOU'RE TOXIC?

In the pantheon of contemporary feminist language, few terms have more bite, potency, or cultural weight than the term "Toxic Masculinity." It's everywhere and ubiquitous, caking the face of feminist discourse. But let's face it: like cheap foundation at the end of a long night, the cracks are starting to show.

"Toxic Masculinity" is a pack of cigarettes. Addictive. Teeming with glamour, nicotine, and sex. Light up and people will know that you're edgy. Throw on your best lycra bodysuit and Sandra Dee leather jacket, tease your hair seventeen inches high, walk right up to a man, and blow it in his face. The ultimate symbol of feminist edge, of a woman who's no longer willing to behave. A social activity, uniting us with other rebels, gathering in the metaphorical alley as we puff. Like cigarettes, we haven't figured out it's bad for us. Secretly blanketing our collective lungs in tar, it can kill.

"Toxic Masculinity" is a gun, capable of causing garish injury. Under no circumstances should it be used imprecisely or in crowded public forums. Wielding it responsibly requires extensive training, practice, and a rock-solid ethical compass. Aimed incorrectly by half an inch, it can harm someone for life. Can it be used safely? *In theory*. Historically speaking, has it been used safely? *Eh*. Like a gun, we'd be best served by simply locking it away.

Investing in and subsequently popularizing the term "Toxic Masculinity" has been one of the great strategic blunders in the last decade of popular feminist discourse. Not because it's wrong to proclaim the myriad ways in which men hurt the world and themselves, but because we're reckless with it. Few people use the term responsibly, in the correct context, or for the right reasons anymore. Most of us who use the term haven't even taken the time to define for *ourselves* what we mean by it. What's more, even *if* we use it correctly, men—the very people the term is intended to engage—can be relied upon to misconstrue our meaning most every time. A feminist Lamborghini, driven drunk, we wield something existentially powerful and spiritually potent like it's nothing.

It's a blunder that we can and should forgive ourselves for. As Roxane Gay reminds us in *Bad Feminist*:

> Feminism is flawed because it is a movement powered by people and people are inherently flawed. For whatever reason, we hold feminism to an unreasonable standard where the movement must be everything we want and must always make the best choices. When feminism falls short of our expectations, we decide the problem is with feminism rather than with the flawed people who act in the name of the movement.

The problem here is not "with feminism." Feminism is an abstract cohort of well-meaning billions across the globe, striving imperfectly in an imperfect world. We're all human. We err.

And since its inception, our movement has faced a near-vertical uphill battle: How do we decry the violence being done by men without decrying men themselves? How can we undertake something so *subtle* on the level of mass discourse without being misunderstood? It's an almost impossible task, one that can never be done perfectly, one that requires constant adaptation, evolution, and linguistic agility.

I agree with Roxane Gay: "We should disavow the failures of feminism without disavowing its many successes and how far we have come." By stating that the term "Toxic Masculinity" is no longer effective and that we have lost the plot a bit, I am not condemning feminism wholesale. Not at all. That would be a mistake. I am simply asking us to reflect and, from a place of sincere love, urging us to continue to grow.

Besides, you know the term is broken, right? On a gut level, I think we all do. But for some reason, we've been afraid to say so. It's my considered opinion that, as a term, "Toxic Masculinity" needs to be retired from our feminist lexicon, likely forever.

Allow me to themsplain.

• • •

The trouble with the term "Toxic Masculinity" begins with the fact that it isn't literal. Masculinity is not a molecule or a chemical. You cannot ingest, inhale, or inject it. Factually speaking, there's no such thing as a toxic gender. You can't slip masculinity in someone's coffee in order to poison them, let alone *hold the stuff.* Gender is an abstraction, folks.

Toxic Masculinity isn't even a metaphor; it's the *suggestion of one.* In order to be correctly understood, it must be correctly interpreted. But how can that happen when neither the word "toxic" nor the word "masculinity" specifies at *which metaphor* the user is expected to arrive? We merely suggest that they should consider *some sort* of toxic or poisonous substance and hope for the best, praying it'll work itself out.

It doesn't. Each time we say "Toxic Masculinity" we are wrongfully assuming people will be able to take those two words and make appropriate meaning of them. We're relying on the average consumer of language—ourselves included—to *infer* a correct metaphor without any further instruction or clarification. Many of us, people who've identified as feminists for decades, struggle to adequately define the term or articulate the metaphor we're alluding to when we describe masculinity as toxic. If we can't, why do we expect others to be able to?

In a dream world (read: a fictional world that does not exist, a ship long since sailed), people would hear "Toxic Masculinity" and immediately arrive at something like the following definition:

Toxic Masculinity (n):

A specific subset of traits derived from conventional, socially constructed masculinity (i.e., aggression, emotional unavailability, violence) that, though they are not inherent to men, are metaphorically toxic (i.e., emotionally and socially harmful) to both men exhibiting those traits and everyone who interacts with men exhibiting those traits.

Then, after correctly defining the term, people would go on to identify an apt metaphor. Something like:

Toxic Masculinity is lead paint. It hurts everyone who comes in contact with it. Men are the painters, compelled to apply lead paint to the walls in order to eat and pay their bills. The rest of us are forced to live in those lead-painted rooms. Everyone, from the painters to the people living within the painted walls, is subjected to lead poisoning. Everyone ends up ingesting the toxin. No one is spared, and it hurts us all.

If we lived in that platonic ideal of a feminist universe, we could responsibly use the term to our hearts' content. We could throw it around everywhere—at town halls and on social media alike—and we'd all be on the same page about what we're actually saying.

But that isn't the world we live in. When we talk about Toxic Masculinity, very few people think to themselves, "Yes. Like lead paint." In order for that to happen, it would've required rigorous definition and a substantial public education campaign *at the time we debuted the term* so that people were using it correctly from the get-go.

We didn't do that work. Or at least we stopped doing it. And so the term took on an imprecise and increasingly destructive life of its own. A gargantuan, society-wide game of telephone wherein the self-image of all men and the future efficacy of feminism were on the line.

The game went as it always does. As knowledge was passed from person to person, it degraded entropically. The term went from something compelling—an avenue that invited men into a conversation about how masculinity was hurting *them* alongside *us*—into a trite accusation that all men are inherently and irreparably bad.

At some point, the meaning got twisted beyond repair. **We went from understanding men as *wielding* a toxic substance to understanding men *as* a toxic substance.**

We went from talking about men metaphorically *using* lead paint to men *being* the lead. In our mind's eye, men are no longer operating the nuclear reactor; they're the uranium.

In the popular imagination, "Toxic Masculinity" has stopped referring to metaphors that leave room for redemption. If a man is a painter painting with lead, he need only switch paint to stop harming himself and those around him. But if a man is the lead, what can he do? Wish himself out of existence? Scrape himself from the walls? A poison dart frog cannot scrub the poison from its skin. A venomous snake cannot will away its fangs.

Though many people would prefer to infantilize men and act like they're devoid of complex understanding, men have picked up on this meteoric metaphoric shift. It hasn't exactly been subtle, and they've felt it. They've heard it, implied from every direction. Across cultures throughout the world, they've been surrounded by it.

It's led to what social scientist Richard Reeves calls "a political stalemate on issues of sex and gender." In his pivotal work *Of Boys and Men*, he spells out the dichotomy adroitly: "Both sides have dug into an ideological position that inhibits real change. Progressives refuse to accept that important gender inequalities can run in both directions, and they quickly label male problems as symptoms of 'toxic masculinity.' Conservatives appear more sensitive to the struggles of boys and men but only as a justification for turning back the clock and restoring traditional gender roles."

What men have heard from us, loud and clear, is that *their very gender,* the sum of who they are, is toxic. That masculinity itself is harmful and dangerous and irredeemable.

What a brutal thing to say. What a *horrible* thing to hear.

For someone to proudly proclaim, in public, that the sum of you is toxic? For someone to say that the essence of you—how your parents raised you and how you operate in community—is poison, living in your very skin? For someone to imply that because you're a man, you are necessarily a fanged creature, burgeoning with venom, beyond redemption, waiting to strike?

And so, reasonably—*protectively,* even—most men have shut down. They've dismissed us. They've left the chat over a game of telephone gone horribly awry. Because of a corrupted metaphor, they've chosen to disengage from feminist discourse altogether.

What's worse is that, as feminists, most of us have been too stubborn, shortsighted, or careless to grasp that it is, in fact, a misunderstanding.

We proclaim that certain aspects of masculinity *can be* toxic. But we do so in reductive (and therefore imprecise and easy-to-misconstrue) terms. Our opaque, easily misunderstood language leads men to (reasonably) hear that all masculinity is toxic. So they shut down or don't engage—you know, because it feels like an attack when someone implies that *your gender is toxic.* We take that as further evidence of exactly how toxic they are. In retaliation, we proclaim, even more loudly, in language that is increasingly acerbic and imprecise, that *all men* are toxic. They retaliate by lashing out at us. We retaliate by lashing back at them. The cycle continues. Nobody learns. No one is healed. And everything just gets worse.

It becomes a negative feedback loop, one that is eating our movement and our world alive. One that puts men in an impossible, irredeemable position, with all the irrational mechanics of an old Salem trial. You've been called toxic. If you admit to the charge? Definitely toxic. If you insist that you aren't entirely toxic? Even more toxic.

If you're silent? Well, that's toxic, too.

• • •

In the process of writing this book, I spent a lot of time in the "manosphere"—the corners of the internet where men gather to rebuke feminist ideology and bemoan the state of masculinity in the world. I marinated in it, listening to speeches and reading articles by Ben Shapiro, Andrew Tate, and Jordan Peterson as I sought to deconstruct their secret sauce.

Which is how I found myself in the uncanny position of being emotionally moved by something Jordan Peterson, the self-appointed True Leader of Contemporary Men, said.*

It was a video on TikTok, in black and white, posted by an account called the Quote Circle. Over stirring piano music, an off-camera interviewer asks Peterson:

> *"Is it okay to be a man?"*

Immediately, he responds:

> *"It's not okay, it's* necessary. *What the hell are we gonna do without men?"*

His voice is hoarse, gravelly, barely there. He's clearly been talking all day. I wonder how long he's been on the road. He looks exhausted, worn down, burnt out. As a public figure who is exhausted, worn down, and burnt out, too, I find myself empathizing with the guy. Really caring about him as a human being. It's a strange sensation. He continues:

> *"You look around this city here, you see all these buildings go up. These men, they're doing impossible things. They're under the streets working on the sewers. They're up on the power lines in the storms and the rain. They're keeping this impossible infrastructure functioning—often literally. And the gratitude for that is sorely lacking, especially among the people who should be most grateful. Failing to understand entirely that there's a massive infrastructure*

---

*If you don't know who Jordan Peterson is or understand his cultural significance, just ask your nephew, uncle, brother, or husband. Odds are, he'll know all about it.

of unbelievably hardworking, solidly laboring, working-class men breaking themselves in half on a regular basis, making sure that everything that always breaks works. And so a little gratitude for that is in order."

Listening to him, I find myself broken in half, too. Half of me is incensed: Surely he is aware that women also work in construction? That women also do impossible jobs? That women also break themselves in service of making sure that everything works?

But the other half of me is *moved*. I care deeply for working-class men. Jordan Peterson and I, uncannily enough, share that as a common denominator. As the grandchild of Southern textile engineers and immigrant Ford auto workers—many of whom had their bodies destroyed or permanently disabled by hard labor at the Cleveland Engine Plant—and a member of a union myself, I want nothing more than to honor the lives and work of men like that. I celebrate them and venerate them and love them because they are my family. I could not be who I am today without the vast contributions of hardworking men.

The background music swells, and as it does, something unexpected happens: Jordan Peterson's brow furrows and he begins to *tear up*. I was not expecting that. Verklempt and clearly fighting back emotion, he says:

"And it's very useful to tell everyone, not just men, that they have an important role to play, a necessary role. And that if they act properly and honestly and forthrightly, they can put their lives together and they can help their families and they can make their communities better. And that's not 'toxic masculinity'—that appalling phrase—it's what keeps the world going round."

And all I can feel is remorse. I have uttered the term "Toxic Masculinity" thousands of times in my life and this man, who I have been taught to think of as a bigot and a sexist demagogue, has been thoroughly broken by it. I feel culpable. I have indirectly ruptured some part of him. He has been so hurt and debased by the term "Toxic Masculinity," by the incessant, unrelenting suggestion that all men are inherently bad, that he is moved to tears. He can barely get out the words without his voice catching. Somewhere underneath his imperfect language and somewhat misguided bombasticism, there are glimmers of a spiritually injured boy who merely wants to be valued, cared for, and understood.

The comments provide me neither solace nor consolation. Underneath the video, people I will never know hurl their aching vulnerability into the ether:

> Only women, children, and dogs are loved unconditionally. A man is loved under the condition of what he can provide.

> Thank you Jordan. Construction worker, get up at 4, get home at almost 7 every day. God bless everyone.

> It's the fact that it feels like he is about to cry that hurts me . . .

> Thank you to my amazing husband. He is a service and repair plumber and goes out at midnight to make sure that your grandma has hot water.

I am bowled over by this, brought to my nonbinary knees. All I can think is *How have we been so misunderstood?* All I can wonder is *How did we get here?*

We must find a way to break this cycle. We must find less corruptible language, language that is not so easily subject to incorrect interpretation. We must begin meaning what we say. And we must lead with compassion as we do so.

• • •

How might we find the motivation to make such a shift in our language? Personally, I am not very motivated by the idea of finding language that "helps men be less defensive." That just makes me feel annoyed.

I am, however, motivated by the idea of helping men find freedom from the confines of traditional masculinity. I'm motivated to help men identify how what they've been taught has hurt them. I want to help men find compassion for themselves, to find freedom from the yoke of abuse that constitutes a non-negligible portion of contemporary manhood.

I want to find language that, instead of consolidating men under the banner of the abuse they've endured, helps them distance themselves from it. As a term, "Toxic Masculinity" does the opposite.

When you tell a man that masculinity is toxic, he hears it as an accusation aimed not at a social structure, but at himself. He feels the need to defend his own masculinity. In the process of doing so, he often ends up defending all masculinity and, before you know it, all men. He's drawn in closer to monolithic manhood—away from us, and toward the abuse he's endured in the process of being "made a man." Our effort backfires. We sought to free him, but in doing so, we scared him further into the cage.

Instead of yelling at them to get out—instead of screaming at men and expecting them to leave the rigid confines of masculinity as they've known it—we've got to give them something worth leaving the cage for. It's proven ineffective to say, *Men, your cage is bad,* no matter how hard we try. Instead, we need language that insists the opposite, that proclaims, *Men, out here is better.*

What happens if, instead of talking about "Toxic Masculinity," we focus on its counterpart? What if, instead of focusing our attention critically—on what we don't want men to be—we focus our attention generatively—on the freedom we hope for them to find.

What if we focus instead on *nontoxic masculinity*? On defining and popularizing masculinity that is hypoallergenic, FDA-approved, and BPA-free? On shaping a vision for masculinity that is organic, non-GMO, cage-free, sulfate-free, paraben-free, free-range, and free of charge?

Admittedly, this approach is less fun. Demolishing a house is a blast. Who doesn't want to smash a toilet to smithereens? Building a house is a lot harder. You have to, like, *actually work*. But if we want to have a warm existential place to sleep, at some point it's what we gotta do.

To facilitate this shift, I'd like to propose that we popularize the term **Safe Masculinity,** instead.

It feels nice to say, doesn't it? Like parting the musty curtains and letting the sunshine in. It feels like freedom to name that there is such a thing as warm, fluffy, safe masculinity.

And yes, I know, the adjective "safe" has been overplayed. The ideology of "safe space" has tinged the word with a certain rancor and oversensitivity. Paradoxically, the word "safe" has been so weaponized against men that it no longer signals safety *to them*. I've certainly been guilty of this: in college, whenever a man was saying something I didn't like, all I had to do was remind him that "this is a safe space," and that would promptly shut him up. Not my best work.

Which renders its reclamation all the more vital for men and all of us. Men deserve a safe world for *themselves* as well. Their safety—both literal and existential—should matter to us, too. We owe it to men to dig the word "safe" out from the neoliberal etymological feminist mud, clean it off, and make it shine like new. A world where men hear "safe" and think "danger" is a world where none of us can heal.

Besides, I know so many men who inhabit the ideal of safe masculinity. In the context of applying the adjective "safe" to real people, it no longer rings trite.

Men like my adopted brother Rick. Rick isn't afraid to express himself, articulate his feelings, or wear silly clothes to a party. He has a six-year-old daughter—my de facto niece—and he is just so good with her. Watching a grown man twirl and dance alongside his daughter, unconcerned about "his manhood," joyous, and free? Watching a man read *Astrophysics for Babies* to his child, teaching her how stars shine and what nebulae are? Watching a father play in the dress-up bin with enthusiasm? That feels like safety to me.

As an engineer, Rick also knows a gajillion practical "masculine" skills that bring safety and joy to those he loves. When there was a bad storm recently and the trees fell and all the power was out, he got the generator from the basement, set it up, and brought power back for the entire house. Even with damp logs, he can conjure a bonfire for us and keep it burning. We often build fires together.

At the end of the day, this is all we really want, isn't it? For men to feel safe? For us to feel safe around them? For us to be able to build community alongside them?

We do not need the abolition of masculinity, merely the loosening and reinterpretation of it. There is still a place for aggression and strength and energy and power and manhood and all of those things that exist within the constellation of our masculine social construct. But by positively identifying what *safe masculinity* looks like and focusing our attention in that direction, we can ensure that we are no longer misunderstood. Sure, we can still talk about moments when masculinity is unsafe, but even the term "unsafe masculinity" is a vast improvement. Identifying the bad aspects of masculinity with the antonym—as *un*safe—still centers the idea that masculinity can be safe and, in its proper form, is so. That safety is its normal, ideal state.

I want to end the psychic torment of a double-negative imperative. "Don't be toxic" is old news. It sends men down a rabbit hole, asking themselves, "Am I being toxic?" on repeat until they're so exhausted and paranoid they give up on themselves and us.

In its place, I want a clear, positive imperative.

"Be safe, dude."

Simple. Elegant. And, I would argue, our path toward a brighter feminist future.

P.S.

Just because we're adopting more constructive language doesn't mean we can't complain sometimes. I love complaining. A bitch needs to whine, okay? Being vindictive and shady and petty on the internet is a blast. That's what the internet is *for*, baby.

But maybe we do so in a way that *doesn't* lead men to dismiss us and believe they're irredeemable?

As your undemocratically self-appointed nonbinary leader, it's my God-given right to suggest a new, gender-neutral term to replace the vindictive, petty energy of "Toxic Masculinity."

I give to you: *icky gender.*

It has all the upsides of "Toxic Masculinity" with none of the baggage. It's fun to say. It's buzzy. And, most importantly, it still allows us to be sassy and silly and poke fun at the people who oppress us. Plus, it allows us to identify moments when anyone, of any gender, is being icky about it. Because, ladies? Y'all got some pretty damn icky gender sometimes, too. No offense.

Here's how it sounds in practice:

"Yeah, they had a gender-reveal party where they exploded a blue grenade. The uncle got hit with a bunch of shrapnel and almost didn't make it. Icky gender strikes again."

"He told you he wanted you to wear something a little more form-fitting and feminine for him? Dump that man. That's some icky-ass gender."

"Did you go to that sorority rush party? Icky gender central."

"All those icky dudes manspreading on the subway need their MetroCards revoked and a swift kick in the nuts."

"Just because she's a woman doesn't mean that her gender isn't icky. She's still a war criminal, Ethel."

"You told our three-year-old son not to cry? Steve, that is the ickiest gender I have ever seen. I want a divorce."

Something like that.

Ninety percent
of American veterans
are men.

One out of every
seven American men
has served
in the armed forces.

Since 2001,
7,000 American service members
have died in Afghanistan and Iraq.

Between 2001 and 2021,
134,000 American veterans
died by suicide.

CHILD SOLDIERS

I'm gonna level with you. This essay is, in itself, a foolish endeavor. The very definition of biting off more than you—than *anyone*—can chew. Trying to address the global, systemic violence of the American Military and what that violence does to the young men who are preyed upon to enact it? I may as well bite a jawbreaker, full force.

If shattering my teeth is what it takes, so be it.

• • •

In 2003, when the United States' invasion of Iraq was beginning, I was in sixth grade. Boy soprano parachuting down toward bass, peach fuzz marching across my cupid's bow, I wasn't paying much attention to world politics. I was far too preoccupied with what my body was up to; the changes were so *sudden,* so vast and expansive, I couldn't keep up. My balls dropped alongside my voice, exploding with hair follicles that, at first, I thought were some sort of skin disease.

I was growing so quickly it *hurt.* When I lay down to sleep at night, my femurs ached. Breaking and rebuilding. Breaking and expanding. Testosterone invading every cell, forcing me to grow. I was "becoming a man" more quickly than I'd ever thought possible, outpacing my peers by a mile.

When I wasn't inventorying the changes in my body, I was attempting to learn Japanese. That summer, I was going to be part of the first cohort from my middle school to visit our sister school, Shinonome Junior High, in Hiroshima, Japan. I knew most of the Shinonome students would speak far better English than I could match with whatever Japanese I'd be able to cobble together that spring, but I wanted to try. I drilled my *hiragana* flash cards diligently while taking lessons at NC State's community program. *Itadakimasu. Gochisousamadeshita.* I watched a lot of anime, too—convinced that, somehow, subconsciously, it was sure to help. *Hai.*

I wasn't sent to Hiroshima naïve, which is where the trouble began. My teachers did an admirable job of teaching us about the history of the city, about the fact that it was the first of only two cities in human history to be annihilated by an atomic bomb. That both of those bombs were dropped by America. We spent a lot of time talking about the story of Sadako Sasaki—a story more American children should know.

When the bomb was dropped, in 1945, Sadako was two years old, living a mile or so from the center of the explosion. Even a mile away, it blew her out of a window and into the street. Her mother clambered to find her body in the burning wreckage, certain that her daughter must be dead. Miraculously, she wasn't. At least not yet. Sadako's mother found her toddler among the rubble outside, seemingly unharmed. As they fled the incinerated city, black rain—a tarlike precipitate created by radioactive particles and ash flung high into the atmosphere—began to fall. It covered their clothes, their hair, their already-charred skin.

After healing from her injuries, Sadako grew up normally. For a decade, it seemed that she would be okay. But at the age of around eleven, the effects of radiation poisoning began to catch up with her. She was hospitalized for leukemia at the age of twelve and given no more than a year to live. In the hospital where she was to die, a friend told her about the legend of the paper cranes; that anyone who folded a thousand origami cranes would have their wish come true.

Sadako wished to live.

From her hospital bed, she got to work. Origami paper was scarce, so she made cranes out of whatever she could find: medicine labels, old hospital paperwork, receipts. Daily, she made cranes, armed with the mystical hope that as she gave new shape to discarded paper, she could give new shape to her discarded future. There's some disagreement in the historical record about how many paper cranes she was actually able to make—about whether she met or exceeded her goal of a thousand.

Either way, the cranes didn't work. Everyone knew they wouldn't, but the striving and trying and yearning of a doomed twelve-year-old girl has a habit of instilling hope, however irrational. Eight months after being admitted to the hospital, she died. They buried the paper cranes alongside her.

Sadako and her paper cranes became a rallying cry for the children of Hiroshima: children awash with grief, in need of a hero, desperate for some way to express their collective, unprecedented lamentation. Following Sadako's death, her schoolmates and young people across the city started fundraising for a memorial in her honor and in honor of the tens of thousands of children whose lives were indelibly destroyed by *Little Boy.*

The Hiroshima Children's Peace Monument opened in 1958, directly across the Motoyasu River from the skeletal remains of the Atomic Dome. Atop a two-story midcentury plinth, a bronze Sadako stands defiantly, thrusting a giant paper crane toward the heavens above. Thousands upon thousands of paper cranes, sent from children around the world, rest in glass cases at her feet.

As middle schoolers, we were taught about Sadako for a reason. For young Americans, war is too often an abstraction. It is something that happens *over there* or *back then,* never *here* and *now.* When I was in sixth grade, the story of Sadako landed powerfully because she was my age when she died. Her death somehow felt proximate. Through the simple effect of chronology, a new pathos took root.

At the age of twelve, I was invited to do something teenagers coming of age in the post-9/11 American South were seldom encouraged to do: empathize with a victim of American military violence. Think of myself in their place.

As Colin Powell was lying to the U.N. and fervent nationalism was swelling, I was in Raleigh, imagining myself in Sadako's shoes. Along with the rest of my sixth-grade class, I folded paper cranes for her, eyes misty as I creased.

A few months later, as war drums were sounding, I was in Hiroshima, visiting Sadako's statue in person, laying paper cranes at her bronze feet.

The statue stands at the very heart of the city, in what is known as Peace Memorial Park. As an American—the grandchild of a World War II veteran who'd been deployed in the Pacific, no less—it felt wrong to be there. The guilt was remarkable. Everywhere I looked, I saw monuments to devastation that was *our* fault.

In the park's museum, I saw a watch that'd been frozen in time, gears melted and fused, perpetually marking eight-fifteen A.M., and thought: *We did this.* I saw a piece of stone, cut from the steps of a bank, on which is forever cast the shadow of a person who was vaporized, and thought: *My country did this.* I saw wax figurines stumbling through rubble, burned skin hanging from their limbs in tatters, and thought: *This, too, is America.*

On a level bordering existential, my time in Hiroshima shattered my trust in almost everything I'd been told. It couldn't be helped. You cannot confront a wound the size of a city and leave unchanged by the experience. You cannot spend three weeks in a monument to your own nation's brutality and not be transformed. Everywhere I looked, I thought: *These are people whose grandparents my grandparents murdered.* For three weeks, I thought: *I am living inside a scar. I am living inside a gash in human history, one inflicted by my ancestors, one I would never have properly acknowledged if it weren't for the random fluke of a student exchange program.*

And for years thereafter, I wondered: *How can I be proud of a country that could do this? What other atrocities is America hiding from me? We do a moment of silence for 9/11—where is the moment of silence for 8/6 and 8/9? No one in America seems to know or care what those dates even mean.*

As an American adolescent, I was told that the bombings of Hiroshima and Nagasaki were victorious. Or, by those who were somewhat more evolved, a necessary evil. That the maimed, irradiated, mangled bodies of children were not *needless* casualties of American bloodlust and imperial greed, they were *necessary* casualties of America's desire for peace. Sadako *had* to die, Jacob. It couldn't be avoided.

I returned to America voracious. Throughout my seventh-grade year, I read. About the Manhattan Project and the end of the war and FDR and Truman and proliferation and the arms race that ensued: *Oppenheimer* in adolescent hands.

I started watching the news, too, and I finally began to care. It was happening all over again. America was murdering and brutalizing and rampaging afresh.

Except this time, I didn't need a student exchange program to humanize the people on the other side. As an Arab American who is half Syrian-Lebanese and half cornbread-Anglo-white, my entire adolescence and adulthood have been characterized by people who sound like my mom's side of the family murdering people who sound like my dad's side of the family. The tension is relentless. After 9/11 and The "Patriot" Act, many of my aunts and uncles on my dad's side simply started lying: we were no longer Syrian-Lebanese, we were *Greek*.

But it is necessary, the pundits said. *Iraq has Weapons of Mass Destruction. We must murder as many Iraqis as it takes; otherwise, we may suffer as we made Japan suffer. Saddam wants to make Washington the next Hiroshima, Jacob. We have to kill everyone we can. The burned, maimed, mangled bodies of Iraqi children are necessary casualties of America's desire for peace and democracy, not needless casualties of American greed. Sadako must die again; it's just that now she talks like your grandmother.*

In seventh grade, I started attending protests against the war with my homeroom teacher. They were held in the large public square across the street from my school. At the protests, I heard from mothers of soldiers who'd died at the ages of nineteen or twenty. I heard from soldiers who'd returned from Afghanistan or Iraq, ripped to shreds by IEDs. I heard from Muslim Americans who were terrified for their safety and the safety of their families. I grieved with them. I yelled with them. We all burned together. But no matter what I did, the feeling of guilt—the guilt that began in Hiroshima and spiraled out, out, *out*, touching almost every part of the world—could never be completely assuaged.

I don't think my feeling of guilt will ever be completely assuaged. Such is being an American with a brain and a heart.

. . .

For years, I've told myself the same story about how and when I "came out" as nonbinary. I published a book about it.

It started, the story goes, when I was a child. I was an effeminate little kid who was socially coerced into putting away their femininity and made to settle for being a boy. Some wanted me to be a sufficiently masculine boy because they hoped to keep me safe in a world that hurts gender non-conforming people. Others wanted me to be a sufficiently masculine boy because they hated trans and queer people alike and did not want me to be one of them.

As a child, the story continues, *I fought those who sought to coerce me, then gave up. I pretended to be a boy for a decade as I grew, then began undoing all the assumptions people made about me.*

My gender rebellion truly began, I have told the world, on repeat, *when I rejected heterosexuality and came out as gay. Circa 2008, men were still not supposed to be gay. To be gay was to be a second-class man or, according to many, to reject manhood wholesale.*

Then, the story finishes, *I began fighting masculinity in earnest and rebuking the mantle of manhood that had been nonconsensually foisted upon my shoulders. I bought high heels and started wearing them privately, then publicly. I assigned language to my disobedience, coming out as "genderqueer," then "nonbinary," and declaring they/them pronouns. I bought dresses and lipstick and nail polish and so on and so forth until the lesson was made clear: Jacob is not a man.*

It's a good story, but one in need of correction.

First: I've gotten the point of departure wrong. Looking back, it wasn't a *trip to the mall to buy high heels* that marked the beginning of my gender defection; it was a trip to *Hiroshima.*

I did not first abandon masculinity by "traditional" queer means. By the time I came out as gay or began painting my nails or bought my first dress, I was already well practiced in the art of rebuking my gender. I'd been doing so since I was in seventh grade. The moment I began working *for* peace and *against* the United States War Machine, I'd fundamentally defied American masculinity.

For any man—let alone a teenager or a boy—to protest war? For someone with a penis to pick up a picket sign calling for a ceasefire? For someone with nascent chest hair to loudly oppose the armed forces? This is protesting gender itself. American Manhood and war, American Boyhood and basic training, American Masculinity and military violence—they are forces as difficult to parse as indigo and blue. In America, you cannot confront one without confronting the other.

Peace is the work of women, they whisper. *War is the work of men.*

How dare you *protest it*?

My queerness did not begin when I came out as gay. It began when I came out as a pacifist. As I stood in Moore Square with my seventh-grade teacher, I was not simply protesting George W. Bush; I was protesting *men,* their desire to prove themselves through violence, and their ceaseless quest to conscript me into it all.

Second: I need to start giving the homophobia and transphobia I faced as a child more depth. More dimension.

Until recently, I told myself that people were forcing me to conform to the gender binary because they were invested in one day making a man of me. Something about that always rang a little hollow, but I couldn't quite put my finger on it. "Being a man" lived in a vacuum. It was the *what,* but it wasn't the *why.* Not really. Yes, "being a man" is important, I guess, but it's a pretty abstract thing to make your child abjectly miserable over.

Why was it so important for them to make a man of me? What lived *underneath* their intense, phobic responses to my gender precocity?

In the mid-2000s, when I was an unwieldy preteen, the justification in public discourse was mainly religion. People hated gay people and trans people because we were sinners and we were going to hell. They had to hate us. The Bible told them so.

Or they'd talk abstractly about "family values." They'd imply that if trans and gay people were to be accepted in culture, "the family" as we know it would fall apart. A man marrying another man? What's next? A man marrying a *goat*?

In hindsight, I can see that neither of these tell the full story. They are merely excuses.

Oh, *the Bible* made you hate gay people? No, it didn't. You still eat shellfish and wear mixed fabrics. You don't give two fucks what the Bible says, especially not Leviticus.

Oh, *family values* made you hate gay people? That one is a little more honest. Conservative men *were* worried about women being empowered to come out as lesbians and divorce them. They were (and still are) scared that they might have to start relying on being good partners—instead of on social and economic coercion—to keep their marriages intact. A lot of conservative men were angry that they *themselves* were gay. But still. This family-values nonsense was also mostly surface-level. Unless you're a homo, gay marriage has nothing to do with your marriage. And no, you aren't *legitimately* worried that same-sex marriage will lead to people marrying goats. I suspect many conservative men were just nostalgic for being able to legally own their wife like they can legally own a goat.

I have a new theory about what was really going on. Underneath all this homophobia and transphobia were deeper anxieties about manhood, masculinity, the military, America, and *violence*.

People didn't discourage me from twirling in tutus or playing with Barbies or doing gymnastics or loving the color pink because they were *just* trying to turn me into a man. They did so because they were also trying to *turn me into a soldier*. They weren't worried that little boys wearing pink nail polish would go to hell—they just knew that the American project of global violence cannot survive gentle boys.

My gentleness was an affront to America, a dangerous dereliction of duty. A happy, feminine boy is a threat to national security.

It's the only explanation I can come up with for the ferocity of gender policing I experienced as a child. People weren't just mad because playing with a Barbie meant I wasn't sufficiently masculine; deep down, they were mad because being soft meant I could never kill. How can we affirm four-year-old Jacob's sensitivity when we may one day need them to slaughter Iraqi or Russian or Palestinian or Chinese civilians for us? How can we encourage gentleness when the destiny of all American male children is, potentially, to hunt other human beings for capital and national pride?

As an American Boy, I was implicitly told, *you must put down the doll so that you can one day pick up a gun.*

· · ·

Nothing illustrates this more bluntly than the toys we give our children. Little girls have Barbie, who lives in a house and hangs out with her friends and wears cute dresses and doesn't eat enough and sometimes goes down the waterslide. And little boys have G.I. Joe, who carries guns and drives tanks over enemy lines and sometimes deploys scatter bombs.

They're both blond, but one does her makeup while the other *murders people.*

It's wild to me how normalized violence was in my life and the lives of American boys. Have we even stopped to consider the term "toy soldier" as an oxymoron? In what universe is it acceptable to make industrial warfare a source of adolescent recreation?

Sometimes I worry that I'm being a bit dramatic about all of this. I have a penchant for drama. It's never outside the realm of possibility.

So I looked into it. I needed to be sure that I wasn't making this up. I needed to ascertain whether it was still as bad as I remembered. I needed to see if much had changed in the past thirty years, since I was a child.

I didn't have to look very far or dig very deep. I simply went to the Hasbro website for G.I. Joe, read the product information for the toy, and all my fears were confirmed. It was as bad as I remembered, if a fraction more subtle:

A highly skilled, on-demand, special operations force . . . tasked with defending the world.

On the website, the action figure is depicted with a big explosion behind him, double-fisting a pistol and an AK-47.

Wherever there's trouble, G.I. Joe is there.

His name is Duke. He has bulging muscles. He's pointing one gun to the left and one to the right. He has a knife strapped to his ankle.

Comes with character art inspired by the classic Real American Hero figure line . . .

In another photo of the action figure—sorry, I mean *military recruitment toy*—there's a close-up of the figurine's face.

. . . perfect for display.

He's scowling. Brows set in a ruthless gaze. Ready to kill.

Figure contains 10 accessory pieces including helmet, binoculars, backpack, knife, peg stand, and weapon accessories.

They will not name the *pistol* or the *assault rifle*. Instead, they are euphemized as *weapon accessories*. It's almost like Hasbro *knows* that what they're doing is wrong and unethical.

This figure makes a great gift for boys and girls . . .

The "boys and girls" reference is egregious. We all know they don't intend this toy for girls, but neoliberalism requires that they give a nod to a perverse type of "gender equality."

. . . who love action and adventure.

And *murder.* You forgot to say *murder.* And *dismemberment.* And *being blown to smithereens by IEDs.* And *PTSD.* And *being aban- doned by the American people and left homeless on the street when you return.*

WARNING: CHOKING HAZARD. Small parts. Not for children under 3 years.

Don't give this toy to your three-year-old. Wouldn't want them to choke to death on small plastic symbols of death.

Appropriate for ages 4 and up.

According to the Hasbro corporation—and, I suspect, by the transitive property, much of the American public—once you turn four, you are ready. You're ready to fantasize about murdering other human beings. You've come of age.

In the United States of America, when a boy is old enough to not choke on small pieces of plastic, he is old enough to begin the recruitment process. He's old enough to begin thinking about bullets and blades entering flesh. He may not be old enough to do multiplication or count to one hundred or form clear, lasting memories or tie his shoes, but he is old enough to fantasize about conquest and war and murder and death.

Start early. Get 'em while they're young. The Military-Industrial Complex needs your boy-child's soul, please.

I'm sorry, but *what is wrong with us?* As a feminist movement, we are obsessed with the fact that Barbie encourages negative body image among little girls, but we say virtually nothing about the fact that G.I. Joe encourages little boys to conceptualize themselves as killers?

. . .

It's time we face it: America *does* have a child-grooming problem. One so normalized, we consider it entertainment; so expansive, we have federal holidays for it; so pervasive and effective and integrated into society, our feminist movement has scarcely noticed it or addressed it all.

In America, we groom our boys to be soldiers. Most especially, the poor ones.

Working-class American boys are little more than indentured servants for the Secretary of Defense. Want to (maybe) go to college? Be prepared to kill for him. Want to (partially) avoid debt? Be prepared to give him your body. Want to get (shitty) healthcare? You must risk your life first. Want (even the slightest chance of) economic ascendency? Then ascend the ranks, boy. The hallmark of indentured servitude is that powerful people force economically desperate people to choose between signing away their bodies and enduring abject poverty. Our Secretary of Defense, arguably one of the most powerful men in the world, is more than willing to take the body of any boy who'll sign.

I switch tabs in my browser, from the Hasbro product page to the young adult version: an official recruitment ad for the U.S. Army, published on YouTube as "Be All You Can Be—U.S. Army's New Brand Trailer."

Trailer: Could they make it any clearer that they are selling a fictional narrative? That they're marketing a delusion?

The ad starts, ironically enough, with drone footage; we're flying over the American Southwest at dawn. Canyons and red rock spill out toward the horizon, yearning for the sun's auburn rays. The voiceover begins, a man's voice, the voice of God *himself*, deep and bassy with a touch of down-home charm: "*What does it mean when people say America is a land of opportunity?*"

The perspective shifts: we're flying over a suburban neighborhood now, a few cars inching sleepily in the early-morning light. America is waking up. "*It means we strive to be a nation of limitless possibilities.*" A dozen recruits run laps through idyllic green pasture in the shadow of a barn.

"*Exploring those possibilities isn't just an inclination. It's our greatest strength.*" We've switched to a diverse chorus of uniformed army recruits, talking heads contributing words to the collective. A woman in glasses with noticeably Spanish-accented English starts with "*The power to discover,*" followed by a Black man with a mustache and a German shepherd. Then an Asian American man: "*To redefine yourself.*" A Black woman: "*To improve yourself.*" A white guy: "*To challenge yourself.*" The next line is broken up between three speakers: "*To realize there's more in you than you ever knew that you could do.*"

I can't help but feel cynical about the gender diversity of the ad. It's obvious pandering—virtue signaling of the most insidious kind. As if actual recruitment is equally directed at women and men. As if our collective vision for the American military really is an army with women on the front lines of active combat. As if the Pentagon has a history of *caring* about American women, their bodies, or feminism writ large.

Neoliberal Greek chorus swelling—a culmination of melting pot fantasia, a rainbow of working-class bodies the army is now willing to exploit—the ad crests to the main refrain. Each person adds a slightly different emphasis to the words:

"*Be all you can be.*"

"*Be all you can be.*"

"*Be all you can be.*"

I toggle back and forth between the tabs in my browser.

Hasbro military toy. Army recruitment ad. Hasbro military toy. Army recruitment ad.

Which one is selling a product? Which one is official state propaganda?

At a certain point, I can no longer discern a difference.

• • •

I switch tabs again—my browser a microcosm of violence—this time to a documentary short from *The New York Times* entitled *The Army We Had*.

The documentary begins in 2003. When I was sprouting pubic hair and traveling to Hiroshima, filmmakers Petra Epperlein and Michael Tucker were following the U.S. Army's 2nd Battalion to Baghdad for their first deployment. The footage chronicles young, foolhardy boys— I hesitate to call them *optimistic;* I hesitate to call them *men*—on the precipice of something they do not yet understand. In their late teens and early twenties, they are callow and brash. Through the camera, you can almost feel the raptorial, succubus-like tentacles of the U.S. War Machine at work, preying upon youthful exuberance, consuming boyish raucousness, extracting nationalist naïveté.

One young man says, unaware of the devastation waiting at his doorstep, oblivious to how the world will view this war two decades hence,

> *"I mean, how many people can say they're combat veterans? That's—that's awesome. Nothing can beat that."*

Another young man freestyles for the camera. His fellow soldiers beatbox:

> *"They got us out here, Baghdad, life is hard.*
> *Got us pulling fucking two hours of guard.*
> *Then they up it up to eight between twelve.*
> *I don't give a fuck, I think I'm stuck in hell. Uh.*
> *But I'd rather be there instead of jail."*

We cut abruptly to a third soldier:

> *"The area I come from is very small. Not a lot of opportunities for people fresh out of high school. So it was either community college*

or go do something: travel the world, get paid for it, experience places like this."

Then, in an instant, the documentary flashes forward twenty years. The boys have come home and become men, faces lined with age. On the tail end of the COVID pandemic, most of them now in their late thirties or early forties, they are asked to offer reflections on their time in Baghdad:

"Now that I have a kid, sometimes I find myself thinking, 'Is he gonna end up going to some war that ends up not doing any good for the world and receive a bunch of shitty care afterwards, too?'"

These are reflections we'd rather avoid.

"We were in Baghdad for a few days and then we were in a firefight outside the Abu Hanifa Mosque and it was just totally bizarre. Just fucking gunfire everywhere. A couple of RPGs. And I was just thinking, 'What the fuck am I doing here?' And that question never went away. I don't know how to explain the war to myself. And have yet to have any clear thought of like 'Yes, we actually made a difference there.' Because we didn't. At all. There was no difference fucking made. Maybe [it was even] for the worse."

Reflections we'd rather erase.

"We're not defending our country anymore. I know we haven't defended our country in a while."

Footage from the past is now interspersed with footage from the present. Time falls apart.

"Once you join, you have no politics. You're property. You go where they send you."

These reflections, I begin to realize, are not just of them.

> *"It was dark out and I couldn't see my fingers, basically. I was hoping I still had my fingers. I couldn't tell where I was shot. I just knew my arm was numb."*

These are reflections of *us all*.
Reflections of how we, as a nation, treat men.
Reflections of how comfortable we are destroying the bodies of mere boys.

> *"IEDs are the scariest. Gunfire and crap like that, that shit don't bother me, y'know? It's whatever. But IEDs? They had shit in garbage, man, and it could be anywhere. . . . I still cringe when I pass garbage. Ask my wife, she goes nuts. I avoid garbage like the plague, on the road."*

At the end of the film, a man who joined the military to serve along-side his older brother dismounts a motorcycle outside a biker bar. His brother is now dead.

Combat didn't kill him—he survived all four of his deployments to Iraq and Afghanistan—but the trauma of trying to *live with what he'd experienced* did. He died by suicide in 2020. The man pats the now-empty seat of the motorcycle—his older brother's old bike—and breaks. Bikers throw their arms around him, protecting him from the camera as he sobs into their chests.

> *"When shit gets dark and you're thinking about ending it or whatever, you call someone. [My brother] Jason was that phone call for me and I was always that phone call for him. So it was hard for me when he did what he did. . . . Why didn't he call me? Why didn't he call? I don't have that answer."*

Tears carve tracks down his face. In the final shot of the documentary, the camera leaves him behind at the bar, driving off into the distance.

· · ·

Take a moment, okay?
Take a breath.

· · ·

The credits roll. I scroll through the comments on the video. The very
first comment has twelve thousand upvotes.

> I don't know one veteran, myself included, who feels like they
> made a difference. We had no mission apart from "wait until
> someone fires at you and then fire back." We didn't bring free-
> dom and democracy; we tore the country apart and left it in
> chaos and ruin. And we treated innocent people like they were
> terrorists. When people call me a hero and thank me for my
> service, I flinch. I feel like I should be punished for what I've
> done, not praised.

I wish I could let myself stop, but I keep scrolling.

> I lost about 20 friends to suicide, drugs, and late night car
> accidents after my service. Hurts . . .

These comments, each bolstered by thousands of likes, are excruciating.

> I spent time in Tikrit, Ramadi, Baghdad International, Mosul
> and a bunch of other places and now I'm living in my car. God
> bless America.

At long last, I close my browser.
When will we claim that this, too, is gender-based violence?

· · ·

American men are angry right now. American men are frustrated: with women, with feminism, with social justice, with politics, with seemingly everything. We all feel it on some level. Whether it's online or at a political podium, their anger is raw, visceral, and everywhere.

It reminds me of something that happened to me when I was living in New York. One day, I began to notice a foul smell in my apartment. It was something like half a whiff at first, subtle enough that you think to yourself: *Did I smell something?* I didn't notice it again for the rest of the day. I figured it must've been a fluke.

But the next morning, after it'd rained and the air was heavy with moisture, it was clear that I *had* smelled something. Somewhere in my apartment, something terrible was amiss. I sniffed and sniffed, following my nose, attempting to figure out what it was and where it was coming from, to no avail. I grew frustrated, trying and failing to locate the stench. I ripped through the apartment, slamming drawers, hurling open cabinets, huffing and breaking things and swearing to high heaven as I scoured. I was incensed.

Not being able to figure out why my apartment *smelled dead* was infuriating and nauseating in equal parts. For three more days, the smell tormented me and my roommates. For three days, we grew angrier and more exasperated, failing to sniff it out. It felt like losing my mind, for something to be so obviously wrong without explanation.

As it turned out, a small mouse had made its way into our hallway closet, nestled itself between the folded layers of my roommate's winter comforter, and died. It sat there for weeks, decomposing under our noses, before we found it.

Men are angry like that. They smell something awful and hypocritical in the world but have yet to find the carcass. They know something is wrong; they just can't quite *locate it.*

Instead of helping them place their anger, I'm afraid we've denied that there's a stench in the first place. We've told men, en masse, that the anger they feel is from nothing. Is illegitimate. That there is, in fact, no cause. That the stench they *think* they're smelling is all in their heads. In spite of how much we protest when they gaslight *us,* I'm afraid we've chosen to gaslight the living hell out of *them.*

That feeling of injustice deep in your gut isn't real, we say. You're a man. Things are fair for you. Stop being angry at nothing, we say. There is no dead mouse. The apartment smells fine.

It's irrefutable that men's present anger is lacking in sufficient specificity and articulation. As a feminist movement, this should not be alien to us. There was a time, half a century ago, when women's anger and frustration were equally inarticulate. In 1963, Betty Friedan wrote *The Feminine Mystique* in search of illuminating what she deemed to be "the problem that has no name," the problem that "lay buried, unspoken for many years in the minds of American women . . . a strange stirring, a sense of dissatisfaction, a yearning." Her words from the sixties still ring true today:

> It is no longer possible to ignore that voice, to dismiss the desperation of so many American women. This is not what being a woman means, no matter what the experts say. *For human suffering there is a reason; perhaps the reason has not been found because the right questions have not been asked, or pressed far enough.*

Might we now, sixty years later, say the same thing of men?

Without a movement to teach them or an analysis to guide them, their present anger lacks the sort of precision that could help us feel comfortable with it. It's anger that stems from abstract knowledge, a gut feeling that injustice is being done: words on the tip of the tongue, but never quite spoken. Men don't know exactly *what* the injustice is, but they perceive it nonetheless. *Something* is off. A stench without cause. An odor emanating from *somewhere*.

Here's the thing: paucity of specificity and inadequate articulation do not render men's current frustration illegitimate; if anything, they bolster the case for further investigation and lay bare the urgency of this historical moment. It's time we entertain the idea that men might be picking up on something real. There *has* been hypocrisy, and it *is* worth being angry about.

Men look at the feminist movement and—subconsciously, I think—

ask themselves: *What is feminism doing to protect me? I need protection, too, you know.*

In general, we dismiss this feeling. *Protect you? After what you've spent centuries doing to us? Protect yourself, asshole.*

Though I understand where it comes from, I'm afraid this sort of terse reaction stops us from asking the important questions. Namely: If we say we abhor the violence of men and want it to cease, what are we doing to *stop boys from being recruited into it*?

We have not embodied gender equality sufficiently. We have worked tirelessly to protect women and girls from the violence that is all too prevalent in their lives but have said next to nothing about the violence facing men and boys. We have fought tooth and nail against institutions that predominantly brutalize women but have done little to combat the institutions—institutions like military bases, prisons, and police training facilities—that so often brutalize men, too. I think that's in part because men operate (and sometimes benefit from) these institutions, but that's no reason to ignore them. Just because a man is in charge, that doesn't mean the institution is *safe for other men*. Men and boys need protection from the violence of powerful men every bit as much as women and girls do. Powerful men—men who are used to enacting violence with impunity—are a threat to us all.

What's worse, we seem to have decried men's anger wholesale. We have labeled angry men as bad men and, in so doing, have lost vital nuance. Because they cannot articulate it to us in sufficient language—because they have yet to locate the precise source of the stench—we have denied any possibility that the anger men feel might be righteous.

Here's the thing: men *should* be angry, and their anger *is* righteous, albeit frequently misplaced. If the culture that raised you sees you as little more than a future agent of military violence, it would be strange for you *not to be angry*. Men have been ignored. They have been brutalized. They have been told that it is *their job* to do the policing and soldiering and brutalizing on behalf of us all. They have endured grave gender-based violence, and rather than help them locate it, we've mostly told them they're making the whole thing up.

Most effective social justice movements are predicated on anger, on people being so fed up and exasperated with how they're being treated, they're spurred to action. Why are we *denying* men's anger when we should be *helping them better articulate it* and then *using it*? The anger men feel at how they're treated by the world is not only productive, it is necessary.

We should not ask men to renounce the anger they feel about the violence they have been groomed to enact; because doing so entails asking them to renounce their belief in their own dignity and person-hood. We should make use of that anger, instead; focus it, hone it, fun-nel it into tearing down institutions that need tearing down, channel it into creating a kinder and less violent world.

What if we encouraged men to trust their noses instead of instruct-ing them to relinquish their frustration? What if, instead of spending energy *denying* that something is amiss, we dedicate our energy to *af-firming* that something is off and join men as they search for the source of the stench? What if we say to men, "We agree. Something isn't right. Your body and psyche *are* being exploited to nefarious ends. You *were* groomed unfairly," and then rage and scream and investigate alongside them?

This is where I am flummoxed and exhausted by contemporary pop-ular feminism, if only because it is so *obvious*. We will volunteer for hours outside an abortion clinic, helping to protect women who are entering from being harassed. We do so because it is both vital and necessary. We do so because we believe in a world where people have agency over their own bodies. But we do next to nothing about military recruitment centers or police academies, institutions whose sole job is to *instill violence in men*—to take their bodies and their minds and ex-ploit them for the violent ends of the ruling class.

Can we stop scratching our heads and pretending we do not know how America became a nation of such violence? Can we stop acting surprised when, after raising our boys as child soldiers, their violence turns back against us? Can we own up to the truth: that we cannot ask boys to conceptualize ruthlessly killing faraway brown people, then reasonably expect them to turn it off when they come home? That we cannot raise boys to fantasize about guns and war throughout their childhood, then act surprised when they shoot up a school? That we cannot raise our boys to be *fine* with abusing Afghani prisoners, then expect them not to abuse *us,* too?

As a feminist movement, it's high time we pick a lane. It's time we take a stand with veterans and against the military. It's time we declare that we're no longer okay living in a violent world. We must decide that the dignity and bodily autonomy of men and boys matter to us enough to fight for them. We must rage against the myriad institutions that insist on making murderers out of our little boys. As a feminist movement, we must categorically decry war, in all its forms.

"But what about when military force and war are necessary?" you might be thinking.

I have not seen "justified American war" in my lifetime. I have only ever seen George W. Bush and Colin Powell knowingly lie to the United Nations in order to provide American corporate interests with an invasion of Iraq. I have only ever seen trillions of dollars go to buy fighter jets when an increasing portion of Americans cannot afford healthcare or buy food. The Military-Industrial Complex has ruled America with an iron fist since the day of my birth. I have never known an ethical American Military, free from corruption. Such an idea is, at this juncture, nothing more than wishful thinking.

What I *have* seen is the way in which the American military preys on all of us and our imaginations. What I *have* seen is the way in which our feminist work is made impossible by the ceaseless child grooming of the U.S. War Apparatus. What I *have* seen is the way in which the Department of Defense sways Hollywood and encourages movie studios to churn out military propaganda, on repeat, ad nauseam, to the entire world. What I *have* seen is Hasbro and G.I. Joe and Tom Cruise and every single person involved in the *Top Gun* franchise knowingly sell you a lie: That going to war is fun. That going to war makes you strong. That going to war makes you *sexy* and *cool.* That going to war makes you *powerful. That going to war makes you a man.*

And I'm absolutely fucking sick of it.

. . .

Caring for men means speaking up against the Pentagon. It means challenging the military and its strategy of predation and perpetual war. It means caring for veterans who have fallen prey to this system and have subsequently been brutalized.

And it means acknowledging that most of us owe veterans an apology.

At least I know I do.

For most of my life, I viewed veterans as nationalist meatheads, brutes who signed up to kill for America and therefore could not be trusted. Because of the violence they were compelled to enact, I didn't feel safe around them. Veterans and people serving in the military made me uncomfortable. And so I was silent.

That's why I owe an apology to veterans, especially men, whose bodies and minds have been so vitiated by the military. I confess: I did not know how to see you as a full person. Men like you scared me. You scared me because I did not connect your childhood to mine. I did not account for the ways that you, too, were molded, that you, too, were coerced. And I did not sit with your suffering because it was too difficult to make sense of.

I'm ready to fix that. I'm prepared to acknowledge that, through ignoring the suffering of veterans, refusing to engage with the violent acculturation of young men, and neglecting to make those things part of my feminist cause, I have diminished the personhood of us all. I'm prepared to say, categorically and without caveat, that there is no gender equality without justice and care for those who, on the basis of their gender, were coerced into enacting state violence. I'm ready to atone for saying next to nothing as millions of boys were indoctrinated and turned into soldiers. I'm prepared to make amends to the boys, now men, whose brutalization my tax dollars funded. Supporting you and caring for you does not mean I support war, but I will no longer let my aversion *to war* become an aversion *to you*. I will no longer demand bodily autonomy for *myself* without remembering to demand it for you, too.

Grooming boys into soldiers is the American Way, but it doesn't have to be. We can change it.

It begins by acknowledging that we live in a nation of child soldiers who became men. It ends by learning to value *and fight for* the humanity of our boys.

We have spent centuries fighting the imperative that *a woman's place is in the home.*

Are we now brave enough to fight its equally oppressive corollary: that *a man's place is on the battlefield?*

P.S.

In case you're thinking, "Well, Jacob, women also serve in the armed forces." Don't think that hasn't occurred to me. Women, queer people, and trans people are also poor. We, too, face economic coercion. Military service is often the only opportunity for us to escape the cycle of poverty as well. Which is why many women and queer people and trans people still enlist.

That being said, we do not build the bedrock of American womanhood on the idea of women (or trans people or queer people) becoming soldiers. American women are, fortunately, exempt from the brunt of that cultural pressure. Luckily for me, the American military is also still ambivalent about queers and trans people serving. They may *tolerate* us serving, but they aren't exactly *hoping* we will. If you are queer or trans or a woman and you enlisted in an attempt to escape poverty, my heart goes out to you. You were forced into making an impossible choice. You deserve to have your economic needs met without having to put down your life, limbs, and mental health as collateral.

But if you are queer or trans or a woman and, without overwhelming economic or social pressure, still opted into the violence of men in order to prove a point? Then we should probably have a separate conversation.

Also: the fact that I can say "he" and refer to every Secretary of Defense in American History should tell you something. Not even Obama or Biden cared to fix *that* gender gap.

Men are
eleven times
more likely
than women
to be killed
at work.

THE RITES OF MEN

I *really* like ritual, okay?

I'm obsessed with the stuff. It's why I excelled at both summer camp and church growing up. *Oh, there's a song we have to sing every morning at 7 A.M. the very moment we wake up? We have to greet the day with a big sing-along? And then there's a little gratitude prayer song, with motions, that we have to sing as a group before we can even eat breakfast?* Sign me up.

It's also why I get along so well at a monastery. Things that would drive others crazy—like starting your day with an hour of silent meditation at 5:30 A.M. with a hundred other people in a giant meditation hall—make me giddy. Do I ever meditate on my own? Nah. Do I *ever* wake up at 5:30 A.M. of my own volition? Absolutely not. But make it a *ritual* that I get to do with *other people* to cement the abstraction of a *collective community bond* and, babe, I am *horny for it.*

You ever signed a blood oath? I have.

Why? Because it was a *ritual,* goddamnit.

Lemme back up.

. . .

Duke University, a school that I am cursed to call my alma mater, is a creepy place. It's beautiful, what with the Gothic stone and gargoyles and buttresses and whatnot, but in a scary way. You set foot on campus and you just *feel it*: this is the kind of place with a crypt. With, like, *actual bodies* buried in it. And you wouldn't be wrong. Duke Chapel has a crypt; the Duke family has stashed a non-negligible portion of their familial bones there.

All the old buildings were funded by tobacco money. All the new buildings were funded by David Rubenstein, Duke's Iraq War profiteer of choice. Add to that the fact that Duke receives a ton of research money from the Department of Defense every year and you'd be correct to assume that the entire place is metaphorically drenched in blood.

Which made my undergraduate experience tense. On the one hand, I wanted to live the "I go to school in a castle and am therefore a hybrid between Hermione Granger and a princess" fantasy; on the other, I knew that humanity would be better off (and probably avoid another financial crisis) if a hell pit opened under the chapel and the entire institution was abruptly swallowed into the earth.

It was a very alienating place to be queer—it was also a very alienating place to *have a conscience,* but I digress—and part of what made that alienation most profound for me was the Greek system. The fraternities and sororities.

The frats ruled everything in a manner that, circa the mid-2010s, already felt anachronistic. They determined who won student elections, who got jobs, who was cool, and who you were supposed to want to fuck. I coveted those things. It would've been nice to have been deemed fuckable *once* during undergrad, when my body and my ass were at their tightest. It would've been cool to have a phalanx of frat boys backing *me*—and also maybe fucking me, but again, I digress—when I ran in a student election.

But the main thing I envied was the ritual of it all. The entire fraternity system had low-grade-fascist-summer-camp energy, and I wanted *in.* They did complex, ornate hazing rituals. They had paddles that they were made to carry around campus for months at a time. They had dress codes and secret chants and pledges they made to one another. They went on trips together and planned parties together and did all sorts of fun, ritualistic shit.

Did I want to do a keg stand while simultaneously being forced to recite the Declaration of Independence? Not exactly. Sure, I'd do that if two hot dudes agreed to hold my legs, but no, that wasn't my primary desire. Did I want *ritual*? Did I want a communal, time-tested *process* whereby I could feel that I truly *belonged*? Did I want a moment where I completed some task and was deemed somehow *worthy* and *part of something*? Absolutely. I wanted that more than anything.

Other than the gender-binary-reinforcing-Goldman-Sachs-teet-sucking-capitalist-fuckity-fuck, *that* was what drove me crazy about fraternities. Those bros got *ritual*. My socialist faggot ass got jack.

Which was why I was stoked when, spring semester junior year, I found a hand-addressed letter in my student mailbox. My student mailbox was usually just filled with junk mail. Or bills or whatever. Boring stuff. Which was what made *this* letter really stand out. The text on the front was *swirly*. I think it was even sealed with wax.

I opened it and found something minimal and delicious, to the following effect:

You have been chosen.
Tell no one.
For further instruction, go to Perkins Library.
F1923 J78 1965
—L.H.

I clutched the letter close to my chest and looked around. Was anyone watching me? Who'd sent this? What was it? Also, *hell yeah*.

That evening, I went to the library, descended into the stacks, and found the book referenced in the note. It was a biography, in French—how did they know I took French *in high school*?—about the Haitian revolutionary leader Toussaint Louverture. When I pulled the book from the shelf, another note fell out, also minimal.

You have been chosen.
Tell no one.

*Be at the corner of Towerview and Science Drive
at 11:37 p.m. sharp on Thursday evening.
Come alone.
—L.H.*

I squealed, caught myself, then did a sotto voce, library-appropriate freak-out.

This was *totally* what I'd thought it was. Bitch, I was being recruited for a secret society.

(Or being really elaborately pranked, but this was a lot of effort for a prank.)

Duke has a longish tradition of secret societies. Not as long as, like, Yale or something where you have secret societies with literal American presidents as members, but a tradition nonetheless.

The two Duke secret societies I knew about were both gender-segregated and gross. There was the Trident Society, a group composed of douchey frat men who were annoying and, circa 2013, definitely didn't know where the clitoris was. And then there was the Order of the White Duchy—a secret society for women that, honestly, I'm still not fully sure exists.

I knew that Trident existed for a fact, because one of my friends had infiltrated it. Their induction ceremony was out of a movie. They summoned inductees to the top of the Duke Chapel bell tower—a 210-foot-high vantage point from which you can overlook all of campus like some sort of frat-boy child-god, a place you can get to only by ascending a medieval, curved stone staircase that spirals as it ascends—and told them they were part of the thing. They got access to the bell tower because they were friendly with the staff who ran the Chapel and they'd unlock it for them.

One of my friends, a reporter for the student newspaper, had done some digging, figured out when the induction ceremony was happening, and literally *snuck up to the top of the chapel after them.* When he arrived, unannounced, and was like, "Hey, secret society, you've been outed—what is this extrajudicial nonsense?," one of the members of Trident, a student who served as the Young Trustee on the Duke Board for a number of years, manhandled him, shoved him back down the spiraling Gothic stairwell, and slammed the door in his face.

So, yeah. These things were real. Real enough that when a different campus reporter friend emailed a prominent administrator who was rumored to *also* be a member of Trident about the matter, the administrator responded by saying, in summation, "No, don't worry, Trident isn't real. I don't know anything about secret societies on campus, and if they existed we would most certainly subject them to the same rules as everyone else and shut them down for operating without university approval." Which would've been a great, perfectly unsuspicious-seeming response if it weren't for the fact that he'd accidentally cc'd the *same student who'd tackled my friend at the top of the chapel* on his response instead of bcc'ing him (which is what he'd clearly meant to do). "There are no secret societies at Duke. Which is why I have, out of nowhere, cc'd the exact student y'all saw at the top of the Chapel on this email."*

It's why I was shocked to be holding the invitation in front of me. I didn't know that a third secret society existed. It was *actually a secret.* And if they were inviting a sequin-sporting punk like me, I figured, it must be real different from the others.

That Thursday, I showed up at the designated spot and was approached by a senior I recognized, who proceeded to hand me a blindfold. I voluntarily tied it around my head and was instructed to wait. A few minutes later, someone's hand was placed in mine, and we started walking away from campus and into the forest. After twenty minutes or so of walking blindfolded through the dark, we arrived at a clearing in the woods, arranged ourselves in a circle, and were each given a candle to hold. Once our candles were lit, our blindfolds were ceremonially

---

*To be fair, this administrator was well known for being an absolute scoundrel, corrupt as hell, and an idiot. A few years after I graduated, he literally *hit one of the dining hall staff with his car,* a Black woman (because it's Duke—so of course almost all the blue-collar workers who make the place run are Black or brown), purportedly called her the N-word because *she'd* gotten in the way of *his car,* and *wasn't even fired,* in spite of widespread student protest.

removed, and we could finally see everyone else who'd been chosen. The leaders explained to us that we'd each been selected to be a member of Lower House, a new, gender-neutral, intentionally diverse secret society founded for those who fought for justice. Or something. They had a great pitch. I was totally in. A start-up secret society for social justice weirdos? Hell yeah.

Then they got out a piece of "parchment," a dozen or so needles, and a lighter. The parchment had some sort of pledge on it that we each had to read and sign. They passed each needle through the flame of the lighter to fully sanitize it, pricked our fingers, and had each of us deposit a drop of our blood on the page next to our signature.

At no point in this entire saga—not even when I was asked to sign a blood oath—did it occur to me that I could've just said no. *That's* how committed I am to ritual.

I could've easily been like, "Yeah, I'm super down for this analysis of power and creating a secret society for the weirdos and Marxists and cool kids, but I am not putting my blood on a piece of paper, dude," and everyone would've been like, "Yeah, no, you're right, that's a little much—we just made up this ritual a few weeks ago, so we've got a few kinks to work out." And everything would've been fine.

But the thing is that I didn't *want* to. I *wanted* to take a lefty blood oath. I *wanted* to be blindfolded and brought into the woods. I *wanted* to stand in a circle with candles, marking our collective commitment to one another. And as someone who'd felt like an outsider on that campus from the moment I'd set foot on it, it felt powerful to finally have a ritual that wanted *me*.

Which, at last, brings me to my point: rituals are fundamental. They are a core, unshakable part of what it means to be human, to live in a society, and to be part of a community. Without ritual, without signposts and demarcations of change, life simply passes us by. Sure, you technically arrived in a new state the moment you drove across its geographic border, but you don't really *feel* you've arrived until you see the sign declaring, WELCOME TO KANSAS.

In the context of gender, ritual is as old as human civilization. In cultures throughout the world and across time, societies, tribes, communities, and metropolises alike have devised endless rituals for demarcating the end of childhood and the beginning of adulthood.

From profound religious rituals like bat and bar mitzvahs to silly ones like sweet sixteens and proms, from going on your first solo walk around the neighborhood and getting your first cellphone to testing for your driver's license and graduating from high school, rituals are everywhere.

Among these rituals of transitioning into adulthood, most have a fundamental flaw. They are almost always vigorously gender segregated and heterosexist. Your mitzvah must be "bat" or "bar." Only young women get quinceañeras—technically a young man can have a quinceañero, but it's rarely ever done. Until just a few years ago, you earned your Eagle Scout designation only as a man, among men, in a men's organization. You get your prom night, but it's only really meaningful if you have a date and "lose your virginity" with them (and until *very* recently, your date needed to be a heterosexual one).

In general, the rituals that do exist around the world for becoming a man involve violence or sex or both. Get circumcised without anesthesia at the age of twelve. Go on the hunt, shoot your first stag, then wipe its blood on your face. Stuff your hand into a glove filled with bullet ants, leave it there for ten minutes while they sting you over and over, and don't you dare flinch. Work your first-ever shift in the mine. Climb into in a canoe, go down the river, and be presented with a sword—which is obviously a metaphor for both your dick *and* the violence you'll do now that you're a man.

I am not fully against all of these rituals. I am okay with the idea that becoming an adult, *in part,* means enduring pain, doing hard work, challenging yourself, pushing your body's limits, and potentially learning to (sustainably, ethically, and safely) hunt.

My objection to these rituals is that they are almost entirely done in the absence of women. Most rituals for attaining manhood are performed only in the presence of other men. And it doesn't take much thought to understand how that makes them breeding grounds for sexism and misogyny. What these rituals imply, in cultures throughout the world, is that what you're doing in the ritual is something women *cannot do* or *are not capable of*. It is the exclusion of women from these rituals that makes them so distasteful, i.e.,

> To become a man, you must kill a deer. You do so only with other men because women cannot kill.

> To become a man, you and the other boys must go into the woods alone and survive. If you make it out alive, you are a man. Only men do this because women simply couldn't manage.

> To become a man, you are presented with a gun by your father. Your sister is not presented with a gun because girls can't shoot.

When done to the exclusion of women, any sweetness embodied in these rituals goes bitter. The sexism burns what could otherwise be a yummy loaf of bread.

In the absence of women, *any* ritual where boys become men will also inherently be a ritual where boys become misogynist pieces of shit. It is structurally impossible to reclaim any ritual of arriving at manhood without also reclaiming sexism. Which is to say nothing of how these rituals affect queer kids and trans kids and weird kids and sensitive kids and kids who are a little socially awkward.

As a culture, we have correctly identified that rituals where boys become men are mostly sexist and shitty. We have grown to have a distaste for such rituals, and they have fallen out of favor in popular media and many social circles. Rightfully so. These rituals are often designed to create violent men who view women as weak; self-actualized men who view women as inferior; decisive men who view women as vacillatory; or cunning men who view women as stupid.

These rituals are designed against us. So, in many cases, we've fought them and defeated them and won.

But then we foolishly threw in the towel. We got rid of the bad thing. We rid ourselves of rituals that encouraged men to see us as weak. That's all we had to do, right? Problem solved, yeah?

I'm afraid that in our quest for postmodernity and gender equality, we've lost something vital. We've dumped the baby with the sexist bathwater. Where we once had meaning-making rituals for marking the pivotal transition between childhood and adulthood, we've simply left a vacuum.

Is it any wonder that boys these days are miserable and lost? Is it any wonder that modern life feels empty? Is it any wonder that boys and men have become so profoundly isolated and lonely? Deprived of ritual—especially *intergenerational* ritual—life as we know it loses most meaning. It becomes drudgery, devoid of magic, glory, continuity, and significance. At some point you stop being a kid and start being an adult. But at which point? When?

When you graduate high school? *What if you don't finish high school?*
When you find a partner? *What if you can't find a partner?*
When you buy a house? *What if you can't afford a house?*

The answer to something bad isn't a vacuum; it's something different. You can't abolish anything ever. You can only ever replace it. And young men have.

Devoid of healthy rituals for marking the difference between boyhood and manhood, many young men have turned to the internet, predatory social media, and fantasies of violence to fill the void. But it doesn't work. Nothing can replace ritual. Nothing. Not money, not power, not fame, not sex, *nothing*. Ritual in a community of care is irreplaceable in the human experience.

When we get rid of sexist practices, we must always offer a replacement, propose a new model, or come up with a better pitch. It must be out with the old, in with the new. Not out with the old, in with the nothing.

Because here's the thing: children must become adults. Boys need a healthy, exciting way to become men.*

It is possible for boys to become men without also becoming mi-

---

*If they want to, of course. Boys can also become women. Or sophisticated nonbinary authors.

sogynists. It is possible to become a man in a way that is good for your soul, sense of autonomy, *and* capacity to love and respect people of all genders.

And it's, like, not even that hard, y'all. Simply stop segregating rituals of adulthood by gender *et voilà!* We've done it. Problem solved. There is almost nothing a boy needs to learn about being a man that he cannot also learn from a woman. A woman can teach a boy to kill. A woman can teach a boy to fight. A woman can teach a boy to make fire. A woman can teach a boy to [insert additional tropes here].

Transitioning from childhood to adulthood is a universal experience, one best undertaken with the knowledge of the *entire* community: men, women, and nonbinary people alike. Every boy needs the wisdom of women, the wisdom of men, and the wisdom of gender nonconforming people. And we owe it to all boys, girls, and nonbinary kids to build beautiful rituals for entering adulthood.

If there's one thing I learned from being inducted into an (ultimately doomed) secret society* in undergrad, it's that you can just make ritual up. Getting blindfolded, walked into the woods, handed a candle, and pricked with a needle was something that no one had ever done before, but that didn't matter to me because, without context, it felt like something people had been doing at Duke for generations.

Tell someone to pick up a rock, then tell them that rock is their special rock, and *presto,* it kind of *is.* Write a poem for someone to read, tell them it's the official thing they must read in order to become an adult, and *wham bam thank you ma'am* that poem will feel like it's been around for ages. Tell everyone that on Wednesdays we wear pink and in two years "Pink Wednesdays" will already feel like a time-honored tradition at your high school or senior center. People are always making stuff up. We've been doing it since the dawn of civilization. We can make up anything we want. Humanity is a treasure. A supple, flexible, adaptable, overly sentimental treasure.

---

*Turns out, it isn't okay to pass around a half-gallon of whiskey in a Drama Department classroom late at night unless you're an *established* secret society with pre-existing provostal relationships and generational nepotism on your side.

And because I am someone who adores ritual with all of my heart, because I'm the type of freak who still pines after spells and incantations as a thirty-four-year-old, because I'm the type of weirdo who adores hokey dances and spiritual rites alike, I've taken it upon myself to come up with some. A few test models. Ways for boys to become men alongside girls becoming women alongside nonbinary kids becoming chaos incarnate.

Use whatever you'd like. I give these to you free of charge.

Option 1: Eighteen Stones

In the eighteen days leading up to your eighteenth birthday, you must go with your parents to collect a stone from eighteen places that were significant in your life. Places that made you who you are today. On the day of your eighteenth birthday, you must carry each of these stones up a mountain, one by one, and place them at the top. The mountain is scaled to your ability. It's a metaphor. If you're in a wheelchair, it can be a longish distance to wheel yourself. Motorized scooter, same idea. It's the accomplishment and time it takes that counts; however you do it, it should take all day. It should push your body to its limits, whatever that means for you. As your body aches and tires with each trip, you are to meditate on the fact that one day, your body will fail you completely. One day, you will die. To live as an adult is to embrace that death is real. To become an adult is to embrace your eventual end. On the last trip, at sunset, your family and loved ones gather alongside you. Everyone in your community. And all together, with your entire community walking behind you, you lead them to the top of the mountain and place the final stone. At the top, each person who took the journey with you lights a candle in your honor, sharing a wish of love and gratitude for you and your life. Then, when you are ready to leave childhood behind and embrace man/woman/personhood, you lead your community down the mountain. You are now an adult.

Option 2: The Meal

On your seventeenth birthday, you are given the gift of seeds and a bow. Throughout the next year, you are taught by members of your community how to cultivate food, grow a garden, kill an animal (optional), skin it (also optional), and dress the meat (if you aren't vegetarian. You can also, like, learn how to make tofu. It's chill). Throughout the year, you preserve food, pickle vegetables you grow, smoke meats, and learn to can things. Then, on your eighteenth birthday, you spend the day preparing a meal. You make everything from scratch, with food you have grown with your own hands. At midday, your friends and family gather around you and celebrate you by eating the feast you have prepared. When everyone has finished eating, they turn their chairs away from the table, facing outward in a giant circle or rectangle or whatever shape your table is. You go around the circle, one by one. As you approach your loved one, you take their hand in yours, breathe eighteen breaths together, then say the following words:

> *For eighteen years, you have nurtured, cared, and provided for me.*
>
> *Through the grace of your love and protection, I was able to be a child.*
>
> *Now it is my turn.*
>
> *From this moment forward, I will provide and care for you, so that with each act of nurture, you may remember the joys of your own childhood.*
>
> *The meaning of adulthood lies in the power to preserve the joys of childhood for those you love.*
>
> *May I do this for as long as we both shall live.*

And each person at the table responds by saying:

You were a beautiful child.

You are a beautiful child, still.

May your childhood live on and on.

Then you both say:

Amen.

And seal the bond with a kiss on the forehead.

You do this with each person gathered at the table. And now, my son, you have become a man. But, like, not a misogynistic one. So that's cool.

Option 3: Skydive, Cliff Dive, or Bungee Jump

On your eighteenth birthday, your parents rent an airplane (if you're a spoiled brat), drive you to a bungee-jumping facility (if you're rich but not *rich* rich), or take you to a cliff/quarry/ waterfall with a large, ceremonial jump into the water (if you're not a brat). Your parents stand on either side of you, grab your hands, and say, "YOU READY KID? ADULTHOOD IS FUCK-ING NUTS." Then you all jump out of a plane or off a bridge or a cliff together. After that you go get burgers and fries and milkshakes to celebrate the fact that you're cool as hell and just jumped off something really tall, and it's a whole metaphor for the abject terror of having to pay your own bills and be a man and stuff.

Option 4: Do Psychedelic Mushrooms (or LSD or Ayahuasca or Peyote)

Take a heroic dose. Get your face spiritually ripped off and your ego shredded to bits, then talk to God for a while. If you do it right, you'll become a man, a woman, a baby, *and* a fifteen-thousand-year-old tree, all in the same night. This is the most economical version. Also, psychedelics have been proven to be pretty much the most effective medicinal treatment for depression and PTSD out there, and being an adult is *depressing and traumatizing as hell,* so it's good to get ahead of that a little bit.

Option 5: Just Run Off into the Fucking Woods

On the day before your eighteenth birthday, your parents drive you out to a National Park and you set off into the woods alone, at the crack of dawn (with, like, a satellite phone or something in case of emergency. And bear spray and stuff. And proper safety training). You bring no food: only water, a journal, and a tent. You hike alone, deep enough into the woods to feel complete solitude, then set up camp. You spend that day, that night, and the next morning in the woods alone. All on your own. No screens, no TV, just you and nature. Quiet. You are to contemplate your life. You are to gaze at the stars. You are to feel the pangs of hunger rumble in your belly and feel gratitude for all the food you've been given over the course of your life. You are to pray. You are to sing. You are to do all of these things in celebration of the miraculous, terrifying gift that is consciousness. The morning of your eighteenth birthday, you are to find the most beautiful flower you can, pick it, and tie it to a tree. This flower is your childhood. You are to gaze at this flower in reverence. You are to watch it wilt. You are to thank your childhood and all those who made it possible. Then you are to say goodbye to the flower and your childhood both. You hike out of the woods and return to your family, who will throw you a big fuckin' surprise birthday party with all of your favorite foods. It is not, in fact, a surprise. Because it's part of the ritual. But you are to pretend to be surprised. Pretending is an important skill of adulthood, as is feigning enthusiasm. You are now a man.

Option 6: Rent a Bouncy House

But *this* bouncy house is an *adult* bouncy house for *adults only*.

I'm telling you, you can make a ritual out of *anything*. What's important is that we *do so*. With intention. With gusto. With the goal of creating a sacred, inclusive, generative space for boys to become men.*

---

*Boys who *want* to, of course. If you're a boy who wants to become a woman or a gender-free demigod or a fairy instead, that's sick, too, and you are my type of people. Hot trans bitches *also* deserve to carry rocks up a mountain. Which is the other beauty of gender-neutral rituals for adulthood. Trans and nonbinary folks like me can participate seamlessly, *without* annoying the living hell out of everyone like we usually do.

In 1990,
fifty-five percent
of American men
reported having at least
six close friends;
today
only twenty-seven percent
do.

One-third
of men over forty-five years old
reported that they've felt
lonely or isolated
from those around them
for more than ten years.

Fifteen percent
of men
have no close friendships
at all.

BIG DICK IDIOCY

Having a penis is a mixed bag. I've pretty much always felt this way.

When I was sixteen, my AP Psychology teacher taught us about Freud's theory on penis envy.

My gut response was: *What does some Austrian dude who wants to fuck his mom know about what women think?* Followed closely by: *Why would anyone* envy *having a penis? Jacking off is cool, I guess, but it's just a body part.**

The only categorical, non–socially constructed benefit of having a penis is being able to pee standing up in the woods. Mostly because it's fun: a Definite Dick Benefit™. Especially when there's snow on the ground. Or when you pee in a creek and it makes that delightful bab-bling sound as your stream joins *the* stream. But, in my estimation, that's where the sole benefits end. From that point on, I think penises and vaginas are balanced. Tat for tit.

This is a fact that most men resist acknowledging. Men like to coast on the misogynistic implication that having a penis is easier and better and totally fucking cool all of the time. That the penis is somehow the better organ. That it is more fun, more enjoyable, and a better time all around.

And, like, sure. That is somewhat true if you've built an entire culture

---

*Incidentally, that probably should've been the moment I realized I'm trans. That's, like, the most trans thought I could possibly have about my dick. But I digress.

and economy around favoring people who have penises. But if we strip away the whole "genitals as economic and social destiny" thing and speak purely on a physiological level, penises and vulvas are equally great.

I think this is one area where cis people would benefit from listening more to trans and intersex people. In the cisgender imagination—where your genitals can never change—it makes sense to get defensive. You want to believe that what you have is the best because it's what you're stuck with.

That isn't the experience that a lot of trans, nonbinary, and intersex people have with our bodies. Trans folks are some of the only people who have really *thought* about our genitalia in depth. Pulitzer Prize–winning trans essayist* Andrea Long Chu wrote an entire op-ed about her vagina for *The New York Times.* Penning probative essays about your genitals for the Gray Lady is not, generally speaking, something that cis people bother to do.

For us trans folks, it's par for the course. We look at our bodies and sincerely interrogate if we like what we have. We look between our legs and see *an* option, not *the* option. I believe that gives us a more sober view of the thing.

I'm friends with plenty of women who were born with penises, decided to get bottom surgery when they transitioned, and now have vaginas they adore. I'm friends with an equal number of women who were born with penises, transitioned in every other facet of their bodies, chose not to pursue bottom surgery, and kept their penises post-transition. For trans people, our genitals are an open question, not a foregone conclusion.

That's why I believe we have unique expertise here. As a nonbinary lady (with a penis, *sigh*) who is constantly wondering if I should pursue bottom surgery and switch up the ol' equipment, I have made the pros and cons lists. I have thought seriously about whether I would be hap-

---

*And, incidentally enough, my college roommate junior year.

pier with a vagina or a penis. I have interrogated at length whether there actually *is* an advantage to one sex organ over the other. On a field where most people are fighting for either Team Pussy or Team Cock, I'm the sagacious, salacious referee.

As referee, it's clear to me that these teams are evenly matched. Both vulvas and penises are capable of earth-shattering orgasms. Both organs feel incredible when you're with a good partner. Being inside someone else's sex organ with yours is, I imagine, every bit as mystical as having someone be inside of your sex organ with theirs. Both require finesse, communication, and care in sexual stimulation. Both have annoying equipment you have to buy and come with health concerns and risks of cancer. Both can be sites of immense pain. One comes with the risk of pregnancy, but I'd argue that risk is balanced pretty equally by the *absolute fucking miracle* of being able to be pregnant in the first place. If you can get pregnant, it's natural to sometimes wish that maybe you couldn't. But the underdiscussed corollary is equally true: if you can't get pregnant, it's completely natural to sometimes wish that you could. Y'know: *womb envy.*

I don't feel comfortable living in a world where one type of body is deemed "better to have" than another. I do not believe such a thing exists. I believe that all bodies are amazing and terrifying and weird to have in equal part, albeit sometimes differently.

In the sex wars, consider me Switzerland. Our bodies are evenly matched. No grass is more verdant; it's a lush, sprawling lawn in every direction, babe. All genitals are great and yummy.

What I will say, as a penis haver, is that the discourse and cultural nuance afforded to penises is, perhaps, inferior to that afforded to vulvas. Which is just another way of saying that the feminist movement has done an incredible job. Feminists have worked for generations to destigmatize talking about vaginas in a complex manner in public. There have been entire smash-hit, global-phenomenon, off-Broadway plays about it.

What I admire most about the discourse we've created about vaginas is *the nuance.* As a feminist movement, we understood that there's historically been a great deal of cultural stigma against vaginas, but in seeking to fight that stigma, we didn't overcorrect. We insisted all the time on nuance, never painting having a vagina as perfect or completely mess-free. We were able to hold the complexity of the human experience: that possessing vaginas and vulvas and clitorises and uteruses is *both* beautiful-amazing-magical-powerful *and* challenging-complicated-annoying-sometimes-downright-scary.

This "both/and" approach—understanding that elevating vaginas requires neither oversimplifying nor undercomplicating them—is laudable. It's something that, as someone who was born with a dick, I wish I also had.

There is no equivalently nuanced cultural conversation about penises. We do not have *The Dick Diaries* alongside *The Vagina Monologues.**

The reasoning is simple: men spent the last, I dunno, *two millennia* brainwashing everyone into thinking that having a penis makes you superior. They spent inordinate energy building entire cultural institutions and legal codes segregated by sex, ensuring that if you didn't have a penis, you barely got anything. They spent generations insisting, on endless repeat: *penises are better.*

It's time we stopped listening to men on this point. Most men are too busy toeing the party line and chugging dicked-down Kool-Aid to be honest about what having a penis is actually like. Asking the average man if he's happy with his penis is like asking Kim Jong Un if everyone in North Korea has enough to eat: just assume that half of them are starving.

• • •

For the rest of this chapter, I'm serving as a whistleblower. I want to blow the lid of this "penises are better" thing clean off and provide an

---

*I should probably write that play.

honest, vulnerable assessment of the things that make having a penis challenging. Most men and penis-having people will not tell you these things ourselves, but, lord have mercy, do we need to. We're being crushed by our own silence.

One of the primary downsides of having a penis is that people act like you have a weapon in your pants. In one broad stroke, penises are often vilified. They are swords. Daggers. Spears. Pikes upon which we impale. As a human being, this really fucks up your psyche. Yes, some men use their penises to do terrible things, but for the love of God, must we cast all penises under this light? Is that the answer? If you're wondering whether men are screwed up by the frequent implication that *their sex organ is a weapon,* the answer is a resounding yes, they are.

My high school principal once taught the entire junior class a little lesson about car safety. In it he emphasized multiple times that "a car is a weapon. When you drive a car, you are driving a weapon." While I understand what he was trying to do, I found that to be mortifying. A car is not a weapon. It is a tool for transportation, required and nonoptional in most American cities. Telling a bunch of young teenagers that a car is a weapon did not make us drive more safely; it made us freak out, get super anxious, and feel far more likely to panic behind the wheel. For the few students who *weren't* freaked out by driving a weapon, it was even more disturbing. They were just like, "Yeah cool, I'll drive a weapon to Arby's. No problem." Yikes.

Equating the phallus to a weapon is a surefire way to cast a self-fulfilling prophecy. When presented with the idea that your body is a weapon, you can do one of three things: you can shut down and completely ignore whoever told you that, internalize what was said to you and become terrified of your own body, or, worst of all, internalize what was said to you and *embrace it.* I can't decide which is worse: young men learning to be afraid of their bodies or young men learning to be comfortable with the idea that they are carrying around a flesh sword with which they stab their lovers. When we weaponize the phallus, we all lose.

Secondly, dicks are oversimplified like crazy. Across cultural production, we tell the same story over and over: that most penises function the same way and achieving male orgasm is easy as pie. We paint vaginas as demanding goddesses that can only be appeased with complex rituals, intricate sacrifices, deep connection, and the utmost devotion, then turn around and paint penises as genie lamps: rub it three times and, presto, out he comes.

This oversimplification hurts men and people with penises. The expectations and double standards around performance are, in fact, ruthless: *Become erect instantly, but don't get an erection at the wrong time or too early, because that's embarrassing. You must be able to penetrate your partner endlessly without coming, but you must also be able to come on command the moment your partner is finished. You must come easily every time in order for sex to be considered successful, but you must never come quickly. You must stay hard for the entire interaction, but when your partner is done, you should go soft because otherwise it's sort of like you're pressuring them to go again. Your orgasm is easy to attain, so you should never struggle to achieve it. Your load should be huge and manly, but also your cum is kinda gross. It's nasty, but there should be a lot of it. Did I mention that you must always be able to go multiple times in a night or you're a failure? Always be prepared to get another erection and go another round upon your partner's request, regardless of what you want. Your cock should be hairy and manly while simultaneously being perfectly shaved and sleek. It should somehow smell simultaneously musky and like nothing. Muster absolute control over a fundamentally subconscious response, please.*

The pressure of having a dick and performing with it is beyond.

What men really need is what some women already have: permission to acknowledge the ways in which their genitals are challenging, vulnerable, and complex. Men need a culture that gives them permission to acknowledge the ways in which they have been made to feel inadequacy about their genitalia, too.

Without this permission, men's sex lives end up being filled with shame. Every time I've hooked up with a guy and he got in his head and couldn't orgasm, I watched the chagrin rise in his face no matter what I said or how many times I tried to reassure him that it was okay. Whenever I've struggled to achieve an erection because I was nervous or uncomfortable or stressed out or thinking about something else or drunk or *just not into it after all,* I still did my best to comply with the pressure to get it up. I feel like an abject failure any time I have to inform a partner that I'm struggling to get hard or don't think I'll be able to come. And they feel like failures, too.

The first time I ever hooked up with a guy who was having trouble orgasming, we were both only twenty. He kept stroking his cock over and over again, faster and faster, desperate for something that, in that moment, wasn't going to happen. He felt too young to be having this "problem." And what did he say to me about it? Instead of just saying "Hey, I don't think I'm gonna cum but you should get back to sucking it that felt amazing," or "I don't think I want to cum right now, but babe you're so hot please keep kissing me," he freaked out and proclaimed, "I don't know what's going on, *this doesn't usually happen.*" The implication being, of course, that this was all somehow my fault. That I wasn't helping him adequately. That I was making him nervous. That I was not performing correctly or wasn't hot enough. Which, like, excuse me. I am *great* at giving head, albeit sometimes a little out of practice (see next chapter).

It's one of the reasons we most need to shift the conversations around penises. Without a healthy cultural conversation, without allowing penises permission to be nuanced and complicated, without normalizing the fact that people lose erections and struggle to orgasm sometimes, men develop deep, abiding shame. And that ignominy becomes a breeding ground for misogyny, vindictiveness, and violence.

. . .

Maintaining an erection isn't always easy. It's something people who don't have penises rarely understand, because those of us with cocks are seldom honest. The truth of the matter is that, for many of us (or at least for me), the ability to maintain an erection is often inversely proportional to how much I am thinking. The more I'm thinking—the more active and engaged my brain is—the harder it usually is to get hard.

There's a medical explanation for this; it's because *I am not in complete, conscious control of my dick.* Erections are complex neurological phenomena highly connected to the autonomic nervous system, the part of the brain that regulates *involuntary physiological processes*—i.e., heart rate, blood pressure, respiration, and digestion. If you recall from AP Bio, the autonomic nervous system is split into a few parts, most notably the sympathetic and parasympathetic nervous systems. You can think of your sympathetic nervous system as caffeine and your parasympathetic nervous system as Xanax. The sympathetic puts your body on alert, increasing heart rate, contracting muscles, pumping out adrenaline, et cetera, while the parasympathetic puts you at ease. Feeling anxious, stressed, nervous, or scared? That's sympathetic. Feeling chilled, relaxed, cozy, and happy? You're feeling parasympathetic, my dear.

What most people don't know is that becoming erect is, medically and mechanically speaking, the opposite of tension. It makes sense that we get this wrong, because lord knows an erect penis certainly doesn't *feel* too relaxed to anyone involved. But the reality is that your dick doesn't become erect because it is *tensing up;* it becomes erect because the smooth muscles surrounding your penile artery—the bouncers to the blood entering your dick—*chill the fuck out.* Normally, those bouncer muscles are all tensed up and difficult and persnickety. No one's getting past them. But when you're aroused, they say *Fuck it* and just let everyone into the club. Your dick fills with blood and gets hard.

It's why you often need to feel parasympathetic—relaxed, comfortable, and at ease—in order to get and stay hard. When you feel nervous or stressed or scared and your sympathetic nervous system is in charge, the muscles blocking blood flow to your penis often won't let go. They can't let the blood *flow.* They won't let your dick become engorged because they're convinced that you aren't *safe enough* to be hard.

But that's where things get even more complicated. Because while erections are *often* correlated with parasympathetic comfort and ease, they don't *have* to be. An erection can also be a purely mechanical response: a result of physical stimulation that overrides your nervous system altogether, causing an erection to occur even when you *do not want it to and would prefer to be flaccid.*

A great deal of men who are sexually assaulted or harassed experience this. In spite of the fact that you are completely uncomfortable, saying no, and withholding your consent, someone can still coax an erection out of you simply by stimulating your penis. All you may want is for everything to stop, but the hardness of your penis is "betraying you" and is beyond your conscious control. Perpetrators of male sexual assault often weaponize this, ensuring that the man or boy they're assaulting becomes erect and orgasms so that he will struggle to be believed by others or even himself. *You must've been into what just happened,* a rapist may say. *You got hard. You came. How could you have done so if you weren't secretly into it?* Not only is this physiologically and medically inaccurate, it is revolting. And it is yet another reason why we must nuance the conversation about penises immediately.

The bottom line is that asking someone to *will* their way into or out of an erection is like asking someone to will their way into or out of constipation. Blaming someone for losing their erection when they felt a little anxious—or getting one when they didn't want it—is no more reasonable than blaming someone for their heart racing. Commanding someone who's feeling anxious to either stay hard or cease being hard is no more effective than commanding someone who's feeling anxious to "just breathe" or telling them "it's all in your head." *Of course it's all in my head, idiot. It's just the part of my head I cannot directly control right now.*

This is likely more physiology than you were anticipating, but it matters because popularizing knowledge about the neurobiology of erections has the ability to completely reshape how we speak about penises and, therefore, how we conceptualize male sexuality and men themselves.

Something shifts when we begin to accurately understand *consensual* erections (and all consensual human arousal) as predominantly the response of a body at ease. When we see an erect penis as a sign that someone feels safe, secure, and relaxed? It changes the tone of every-thing. For most of my life, I've seen a hard dick solely as a sign of mas-culinity or confidence or virility or aggression or power. No longer.

The next time you're with a consenting partner and their dick gets hard, you can think to yourself, "Wow. They feel *safe* right now, with me. They feel relaxed and comfortable and at ease." Knowing that you are responsible for their sense of safety? That they feel fully present and secure with you? That's hot, but in a way that contradicts heteronorma-tive, misogynistic norms.

And the next time you're with a consenting partner and their dick isn't getting hard, instead of thinking, "Oh god, am I bad at sex? Am I ugly? Am I a failure?" You can think to yourself, "Huh. This probably has nothing to do with me. I wonder why he's having trouble feeling safe right now? I wonder why he's struggling to relax. He might be struggling to relax precisely *because* I am hot as hell and he can hardly deal. There might also be some trauma there or some untreated mental health stuff, huh? That makes complete sense because, damn, it *is* hard to feel safe in this world. It *is* difficult to feel at ease. He also might just be taking a medication that makes erections more challenging." And then, maybe, if you like him, you can kiss him and hold him and stroke his hair and focus your attention on creating a sense of safety with each other for a while, because (a) what is hotter than holding a man in your arms and petting his head and giving him little kisses everywhere? and (b) that's probably what he needs right now, anyway.

· · ·

All of this is to say nothing about the way sexuality and arousal re-sponses themselves are conditioned. In addition to the autonomic ner-vous system's baseline functioning, erotic/sexual conditioning also has a disproportionate impact on someone's ability to get hard. You don't *have* to be sexually turned on in order to get an erection. As we've dis-cussed, erections can be completely involuntary—I got hard the other day because I was sleepy and the car I was riding in was sorta bumpy—but eros is irrefutably a central component.

Which gets me all steamed up, because the reality is that I had virtually no agency over how my erotic consciousness—and therefore, to a large extent, my dick—was programmed. None of us do. My eros, and therefore my dick's *ability to get hard*, was set into my autonomic nervous system so early in my childhood, I had no say whatsoever. I was fed a perpetual onslaught of handsome Disney princes saving damsels in distress and big strong traditionally attractive hypermasculine miserable aggressive James Bond types and Brad Pitt and Tom Welling as Clark Kent in *Smallville* and abs and pecs and buff arms and *more* abs and Abercrombie catalogs and shirtless men in cologne ads and Zac Efron dancing in that basketball uniform and Chad Michael Murray looking off poetically into the distance and an endless parade of other tall, conventionally attractive white boys *and then my autonomic erotic response was seemingly sealed forever.*

Then, immediately on the heels of all that, I got my first laptop and porn entered my life. At around the age of twelve, I started watching men in the ninety-ninth percentile of dick size rail twinks with three percent body fat or nineteen-year-olds with 34Ds and learned that this was what it meant to have hot sex. That dicks that large were normal and expected. That fucking someone for fifty minutes straight and staying hard the entire time and not coming until at least forty-five minutes in was par for the course. That abs were non-negotiable and huge pecs with virtually no chest hair were a requisite if you wanted to fuck. That an average-sized dick simply wasn't good enough or big enough or hot at all and getting hard should be instantaneous.

If conventional Disney movies first programmed my subconscious sexual inclinations, conventional porn sent them into overdrive; neural pathways seared so deeply into my brain, I still struggle to escape them.

Whether I like it or not, a huge portion of my subconscious sexual self was programmed by others. My desires were formed before I had any power to choose. The tomb was sealed, socially prescribed corporate-approved eros burned into my neurons right alongside my body's regulation of anxiety and defecation.

Or at least that's what it feels like, sometimes. And I bet if you asked most folks with dicks to be honest, they'd tell you the same.

Which puts you in a terrible conundrum. You get a little older, learn to challenge or outright resent the ways your erotic consciousness was formulated by corporate media and porn, and want to change it. But you barely can, because you have this snitch in your pants. A sex organ that refuses to update the iOS, like, *ever.* In 2025, mine is still mostly running Windows 98.

Yeah, I could (and do) try to fuck people who are outside my erotic comfort zone, I could (and do) try to desire a wider swath of bodies and people and sexual power dynamics, but my dick will rat me out almost every time. We'll make out, I'll actually be getting into it with the part of my brain *that I control,* and then my pants come off and it's all out in the open: my Disney-Channel-Circa-2002-Pornhub-Circa-Now-programmed dick isn't actually into you. I consciously *want* to fuck you or have you fuck me, but you didn't hit the Abercrombie Catalog Points™ or OnlyFans Index® quite effectively enough for my cock to get on board. To have a body that does that to me? That makes experimentation and learning and getting out of my comfort zone so difficult? Ridiculous, absurd, and *cruel.*

I often just rely on getting stoned in order to have sex. My erections are more reliable when I'm stoned, because marijuana turns my brain off. My sympathetic nervous system can't be bothered. I can stop worrying about who built my desires and try to enjoy them instead.

I think this is true for many penises. The more you think, the more difficult it is to get or stay hard. The more you try to challenge what you were programmed to want, the more you try to interrogate the sex you usually have or work to expand your sexual horizons, the greater chance you'll lose your erection or never attain one in the first place. If an erection is required, your brain—or at least your prefrontal cortex—becomes your enemy, not your friend.

I'm stunned that we have the audacity to call it a dysfunction. *Erectile dysfunction.* As if people who cannot conjure an erection when they're feeling anxious or stressed or outside their comfort zone are flawed. As if our bodies are wired wrong for not being able to *accio boner* anytime, no questions asked. As if our bodies are dysfunctional for something that is mostly out of our control.

As part of a feminist movement, should we not riot at scientists deeming any sexual challenges "dysfunctions"? At the implication that it is a *dysfunction of our bodies* if we are not able to get sufficiently hard/wet/open prior to penetration? That it is *our responsibility* to figure out how to coerce our bodies and minds into becoming aroused, regardless of whether our partners are actually helping us to do so, regardless of whether we've been able to process the trauma or anxiety that led to these challenges in the first place? As if the responsibility for helping us get excited—and, paradoxically, *relaxed*—enough to create arousal is all our own?

Ironically enough, in the process of diagnosing "sexual dysfunction," I believe we are likely compounding it. The moment you label someone's dick "dysfunctional," they're probably going to have an even *more* difficult time relaxing enough to become hard. A doctor telling you your vagina is "dysfunctional" is likely going to make it even scarier to achieve pain-free penetration.

All of this is to say that when we make an erection and orgasm the only standards for successful sex with be-penised folks, we are encouraging a race to the lowest common denominator. We are asking people to think less, be less critical of their desires, be less thoughtful during sex, and focus on doing whatever they need to do in order to just stay hard and come.

This leads men to be exceedingly risk averse. Many operate in consistent fear that they won't get hard, so they only go for what they were taught to go for when they were adolescents. They do whatever they must in order to maintain their erection as consistently as possible. They re-create the porn they grew up watching, on endless repeat, without much regard for whether that's the type of sex their partners actually *want*. Which often means having self-centered, aggressive, boring, unidirectional sex.

Is that really what we want? Do we really want to back men into a corner like that? Where men must maintain an erection at all costs? I'm interested in creating different scripts. Ones where maybe he doesn't even get hard or stay hard and that's okay and he focuses on pleasuring you for the evening. Ones where he doesn't achieve orgasm and the sex was still worthwhile and wonderful. I'm interested in creating sexual paradigms where there is no pressure to do any one particular thing, where we can explore openly and allow people the chance to get comfortable and feel no shame in not getting erect or wet right away. Where we can allow people to *heal* from sexual insecurity, dysmorphia, and anxiety instead of *compounding* those things.

. . .

Men are hurting right now en masse. Lost in a cultural conversation that doesn't allow their sexual organs to be sufficiently vulnerable or nuanced, that creates consistent pressure and performance anxiety, men are foundering.

Which brings me, at last, to Big Dick Energy. Because all the fucked-up discourse in the world on the *performance* of penises can't hold a candle to the fucked-up discourse on the *size* of them.

When the whole Big Dick Energy phenomenon first started, it felt like whiplash. I blinked and all of a sudden, the entire internet was ablaze, discussing the size of Pete Davidson's dick. Because speculating in public about the size of someone's dick is okay and, clearly, the only explanation for why someone like Ariana Grande would be dating a guy like Pete Davidson is that his cock is huge? Not because he's just, like, cute? Cute in a weird way that somehow defies articulation, but empirically super cute? From there, we started defining someone's "energy" by whether or not it seemed to be consistent with "the energy of someone with a big dick." The term spread like a virus—out of control, dangerous, infecting everyone it touched.

The term "Big Dick Energy" was and is antithetical to everything we stand for as a feminist movement. We can never build a feminist future if we don't do away with size-shaming men and their cocks. Whenever we treat smaller penises as culturally, erotically, or socially inferior, we bolster patriarchal power structures afresh. Whenever we talk openly about the size of a man's penis—big or not—it is a violation.

It's a violation that men perceive. For many men, it spirals from a general insecurity into full-blown clinical dysmorphia. Our culture's fixation on large dicks has created a real, if underdiscussed, mental health crisis. Men with Penile Dysmorphia Disorder believe that their penis is inadequate in size, and no amount of evidence, compliments, or logic can easily convince them otherwise. These men, men who often have statistically average-sized penises, somehow become *convinced*, against all reason, that they are embarrassingly small and start avoiding sex wholesale. It's an intense disorder in the general family of obsessive-compulsive disorder. It can require years of therapy and psychiatric treatment to overcome. Like all dysmorphia, if left untreated, it can end in serious self-harm or suicide.

And it's a disorder I completely understand. I am no stranger to dysmorphia. Though I have never received an official diagnosis, I know I have a serious case. I'll look at my not-all-that-big belly in the mirror for hours, tell myself that I'm "skinny fat," revile any photo or video that shows my belly, inspect the shape and contour of it in every single picture of myself I've ever seen *in my entire life,* and get angry when people try to tell me that my belly is fine. For years—before I knew that this was a common symptom of dysmorphia—I thought that anyone who told me that I wasn't fat was just *lying* to me. They were patronizing me, surely.

Dysmorphia is serious business. And living in a world that openly ridicules you if you *do* experience shame, insecurity, or dysmorphia about the size of your penis? It's brutal. Men who are insecure about the size of their penis do not need to be shamed or made fun of; they need to be compassionately helped.

Stigmatizing the size of someone's penis is also a unique type of violation because *there's barely anything you can do about it.* You cannot change the length of your erect penis, not really. But, because I am an author who does my research, I want to walk you through how people are trying nonetheless.

Before I do, I want to name that I am not encouraging anyone to try to change the size of their penis. Honestly? Be careful as you read this.

Simply reading about the lengths—miserable pun intended—people go to try to change their penis size sent me down a dangerous path.

Researching for this chapter, I found myself drawn into irrational insecurity about the size of my own penis. Reading the testimonials on websites about how much *happier* people were about their "increase in size" made me look at my own penis differently. Ironically, composing an essay about the shame people feel about their penises almost pushed me over the dysmorphic edge. I found myself borderline entertaining the idea of contacting some of these doctors or purchasing some of these products.

So just be gentle with yourself, okay?

First, there are the scams. Snake oil "penis growth pills" that do nothing. The type you heard about in spam email blasts from the early 2000s.

Second, there are injections—something that's becoming far more common than you might think—wherein a doctor injects hyaluronic acid directly into your dick, using a needle. The acid doesn't do anything for the length of your erection; instead, it increases the thickness. And because the acid injected into your penis remains—regardless of whether you're erect—it increases the girth and length of your *flaccid* dick.

(Apparently the size of my *flaccid dick* is something I need to be insecure about now? *Jesus.*)

Third, there's an approach known as "traction," which is essentially attaching a device to your flaccid penis that pulls and holds it taut. You leave your penis in this splint/band/device for six to ten hours *per day,* and in a few months, hypothetically, you should see some increase in length and girth. By keeping your flaccid penis stretched for hours and hours, you're hypothetically creating microtears that your body hypothetically fills in with more hypothetical muscle. The medical literature is not conclusive on whether this actually works.

Fourth, there's good ol'-fashioned liposuction. When you gain weight, the additional fat surrounding the area where your penis joins your pelvis can make your penis look shorter than it is. So you can pay a doctor to suck the fat out from around the base of your dick so that it can *appear* bigger and more prominent.

Lastly, there's surgery. There is no surgery that can actually add *real* length to your erection; that dimension is—at least so far—impossible to change. (If anyone *were* able to come up with a surgery that could add real inches to your erect dick, trust me, we'd all have heard about it.) What *can* be done is a surgical procedure called Suspensory Ligament Detachment, where you essentially cut the muscle directly on top of your penis—the suspensory ligament, which joins your penis to your pelvis—so that you reveal more of the underlying penis muscle and it can *appear* to hang lower by *maybe* an inch or so. It leaves a permanent, highly visible scar, but doctors argue that you can just cover that up by growing out your pubes? But *that's* stupid because growing out your pubes will just make your dick look smaller again, so I really don't understand. Apparently a surgically scarred penis is worth having a slightly bigger-looking one?

Other than that—and, Lord, that is mostly a lot of horseshit—there is nothing you can do. There is no real surgical or medical way to alter your erect length. No treatment can substantively change what you were given at birth. Nada. Zilch. And that complete lack of control, that absolute inability to do anything about it whatsoever, should impel us to even greater kindness, discretion, and gentleness.

But it hasn't. Everywhere—both behind closed doors *and* out in the open—we talk about how big people are and whether we're satisfied with their size. We reserve Big Dick Energy as the ultimate praise of a man who seems powerful, self-assured, and in cool control of his life. And we mock men we hate—men like Donald Trump, for example—by saying that their dicks must be small. I cannot count the number of times I've seen people openly ridiculing Trump on Twitter* by suggesting that he must have a small penis. *His dick must be tiny. That's why he's a fascist.*

I've been guilty of it myself. I am still a work in progress. The other

---

*Until the owner and (former) CEO of Twitter acknowledges that trans people—including his *own daughter*—have the right to rename ourselves, I refuse to acknowledge his right to rename his company.

day, a man drove by on a loud, obnoxious motorcycle, and without thinking I yelled, "WE GET IT, YOU HAVE A TINY DICK!" just to get a laugh from my friends.

I recently started seeing a guy, a cutie who is charming and hot and *connected* in bed.* He also happens to have a larger-than-average penis. When we had sex, I found myself slipping into the old pattern as I was blowing him, praising his dick for being "so big." And, like, it is, but I'm starting to think that maybe I shouldn't have commented on it like that. I want to do better myself. I don't want to necessarily praise my lovers for having penises that are large or hard. I want to choose different, more exciting, hotter words. I want to celebrate someone's body and their cock without focusing so much on its hardness or size. I'd like to get better at that. I think we all should.

We need to create space for men with larger penises to share their vulnerability, too. I've spoken to people who have really struggled in relationships because their penises are too large for their partner to comfortably enjoy on a regular basis. Saying this in our culture—a rape culture—has a weird, erotic edge, but it shouldn't. Having a penis that wears out or *injures* your partner is not a hot thing. It limits how much you can have sex and, in some cases, *whether* you can have sex at all. Men confronting this challenge need compassion and empathy without their very real sexual health problem being eroticized. Having a dick that cannot fully enter your partner without *hurting them* is not a blessing. It can be a heartbreaking reason to have to end a relationship or settle for less regular sexual intimacy.

Plus, when I've hooked up with guys who are on the smaller end of things, I've generally had more fun. As much as it can be great for sex to feel like a physiological challenge, it's equally amazing for sex to feel playful and easy like Sunday morning. I love when I can fully engage

---

*The last time I hooked up with him, he held me in a demi-headlock, stared deep into my eyes, and wouldn't let me look away as I came. He watched my soul temporarily leave my body and fed off my ecstasy like a vampire. It's the most vulnerable and *seen* I've felt in a long time, and I still twitch just thinking about it.

with someone else's body without struggling so much to adequately open up my own. It's honestly amazing.

It's sad how inadequate men like this have been made to feel. Men who are easier and, often, more nuanced lovers. I wish they could see themselves the way I see them. I wish they could unveil their perfectly sized, perfectly adequate cock with pride and excitement instead of trepidation and shame. I wish they understood that, yeah, a corseted dress that contorts my body and reshapes me on the inside can be cool once in a blue moon, but I will take a flowy sundress any day. Why don't men who are on the smaller size see themselves like that? As comfortable? As a glorious, fun, oftentimes *preferable* type of lover?

• • •

It's time we confront our own hypocrisy head-on, hypocrisy so obvious it almost feels asinine to point it out at all:

Publicly shaming *or* praising a man for the size of his penis is no more acceptable than publicly shaming or praising a woman for the size of her breasts. Period. End of story.

Ultimately, it's about reciprocity. We should give only what we're prepared to take. We cannot objectify men's bodies and then forbid them to objectify ours in return. We can't shame men for the size of their genitals and expect them not to shame us for the appearance of ours. We can't expect men to take our calls for body positivity seriously if we don't treat *their* bodies positively, too.

If we want people to understand vulvas as complex and nuanced, we have to work on understanding penises in the same way. If we expect people not to dissect the size, shape, or color of our genitals, we cannot dissect the size, shape, or color of theirs. If we want people to understand all vaginas as beautiful, we must, in turn, understand all penises as beautiful. If we want men to be open to dating women who are taller than them, we must not be afraid to date men who are shorter than us. If we want people to have compassion for our sexual health challenges and the diversity of our genital function, we must have equal compassion for theirs.

I hope we can learn to desire men as diversely as we wish for them to desire us. We must create a body-positive culture that makes this easier for everyone and raises future generations differently. We must practice what we preach and do our best to embody the Golden Rule.

It's time we create a space for penises and men alike to be understood for the complex, vulnerable, beautiful, sexy, peculiar, challenging, complex, diverse organ(ism)s they are.

P.S.

On the off chance you think this is something exclusive to hetero-sexuals, know this: Gay men, y'all are even worse. Despicable, even. Y'all treat dicks like so many trout on the line, as something to entice, hook, reel in, catch, take a photo of, and show off to your friends. The bigger the dicks you can catch, the more successful a gay you are. Y'all boast openly at brunch about how big a dick you were able to lure into your bed. Y'all disclose private, personal information about someone else's body on a Sunday morning over mimosas as if it's nothing. And you'll often go so far as to ridicule someone when their dick *isn't* big enough. It's part of why I've given up gay brunch altogether. I hate that vile, vapid, competitive shit. I also hate day drinking and overpriced eggs and talking about Gay Sports (a.k.a. *Drag Race*), but those are sep-arate issues.

Thirty-nine percent
of men
reported experiencing
penis shame.

The first time they'd felt
penis shame
was age seventeen.

Forty-six percent
of men
reported experiencing
sexual anxiety
due to the size
of their penis.

INCELOPATHY

When I tell people I'm writing a book about having greater compassion for men, the first thing a lot of them ask me is "But what about incels?"

If you don't know what an incel is by now, congratulations. You have somehow carved out an existence disassociated enough from mainstream discourse that you've missed out on one of the more acerbic and intractable cultural phenomena of the last decade.

"Incel" stands for "involuntary celibate" and it is, in essence, an internet movement of young, lost, predominantly heterosexual men who have struggled so enormously to form partnerships with women that they've crafted an identity around it. They find it so difficult to access sex, intimacy, and partnership that they have deemed themselves "involuntarily celibate." They believe that they are being forced into celibacy by society and the women who are refusing them sex. Many believe they are being denied their *right to sex*.

At its worst, it's an ideology filled to the brim with misogyny. "No women want to fuck me" turns into "Women are overly picky and unrealistic in their expectations of sexual partners and are wrong for not wanting to fuck me" turns into "I hate women and want to force them to have sex with me or kill them," in the blink of an eye. It's an internet-born movement that is channeling young men's sexual frustration into a hatred of women. *There's nothing wrong with you*, incel ideology tells struggling, lonely, isolated, vulnerable young men. *There's something wrong with women for not wanting you.*

Which, for a struggling, lonely, isolated, vulnerable young man with acute body-image issues and an inability to socialize well, is a really great thing to hear. For those young men, incel ideology promises psychic relief, freedom from insecurity, and a way to absolve yourself of blame. *It's not that you're ugly, it's that women are too picky. It's not that you struggle to maintain conversation on a date, it's that women are expecting too much. It's not that you are inadequate, it's that women are asking too much. You're not a loser; she's a bitch. You're not to blame; it's her fault.*

These struggling, lonely, isolated, vulnerable young men have flocked to incel ideology like flies to a corpse. It is the ultimate release from responsibility and self-doubt. Ironically, incel ideology is often a path toward a convoluted type of self-love. Because if everything is someone else's fault—if everything is the fault of women or society or both—you can finally stop hating yourself.

More than that, incel ideology provides these young men with an *explanation for their suffering*—suffering that is, much as we are loath to admit it, very real.

Not being able to find partnership, feel desirable, or explore your sexuality with another human being is excruciating. It's terrible to feel that you will die alone and a "virgin." It's terrible to feel ugly on a structural level. It's terrible to sit by and watch everyone else in your life form secure partnerships while you struggle and spiral further into loneliness. People of any gender who feel lonely or sexually isolated are people who are suffering.

I say that because I, too, have struggled seriously with these feelings. I didn't have my first boyfriend until, like, a year ago, at the age of *thirty-two*. I published my *first book* before I had my *first real relationship*. The main thing that makes me uncomfortable with incels, other than the blatant misogyny and the whole mass-shooter thing, is the degree to which I can relate to them.

• • •

In researching this chapter, I spent a lot of time on Reddit. Where else? Incel ideology was born on platforms like Reddit and 4chan. These online threads are where the fabric of incel discourse is still being woven today. For a moment, I want us to witness their words together.

> *I give up on relationships. . . . I want to know how to stop thinking about sex and to no longer desire romance or love.*

The anonymity of a faceless username allows broken people to be honest. For most incels, anonymous online forums are the only place they have to share their deepest fears and anxieties.

> *I want to know how to destroy my libido, to never care about women or about being unchosen and undesirable. I want my libido to die.*

I thought I could approach the world of inceldom as a voyeur.

> *I am legitimately very ugly. So ugly I have made the choice to not see my face unobscured for the last few years. I was mocked for the way I looked from the time that I was a child and up into college. I had 2 women explicitly tell me they would date me if I was better looking. But when I express that I feel the only thing hurting me when it comes to trying to have sex or date is the way I look, I get called an incel. I just am not getting it.*

As a scientist. Objective.

> *Why is it that it's commonly accepted that a person can be so physically attractive that it carries them in a relationship, but denied that a person can be so ugly that it prevents them from finding a partner?*

Removed.

> *My depression from being single has gotten pretty bad to the point that I've contemplated ending my life multiple times. Imagine being on Mars by yourself for years, that's how I feel.*

Analytical.

> *People say to just be yourself, but also imply that I need to become somebody I'm not [in order] to be successful in this part of life. This is the great irony.*

I'd do a little googling, read an article or eighty, and observe these broken young men from afar.

> *I've pretty much made up my mind that most incels, myself included, will die single, the only thing we can control is how fast we die.*

I wrongly assumed that reading the innermost thoughts of someone who identifies as an incel would feel like looking through a telescope at something strange, alien, and far away.

> *When we come to spaces like reddit looking for the reason why we're unwanted, we're met with statements like "You're not unwanted, you just haven't tried hard enough or met the right people yet." which flies in the face of years, if not decades, of experience to the contrary.*

Instead, I found myself looking into a brutal mirror.

> *I've made so many posts along the vein of "How do I accept that I will be alone forever/am unwanted romantically?" and no one has ever answered that question.*

A mirror that concealed neither flaw nor blemish. A mirror that showed me the worst, the scariest, and the ugliest in myself.

> *My experiences prove that I am less desirable than other men. It's been that way for a decade and isn't changing. I can't get what I want.*

As I read the testimonials of these broken young men aching for intimacy, I felt seen.

Just give me a lobotomy please and thank you.

On a level that rattled me, I felt *understood*.

Do you know for certain that you will be alone forever and are unwanted romantically?

Yes.

. . .

I'm a feminine person who has a male body, likes wearing dresses, and is covered with lots of body hair. I have mostly navigated the world as someone sexually abject. There are no cultural representations where people like me are depicted as beautiful or attractive. There are virtually no people who look like me in magazines or on television. When we *are* there, we're mostly desexualized, campy, and not represented as beings worthy of sexual interest or love. There is no television show where a "hairy man in a dress" like me is the object of pining or desire.

Things are changing on this front—rather, advocates like me are *making things change*—but not quickly enough for me to personally benefit. I spent pretty much the entirety of my teens and twenties— years I will never get back—without sex or dating. I barely fucked at all, because unless I butched it up and *fundamentally altered my gender,* seemingly no one would entertain the idea. I went years between kisses, let alone sexual encounters; dry spells so long they no longer qualified as spells.

It felt like I was being marginalized because I was being marginalized. Existing in a culture that sexually erases you is existing in a culture that marginalizes you. I sat by and watched as my gender-conforming friends had raucous, joyous sex all over the place, sat idly by as they started seriously dating, then getting married. It was always my gender-conforming friends who got to do this. Freaks like me—us hairy, unruly, nonbinary ladies, us trans weirdos who can't manage to convincingly "look the part"—had to observe from the outside, mostly unable to explore healthy sexual pleasure or romantic partnership for ourselves.

Being perpetually lonely, sexually abject, unable to find partnership or intimacy, and touch starved to my very core, I became more bitter and hateful than I'd like to admit. For over a decade, it made me hate men. I hated them for not wanting to date me. I hated gay men for being ashamed of having a partner who wore lipstick. I hated straight men, too: Why couldn't they understand my femininity and celebrate it? I hated bisexual men the most. In my mind, they were all cowards who were too afraid of losing their straight-passing privilege to come out. *You're the ideal partner for someone like me—you are someone who is attracted to people who wear dresses and people who have male bodies— but you're too chickenshit to face the social stigma associated with dating me. Go marry a woman, make your parents proud, and live a heterosexist shadow life. Leave the bravery to the rest of us, coward.*

It was a dark time in my life. There are still moments when it all flares back up again. It scares me to put it on the page, but here we are.

More than hating men, it made me hate myself. Why couldn't I find someone? What was wrong with me? Why wasn't I worthy of love? Why did I even *have* a sexuality if I could never put it to *use*? What sort of operation could I get to rid myself of the scourge that is desire? How could I obviate any yearning for romance or love? Was there some sort of pill I could take?

And it's not like I wasn't trying. I was putting myself out there constantly. I was asking people out left and right. I was going out clubbing and making moves and hitting the dance floor and doing my best to flirt. But I couldn't hack it. Romance remained arcane. An alchemical reaction, mystifying and beyond my grasp. Nothing I did seemed to be able to overcome the simple fact that my unruly gender made me ugly in the eyes of almost everyone I knew.

I'd share with friends—most of whom regularly dated and had sex and partnerships—how awful this all was, but they could rarely face the darkness with me. They couldn't acknowledge that I wasn't making this up. That we *do* live in a world that makes dating exceptionally difficult for trans and gender nonconforming people like me. That we *do* live in a culture that categorically considers people like me to be undesirable. That I *should* go back in the gender-conforming closet if I ever wanted a real chance at love. That some people never find partnership in their entire lives. That many, many people die alone. That their friend—someone outgoing and gregarious and intelligent and empathetic and accomplished—might become one of those people who breaks their hip, cannot get up off the floor, and dies there, simply because their gender expression made them undatable.

At that time in my life, I was desperate to be seen and heard. I needed one person in the world to *hold the heartbreak with me*. I needed a compassionate ear and an empathetic heart to listen without advising, someone to hold the brokenness without always, always attempting to fix it. No one could. Not really.

Instead, I got advice. Over and over again, I got advice. Every time I began to share how painful it was to envision a lifetime of romantic loneliness, I got pointers. I'd say something like *I don't know how to live in a world where I can't be loved,* and my friends, people who were otherwise emotionally intelligent and supportive and present, would respond dismissively, spouting trite clichés like:

> You've just gotta be confident, Jacob.

> Fake it 'til you make it.

> You'll find someone, just hang in there.

> Have you tried other dating apps?

> It sounds like you don't love yourself. Maybe that's your problem?

> Gotta put yourself out there more.

The implication of giving someone advice is that their problem is solvable—that it is something *they themself can solve*. Every time a friend gave me dating advice, what I heard reverberating in the under-tones was something like:

> You should've been able to fix this. The structural barriers
> you've experienced are not what's stopping you. They aren't
> real enough for you to deserve to give up. The overwhelming
> feeling you have that the world has made love impossible
> for you is not real. Your lived experience is not real. You know
> very little.
>
> Rather than hold the cruelty of the world or acknowledge that
> sex, dating, marriage, and romance are in fact competitive,
> capitalism-bound, patriarchally rooted, heteronormative pur-
> suits that leave billions of people behind, I am going to blame
> you, my friend, someone I purport to love, for your loneliness.
> You are not single because nonbinary people are discriminated
> against on a cultural level so complete and total it has rendered
> you an unlovable erotic void. You are single because you have
> failed at the endeavor of romance. Because you aren't trying
> enough. Because you're lazy and pathetic. This is, in fact, your
> fault, Jacob.
>
> Anyway, you're coming to my bachelorette, right? Can you
> pick up the dick straws on your way?

Everywhere I turned for compassion and support, I was given the same insufferable bootstraps bullshit. Tired of being single? Simple. Stop being single. Tired of being depressed? Easy. Stop being depressed. Tired of being poor? Just stop being poor.

Through encouraging me to keep trying, my friends were not only implying that my lack of effort was to blame, they were also denying that *trying itself had become anguish*. Ask anyone who has been single for most of their life: trying and failing to find love is a death by a thou-sand cuts. One that I'd *already died*. And you'd like me to die it all over again? *That's* your advice? To avail myself, once again, for the ump-teenth time, to the cruelty of the gay boy meat market? Isn't the definition of insanity trying the same thing over and over again and expecting a different result?

My friends told me to put myself out there, as if putting oneself out there isn't a traumatic process. As if it didn't wreck me. As if rejection doesn't add up and pummel you into the floor.

It got so bad that desire and rejection were no longer separable for me. After a lifetime of romantic rejections, I was little more than a Pavlovian dog, conditioned beyond reclamation. Every time I liked someone, it managed to end in despair. At a certain point, my mind cut out the middleman for me. For efficiency's sake, my brain fused the neural pathways together and made it so the moment I experienced desire for someone, conditioned feelings of rejection immediately followed suit. Against my will, they were hardwired, welded, bonded with superglue. Consciously or not, when I thought someone was attractive, I preemptively put them at a distance, because the simple act of desiring *at all* hurt. It stung. Eros ripped my nervous system apart.

I should add that, most of the time, I don't actually think I'm ugly or unworthy of love. I swear to God I don't. I don't look at my reflection and see an ugly person staring back. I earnestly think I look beautiful in a dress, chest hair and all. I find myself stunning in lipstick, five-o'clock shadow be damned. I have a little bit of a tummy, and I think it makes me even cuter. If anything, vanity is my problem. Sometimes when I'm stoned, I'll look in the mirror recreationally, just for fun. I love myself. I celebrate my body and the multitudes of beauty it contains. I do.

But I'll be damned if I don't *feel ugly* the moment I walk outside. And that's always baffled me. Why don't I get the same things other pretty people get? Am I not pretty? Why don't I have boys lining up around the block? Am I not sufficiently slutty and fun? Why am I being treated like I'm ugly and unlovable when I'm *not*?

No amount of self-love can change the world I am cursed to live in, not really. No matter how much I advocate for nonbinary people to be treated like human fucking beings, I will likely *still* die a freak. And in our world, dying a freak often means dying romantically alone.

When I tried to express all of this to my closest friends, I was left with blame, not support. I was erased by the people I love over and over again. And so I withdrew. I stopped sharing how I really felt. I stopped trying to be understood altogether. It was one of the darker shades of loneliness I can imagine.

To this day, I haven't been fully honest with anyone, not really. I've never once said to any of my best friends how terrible it felt for me to attend their weddings—to stand up there at the altar, having never had a partner or boyfriend in my entire life, as they joined a patriarchal, normative institution I could not access. To try to fake my happiness at the fact that they were leaving me behind to fend for myself.

Each time a friend got married, I did my best to look the part, plastering on a smile as I sat in the pew, quietly disassociating as I twirled across the dance floor, taking great care not to roll my eyes when their parents wept for joy. To someone in my shoes, the whole ritual just felt like gloating. At the time, their normative desirability made me feel ugly and awful and alone, and I hated it. I felt like a nonbinary circus act, put on display by the happy couple as a signal of how wonderfully inclusive they are.

I promised myself that when it was all said and done, I would find a time to talk to my friends about how I felt. But I never have. To this day, I don't know how to tell someone I love that on the happiest day of their life, I was miserable. I don't know how to ask why, during the entire ordeal that was their wedding, with all the preparations and expense it entailed, they never once acknowledged how hard it was for me. I don't know how to point out that they chose to publicly perpetuate, in a church, before God, a world where single people like me are left to crumble and flail. I don't know how to ask if, as they forever pledged their love to someone else, it even occurred to them that I might never find someone with whom to make an equivalent pledge.

Thankfully, I am no longer so bitter about the whole ordeal. My feelings on weddings, partnership, and marriage have evolved since my twenties. I'm old enough now to recognize that getting married sometimes means my friends will have *more* bandwidth to support and love me, not less. I see that the consistent support of a spouse often helps. I understand that part of the reason I was up there during the wedding was because I was low-key joining the family, too. That by having me up there, my friends were making an (unspoken) commitment to me as well. At a bare minimum, a good friend getting married means a guest room I can crash in when I visit, at least until they have a kid.

But I didn't always know those things. In my twenties, the entire ritual was about romance and power and social standing and forever. Every Kiss Begins With Kay. He Went To Jared's. Things I could never have.

At that time in my life, when I went to my (mostly partnered) friends, heart on my sleeve, and confessed that my loneliness had become so painful I was trying to find ways to rid myself of sexual and romantic desires altogether, I did not need dating advice. When I shared that I was terrified I'd never find anyone to build a family or buy a home with, I did not need pointers about how to talk to men. When I shared that I was terrified of figuring out how to subsist in an economy designed to punish single people, I didn't need a pep talk on self-confidence. When I snarkily declared that I don't think I'll receive adequate medical care as an elderly person because gay boys don't think my stomach is sufficiently toned or my arms are sufficiently big, I needed neither foolhardy encouragement nor abject pity. I needed something else entirely. I was desperate for anyone to say something real. Something like:

> First, I am sorry. I cannot imagine how painful this must be for you. To be someone so deserving of love, living in a world that has made it almost impossible for you just because of who you are? I can scarcely imagine. You're right: the world is cruel. You may never find partnership. The world simply may not change quickly enough for you to find love in your lifetime.
>
> But I'm here. You have me. I know I cannot take the place of a romantic partner, but I can promise you this: I will be there to care for you when you are old. I will be there to support you and help you find housing. I'm here to strategize how you can lead a fulfilling life that does not include romance. I will help you find

ways to cope with your sexuality and how painful it's become. I may not be able to love you erotically or romantically, but our platonic love can provide much of what you need.

Even if I do get married, I will not abandon you for them. I will simply place them alongside you. I will care for you like a partner if you will care for me like a partner in return. And whoever else wants to love me or be my partner or spouse? They'll just have to share, because we're in this together, bitch. Because we are, in fact, getting old together. I will pick you up off the floor when you break your hip. I will call 911 and ride with you in the ambulance and sit next to your hospital bed as you recover and hold your hand as you learn to walk again. No infatuation or relationship or fling or romance will ever replace the love we share as lifelong friends. You may never have a romantic partner so long as you live, but, kid, you have me.

· · ·

Underneath all of the pain, fear, and despair that I'd never find my person was a deep reservoir of anger at the world. Anger that almost ate me alive. Anger at the men who didn't like me and the friends who didn't understand me and all the people who dated and married and fucked like it was nothing. For years, I told myself I was a bad person for feeling this anger. I denied it, then denied it again: convinced that if I could deny hard enough, I'd be set free.

That isn't how anger works. Through years of hard work, I've learned that denial makes anger worse. I can't ignore my anger or wish it away; but I *can* redirect it, channel it, and make it productive for myself and others.

These days, I direct my anger accurately. Missile-like, I hone it and perfect its course. Rather than letting my anger break *me*, I use it to challenge injustice and break *that*, instead.

Because, in fact, I was not angry at my friends for getting married or dating or having sex. I was not angry at all men or even most men. I was actually angry at a very small group of extremely powerful people—

predominantly men—who control the cultural institutions of fashion, social media, and Hollywood. The first two determine which bodies people understand to be sexy, attractive, datable, and hot. The last one determines who people understand to be normal, conceptualize as worthy of stories, and, on a fundamental level that should mortify us all, see as *human beings.*

You may think this is an exaggeration, but it is not. Nothing encapsulates this phenomenon more perfectly than a scene in, of all movies, *The Devil Wears Prada.* Anne Hathaway's character, Andrea, lands an internship at a major fashion magazine that she believes is vapid and inconsequential. Then one day, she walks into her boss Miranda Priestly's (iconically portrayed by Meryl Streep) office in a blue sweater. She laughs at another editor as she compares two belts, thinking her stupid, and Miranda gives her the dressing-down of her life.

The exact speech goes:

> "I see. You think this has nothing to do with you. You go
> to your closet and you select, I don't know, that lumpy blue
> sweater, for instance, because you're trying to tell the world
> that you take yourself too seriously to care about what you put
> on your back. But what you don't know is that that sweater
> is not just blue. It's not turquoise. It's not lapis. It's actually
> cerulean. And you're also blithely unaware of the fact that,
> in 2002, Oscar de la Renta did a collection of cerulean gowns.
> And then I think it was Yves Saint Laurent, wasn't it, who
> showed cerulean military jackets? . . . And then cerulean
> quickly showed up in the collections of eight different designers.
> And then it filtered down through the department stores. And
> then trickled on down into some tragic Casual Corner, where
> you no doubt fished it out of some clearance bin. However, that
> blue represents millions of dollars and countless jobs, and **it's
> sort of comical how you think that you've made a choice that
> exempts you from the fashion industry, when in fact you're
> wearing a sweater that was selected for you by the people in
> this room.**"

Fashion, Hollywood, Big Tech, and desire work like that. As institutions, they exert an undue influence over what we want, what we crave, and what we dream about at night. They control us in ways we often do not understand. They limit our collective possibilities with the myopic nature of their vision for humanity.

Deny it all you want, but unless you've somehow managed to never watch a movie or use social media or look at a magazine cover in your entire life, you're not exempt; no one is. *They* decide who gets to be pretty. *They* decide who is deemed ugly. *They* decide what normal love looks like. *They* teach us what romance should feel like in the first place. *They* shape, from our earliest years, who we become as sexual and romantic beings. And now, through the power of social media algorithms, they often determine *who we even see.*

It's sort of comical, one might say to a skeptic, *how you think you've made a romantic choice that exempts you from Hollywood and the fashion industry, when in fact you're marrying someone who was, in large part, selected for you by the people in those very boardrooms.*

I care about this so deeply—and obsess over it so often—because the people who run fashion and Hollywood have thoroughly rebuked almost all people like me. I know this for a fact, because I have spent the last decade of my career struggling to be taken seriously by them. A terrifyingly large part of my economic and professional destiny has been shaped by the fact that the men who run those institutions deem people like me ugly and refuse to celebrate our beauty.

This may not be a particularly relatable story, but I once had a meeting in New York with someone who worked at Ford Models—a gay I went to college with and liked—about potentially being signed as a client. I'd just been named the face of a new brand of gender-neutral makeup, been shot in canary-yellow Oscar de la Renta alongside Michaela Jaé Rodriguez from *Pose* and Nyle DiMarco from *America's Next Top Model* for a Diet Coke Pride Month campaign, and had a debut memoir coming out with a major publisher. I thought that might be enough to convince them to sign me. And for what it's worth, I'm good at modeling. I can smize, take direction well, and, if given the chance, take a runway by storm.

My friend passed my portfolio up to his boss, some guy who'd "discovered" Kendall Jenner or whatever, and the response was an instant no. When I asked why, the brutal answer was that the "trans moment" was already done, there was no place for a "plus-size" nonbinary model like me (which, because I have a *rib cage,* I am deemed; even at my skinniest, I can't get anything smaller than a size 10 to zip around my big ol' chest bones), that I needed to be sample size, and the only reason a few trans models got signed in the first place was because they'd "starved themselves." Oh, and I should probably shave my entire body and get electrolysis, too.

Translation: *We at Ford Models refuse to believe in a world in which nonbinary bodies—at least hairy, "larger" ones like yours, with rib cages and internal organs—can be understood as beautiful.*

When I try to sell shows in Hollywood, I run up against the same challenges. I can always make it to the final round—get producers on board, pitch the hell out of a show starring a nonbinary or trans character like me, sell it to a major network, write the pilot script, and submit it to the powers that be—only to have it rejected in the eleventh hour. They give their reasons: they "don't have room for it on their slate," the script "just wasn't singing for them," they "can't see enough of an audience for the project," et cetera.

Translation: *We at [insert major TV network here] refuse to create a world in which nonbinary people like you can be understood as the romantic lead or main character of any story.*

All of which is to say that I have not just come to understand the ways in which arbiters of dominant culture have categorically excluded bodies like mine from desirability, I have *made a career out of gladiating against them.*

That's how you redirect your deepest pain and render anger as a force for good. That's how you heal yourself and the world around you *without* denying or downplaying the harm the world has done to you. When it comes to shifting representations of gender nonconforming people and the desirability of our bodies, I'm just getting started.

. . .

At this juncture, I want to ask you, the reader, a question: As you've read about me struggling to feel beautiful or fuckable or datable as a nonbinary person, how have you felt?

Odds are, you've been reacting compassionately. Odds are, you've thought something along the lines of: "That's a terrible way to feel. I'm sorry. You are worthy of love, and it's horrible that the world has made you feel otherwise."

This is the right way to respond. When someone tells you that they feel ugly and unlovable and undatable, it's a vulnerable confession, one that should be handled with the utmost care.

Why, then, have we almost entirely excluded incels from the same sort of compassion? On the level of popular feminist discourse, especially on social media, our response to incels hasn't been:

> These poor, misguided boys. They are suffering and lonely and need our help. How do we help them?

It's been something closer to:

> Fuck them. Fragile-ass terrorist woman haters. No one owes you shit. Can you imagine being such a loser that you form an entire identity around the fact that women don't want to fuck you? You're right, women don't want to fuck you. You're a misogynist and a creep and we hope you die alone. Also, you are terrifying. Stop murdering people because you can't get laid, sweaty.

I understand, on a gut level, why most of us have responded this way. Incel ideology is grating and misguided and hurts. Incel ideology supports rape culture and patriarchy both. It's an ideology that has been brought to the general public's attention in large part through the mass shootings it has inspired. It is dangerous, and we cannot allow it to be normalized.

But we've lost the forest for the trees. Behind every incel spewing hateful misogyny on the internet is a broken person, someone like me who feels terminally ugly and needs help to find their way out. I wouldn't condemn an incel any more than I would condemn a person who finds themself trapped in the clutches of a cult. People under the spell of cult ideologies do not need shaming or condemnation; they need honesty, compassion, a listening ear, real relationships with people who aren't subject to that same ideology, and *a path to freedom.*

As a feminist movement, we owe it to ourselves to find a way to help young men escape incel ideology. It's work that we've barely begun.

Google "incel deradicalization" or "how to help an incel" and the results are abysmal. There's no landing page from the National Institute of Mental Health, no toolkits from leading feminist organizations, no real conversations to speak of—almost *nothing* that would help an actual person begin a dialogue with their friend, child, or nephew who's trapped in the ideology.

What you get instead is a litany of alarmist experts discussing counterterrorism. The public policy response to a bunch of young men becoming so depressed and isolated that they've started shooting people has been the FBI and a bunch of academics trying to figure out how to detect and incarcerate them. It's a weird day in feminism when *Ms.* magazine is implicitly praising the Federal Bureau of Investigation.

And what do all these "counterterrorism experts" say? Next to nothing. They sit around scratching their collective heads in an article for *Wired* and act like that's activism. They have spent their entire academic lives studying *counterterrorism* and *deradicalization,* but when it comes to incels, they have no idea what they're doing and readily admit it. They run studies and regression analyses and surveys and walk away with meager epistemological handfuls of sand.

I read a study from a group of academics—"Beyond Violent Extremism: A 3N Perspective of Inceldom"—where their big "accomplishment" was coding incels into three types: incels who are probably going to get out of the ideology, incels who want to kill themselves, and incels who want to kill other people.

That was it. That was the whole study.

Like, congratulations? You've created a schema for organizing incels?

Now we can hypothetically understand if they're just going to shoot themselves in the head or shoot their classmates, too? The study concludes with the following:

> The present research suggests that painting the incel community and movement with a broad brush is perilous indeed. A minority of the respondents in the present study expressed violent ideation and intentions, and this cluster of externalizers should be the focus of work intending to prevent and counter violent extremism among self-identified incels. Additionally, it may be that incels move along a spectrum from hope to despair as they take on the black pill ideology and potentially come to believe that violence, toward themselves and others, is necessary to gain significance. It is important, therefore, to aim interventions at hopers, helping them to "ascend" from inceldom and gain significance in a prosocial manner before they fall into depression and violent expressions of despair. Interventions for internalizers should also be available to them online and should focus on acknowledging their grievances and feelings of significance loss and helping them to gain significance in nonromantic domains if they believe that such relationships are impossible for them.

Ah, yes. Interventions *should* be available to incels online. What interventions? The study does not specify. How should we acknowledge incel grievances and "feelings of significance loss"? No answer. And *obviously* we should help incels gain "significance" in nonromantic domains—any ideas on how we go about that? What do you *mean* you didn't study that part yet? Isn't that *the part* worth studying?*

Even those who attempt to give pragmatic suggestions mostly just

---

*I found another study, this one titled " 'I'm Better Than This': A Qualitative Analysis of the Turning Points Leading to Exiting Inceldom." Sounds important, right? It must be, given that an academic journal demanded I pay $53 to access it for forty-eight hours or $165 to access it for a month. Let's figure out how to help incels leave inceldom, then charge people more than their monthly internet bill to learn what we've learned. *Great.*

flail. Take the New America think tank. They have a page of recommendations for dealing with incels that includes stern pointers such as:
"Support improved mental health services and access as a social good—
but do not mistake this for a solution to ideological violence" and "Interventions should draw on examples of programs designed to deal
with domestic abuse perpetrators and counter racist violence for spe-
cialized counseling" and "Avoid interventions that reinforce boys' and
men's entitlement—collaborations with gender justice organizations
can strengthen program design."

How do these jargon-fueled statements help a parent whose child is
being lost down the incel rabbit hole? How do these policy-wonk dec-
larations help a senator decide what to *actually do* in terms of public
policy? How do these SAT-word-jumble imperatives help any actual
person make sense of the spiritual and emotional stakes posed by incel
ideology?

Approaching incels as an "academic problem" or a "counterterrorism initiative" is destined to fail. The moment you are "studying incels"
as "a population" you've likely already so dehumanized them, there's no
turning back.* Our desire to make this an academic concern or a public
policy problem belies our true feelings: that we do not know how to
approach this as an actual human problem. One with a beating heart
and the dignity of millions of men and boys on the line. In our attempt
to insulate ourselves from the sheer discomfort of it all, we've confessed
the truth: we'd prefer to understand incels as a *cultural problem,* not as
individual human beings.

. . .

We cannot violence our way out of violence. The answer isn't going full
Waco. When your teenage son is struggling with intense feelings of ro-

---

No one on earth wants to hear themself referred to as "a population." Trust me. My nonbinary ass should know. Every time I read academic studies by cis people that talk about trans
people like me as "a population," my eyes roll so far back in my head, my optic nerve threatens to snap.

mantic isolation and suicidal ideation, who do you need help from? Not the FBI or the Department of Homeland Security, that's for sure. By deploying firepower and intimidation and counterterrorism initiatives and ridicule and incarceration, all will be lost. Women and children and men and boys alike will be swept up in the inferno.

Many already have been. Ask the six people that Elliot Rodger murdered in Isla Vista in 2014. Or the eleven people murdered by Alek Minassian in Toronto in 2018. Or the eight people killed by Mauricio Martinez Garcia in Allen, Texas, in 2023. Each of these mass murderers identified as an incel. Lost to an internet cult, they each killed a lot of innocent people. And, as a society, we abandoned each of them. Our inability to substantively engage with and transform the valid, prolific suffering of lost young men contributed, in part, to the deaths that followed.

We have to help young men leave incel ideology of their own volition. It is life-saving, consciousness-redeeming, humanity-reclaiming work. And the only way to do it is to engage with them, care for them as human beings, and seek to understand their suffering.

I'm probably naïve, but I don't think it's impossible. People leave cults all the time.

Take, for example, my good friend Megan, who grew up in the Westboro Baptist Church. At the age of eight, she was hurling anti-Semitic vitriol, condemning people to hell, and carrying picket signs proclaiming GOD HATES FAGS. She grew up steeped in an intense, hateful ideology, as did her entire family.

But she got out. She learned. She healed. She grew.

She didn't leave the Westboro Baptist Church because she was *bullied out of it*. She left the church, her family, and life as she knew it because people outside the church extended kindness, compassion, and friendship, in spite of her support for Westboro's hateful invective. No amount of ridicule or slander would have been enough to help her leave; if anything, these things *fueled* and *deepened* her commitment to the church. But the teeniest slivers of friendship—mostly friendship with compassionate strangers online—worked wonders.

And now she gets tacos in Santa Monica with my gay ass whenever she visits L.A. We talk about our families, process our grief and religious trauma together, and luxuriate in the sheer improbability and fabulosity of our acquaintance. Through our friendship, I've seen firsthand that people can transcend even the most bigoted, firmly held ideologies. Myself included.

• • •

I'm going to end this chapter by spitballing, but all the leading academics and counterterrorism experts essentially are too, so you may as well hear me out.

I am going to give you something that few experts in this field seem able or willing to provide: a proposed theory of change and a simple conversation that we could actually have, en masse, with incels, right now.

My hypothesis is simple: I believe the young men who identify as incels are only one or two logical steps away from becoming our allies. Especially if we can intervene early and engage before they've finished brewing.

My hunch is that it comes down to something like the Socratic method. If we were patient enough to ask incels a few more questions, could they arrive at similar conclusions I did about desirability and culture? Could they come to recognize that they aren't angry with *all women* or ordinary, everyday people? Could incels realize that they, too, are mostly angry at a small group of powerful people—predominantly *men*—who built a culture that works against them and who refuse to celebrate a wider swath of people as worthy of intimacy, romance, and desire?

I have yet to attempt this strategy in real life—I'm not even sure I know an incel irl—but it's a thought exercise worth conducting. In my rose-colored mind's eye, that conversation could go something like:

INCELS: None of us can get a date. Most of us have never even had sex. Women only want to have sex with traditionally attractive, athletic, aggressive, socially dominant men. Women are the problem because they don't want to fuck guys like us. We hate women.

US: That must be really isolating.

INCELS: It is. It makes us so fucking mad.

US: And sad, we imagine.

INCELS: Yeah. That, too.

US: Feeling like sex is something you cannot experience sounds misery-making.

INCELS: It is, for all of us.

US: Are y'all afraid that you're never going to experience sex? That you're going to die before you get the chance?

INCELS: Probably, yeah.

US: Fuck, that's dark. Why do y'all think that?

INCELS: We already said: because women think we're ugly and socially awkward. We've never been able to get women to have sex with us. They don't want to.

US: It sounds like you guys find yourselves unattractive, too.

INCELS: Of course we do. Look at us. We *are* ugly. But women are the problem. They don't want men who look like us.

US: Are women the problem?

INCELS: What do you mean? Of course they are.

US: You said women don't want to have sex with guys like you because they think you're ugly, right?

INCELS: Right.

US: But why do women think you're ugly?

INCELS: They just do. It's evolutionary.

US: You sure about that?

INCELS: Look at us. How are we supposed to compete when all women see everywhere are these jacked, alpha, traditionally handsome Chads? We're not Chris Hemsworth. They don't want to date guys like us.

US: Bingo.

INCELS: What do you mean, "bingo"?

US: You grew up consuming media that told you that you were ugly. Women grew up consuming media that told them y'all were ugly, too. We all grew up consuming media that told us that most people are ugly, and at some point, we all started to believe it was true. It's not the only reason, but that's probably a large part of why guys like you are lonely and have so much trouble feeling confident and finding partnership.

INCELS: What?

US: Everything y'all watched from the time you were children reinforced the idea that there was only one way to be an attractive man or an attractive woman. In advertising and movies and TV shows and social media alike, y'all were told that you were not enough, weren't you?

INCELS: Yeah . . .

US: But who made those movies? Who wrote those TV shows? Who programmed those algorithms? And why did they want to make you feel ugly?

INCELS: We haven't really thought about that.

US: For the most part, it was a group of super-wealthy men who own major media corporations, tech companies, and marketing firms. Marvel movies? Mostly directed by men. Disney? Run by mostly men. HBO? Men. Major advertising firms? Operated by men. Abercrombie & Fitch? Owned by a man. TikTok? Instagram? Twitter? Some women involved, but still mostly men, men, and more men. Across cultural production, these images of the "ideal man" were predominantly created, funded, and orchestrated by men, right?

INCELS: Yeah, okay.

US: And they created these images with the express intent of making each of you (and most people) feel ugly. Why? Because the uglier and more undesirable they can make y'all feel, the more stuff you will buy to compensate. Clothes, sports cars, alcohol, guns, gym memberships, protein supplements, diamonds, a house, life insurance—people will buy anything and everything to make up for the inadequacy they've been made to feel.

INCELS: Whoa. Yeah.

US: So why are you angry *at women*? Pretty much every woman has been subjected to the same marketing forces you guys have, to the same corporate messaging, the same algorithms, and the same generalized feeling of inadequacy and ugliness designed by a few men at the top. Women are no more to blame for how Hollywood casts male action stars than you guys are. They've been manipulated into a narrow view of what makes a man attractive in the same way you guys have been manipulated into a narrow view of what makes a woman beautiful.

INCELS: . . .

US: This whole time, y'all were correct to be angry and hurt. The world has in fact been built in a way that makes it terribly difficult for each of you to feel confident in your own bodies. You were made to feel ugly and unlovable by design. But women were not the architects of this plan. Greedy men, men who would do anything to make a profit—including building a culture predicated on the lowest common denominator where they themselves are perceived as ugly and unattractive (I mean, have you looked at the CEOs of all of these companies? They aren't exactly Ken dolls)—architected this. At some point, these men decided that earning cheap clicks with abs, tits, and "pretty faces" was worth making everyone feel undatable and ugly almost all of the time.

INCELS: Wait . . .

US: And we get it. It was easier for y'all to just hate women. But it was overly simplistic and based on a misguided, unsophisticated analysis. It's easier to hate the thing that's right in front of you than to acknowledge that everything you feel—everything you have ever felt over the course of your lives, even your most intimate feelings like romance, sexuality, and love—was subject to the control and manipulation of a complex power structure run by people whose names you don't even know. It's scary to direct your collective anger at obscenely wealthy, powerful, faceless people. It's easier to direct anger at people on your level, in your own lives.

INCELS: Huh.

US: Greedy men who run fashion and culture and Hollywood and tech are your real enemies. That's your real fight. Collectively, we should direct our anger at those men—not at the women in your lives or the women you encounter online. Those men are the ones who've hurt y'all and made your lives hell, dude. We know because they've made our lives hell, too.

INCELS: Okay. So what do we do about that?

US: What if we told you there's already a group of people who are fighting this battle? A group of people who have decided that they're also done being represented in such restrictive ways and want all bodies—including each of yours—to be celebrated as worthy? Would y'all be interested? You guys down to fight for a world where you aren't made to feel ugly and insecure by design?

INCELS: Maybe, yeah.

US: Well, we're called feminists.

INCELS: Prolly should've seen that coming.

US: Welcome to the struggle, my dudes.

• • •

I know what skeptics must be thinking: "Jacob is a neophytic idiot. This will never work. Incels are so lost we can never reach them, no matter what."

And my gut response to that is: we actually *can* reach them. For all their anonymity and fearmongering and mystique, incels are the easiest people in the world to reach. They are chronically online. They are constantly posting. The totality of their discourse and community exists on, like, four or five websites. They take new ideas—ideas like "looksmaxxing" and "mewing"—and popularize them almost instantaneously, spreading them across the globe and into the cultural lexicon as fast as those giant undersea fiber optic cables can carry 'em. If a single leading feminist writes a cogent op-ed about creating a different paradigm for speaking with incels, pretty much every one of them will have read it within forty-eight hours of publication. Though we may not realize it, incels read almost *every single thing we say about them.* If we start saying something different, I'm willing to bet good money that they'll hear about it.

Furthermore: How can we know whether this approach will work *if we've never even tried it*? I'm open to being wrong about it, but to my knowledge, there has not been a mass feminist response to incel ideology that centered compassion. That is, in part, because as a movement we've gotten rusty when it comes to critiquing the social construction of desire. As leading feminist scholar Amia Srinivasan adeptly articulated in the *London Review of Books,* "It used to be the case that if you wanted a political critique of desire, feminism was where you would turn. A few decades ago, feminists were nearly alone in thinking about the way sexual desire—its objects and expressions, fetishes and fantasies—is shaped by oppression."

We have since lost that thread and somewhat squandered those skills. In their place, we've chosen unqualified sex positivity and the liberation of desire over everything, refusing to acknowledge that, as Srinivasan puts it, "the sex-positive gaze risks covering not only for misogyny, but for racism, ableism, transphobia, and every other oppressive system that makes its way into the bedroom through the seemingly innocuous mechanism of 'personal preference.'" I'm afraid our "personal preferences" are now also covering up the crushing, unattainable norms of attractiveness leveled at increasingly dysmorphic young men.

Srinivasan summarizes the incel dilemma perfectly: "The moment their unhappiness is transmuted into a rage at the women 'denying' them sex, rather than at the systems that shape desire . . . they have crossed a line into something morally ugly and confused."

Which begs the ultimate question: *Can* we help incels direct their unhappiness at the systems that shape desire, instead of at us?

When these lost young men arrived on the digital scene and subsequently started shooting up crowds, we greeted them as they greeted us: with enmity, condescension, hatred, ridicule, and vitriol. All we know, at this juncture, is that those approaches have accomplished nothing. They've fueled the fire and made things worse.

What would happen if we approached incels with the compassion we want for ourselves? What if we treated them as human beings with delicate, aching hearts? What if we began not by hating them but attempting to care about them?

Many incels have given up on the pursuit of romantic love. For the time being, might we help them take all that energy and pain and heartbreak and frustration and direct it like I have—toward creating a culture that builds desire more equitably and a world that makes love more attainable for us all? And in pursuit of that righteous endeavor, might they find a new way to love others and, ultimately, themselves? Would fighting against the cultural institutions that created their dysmorphia and insecurity in the first place help incels get back some of their human dignity?

It certainly helped me.

I have to believe that it might help them, too.

Forty-three percent
of men
are dissatisfied with
their overall appearance.

This number has tripled
in the past twenty-five years.

In just three years—
from 2019 to 2022—
surgical and cosmetic procedures
among American men
tripled.

Forty percent of people
with body dysmorphic disorder
are men.

Of those, an estimated
eighty percent
have contemplated suicide.

Twenty-five percent
have attempted it.

GET FUCKED

I've been thinking a lot about *Green Eggs and Ham* lately. You know the book. The one with the dour little guy with his dour little jowls in his dour little hat who's positively convinced: he does *not* want to down those viridescent yolks, no matter what Sam-I-Am says. He takes one glance at them and his mind is made up. He will not try them here or there, he will not try them *anywhere*. He doesn't like them, *capisce*?

But then, of course, he tries them. He takes a munch of that green meat and a gobble of those chartreuse *oeufs* and he's like, *Excuse me, why didn't I try these ages ago—they're delicious?* And Sam is like, *I've been telling you that for an entire children's book, you disconsolate buffoon.*

It's a simple enough lesson, but one that we seem to forget by the time we reach adulthood: just because you think you won't like something, or have told yourself that it isn't for you, that doesn't mean you shouldn't try it.

So it goes with most men and being sexually penetrated. Men will not try it here or there, y'all will not try it anywhere. Most of you refuse to put something inside your body under any circumstances. You know, because you're *big, strong men*. And *real men don't take it up the ass* or whatever nonsense y'all tell yourselves.

But y'all should give it a try. And it's my personal view that you can't have an actualized masculinity or a fully realized sense of self—and *we* can't have a world devoid of misogyny—until most of you do.

There are a lot of reasons why every man on the planet should explore his butt—and why every woman who has sex with men should play with a man's butt at least a few times in her life—but we'll start simply with the physiological.

Male bodies are hardwired for anal pleasure. Most obviously, there's the prostate: a magical walnut just past your anal sphincter that is chock-full of nerve endings. And it's not far inside. It's basically right there. Open the door, take two steps into the foyer, and you'll see it hanging on the wall. A masterwork. A beautiful piece of art. A gift from God herself.

It's a gift that doctors and cancer have given a bad name. Getting your prostate examined for the first time is enough to throw most men into a full-on midlife crisis. Having a doctor stick a finger up their butt is the scariest thing they can imagine. Seemingly, every man in America is petrified.

Of course you are. The way doctors do it is gruff and stupid and perfunctory and not hot at all. Men: please do not deduce anything about whether or not anal play is for you based on whether you enjoyed getting your prostate examined. I'm still too young to have had a prostate exam, but I have had doctors poke around in my butt because they needed to check on a hemorrhoid, and let me tell you: having a doctor stick their finger in your butt is *absolutely nothing* like getting fingered sensually by a lover.

Men, I am now going to use a *car metaphor* because I want to make absolutely fucking sure you understand how ridiculous y'all are being:

Letting a doctor be the first person to touch your prostate is like buying a convertible Corvette and taking 25-mph suburban roads to Walmart *in the rain* for its inaugural drive. It's disrespectful to the car. Why in the world would you mistreat a Corvette like that? If you have a new, never-before-driven 3LZ, you should wait for a sunny seventy-five-degree day and *then* go to the dealership and sign the paperwork, so that when you drive it off the lot, you can immediately hit the highway going ninety with the top down and make your way to a stunning mountain road and/or drive along the ocean. *That's* how you experience your convertible for the first time.

In addition to your prostate being located inside your butt, you should also consider the fact that *the literal muscle of your cock* runs right up to the front door. The base of your dick is physiologically attached to your anal sphincter. They're intimately and beautifully connected.

But don't take my word for it. The next time you're hard, feel down your shaft, go past your balls, then keep going. You'll notice immediately that your erection keeps going, too. Your dick muscle continues along the perineum—the taint—bridging the space between your balls and your hole. When you're hard, you're hard there, too. The next time you're having sex or jacking off, press there. You will feel your cock get even harder, because you're pushing on your dick muscle, just the part *behind* your balls, stupid.

All of which means that if you want to stimulate *the full length* of your cock, you have to go all the way to your hole. They're buddies. The best of pals. Fingering your hole or applying a little pressure on the outside of it is basically just another way of pleasuring your dick. It can elevate any sexual experience.

Which is to say nothing of having your ass eaten. Better pack an oxygen tank for *that one,* my friend, because you just bought a round-trip ticket to outer space.

At this juncture, I'd like to encourage anyone with a cock to take a break, put this book down, drop your pants, and get to exploring before we tackle the existential stuff.

• • •

Okay, you're back.

Pleasure aside, there's a more fundamental truth to all this. It's the real reason for this essay.

Being penetrated as a man is one of the most glorious things I can possibly imagine. It is beautiful. It is spiritual and sublime. It can be the source of *intense, earth-shattering* pleasure, but more than that, it can help you redefine gender itself and provide existential relief like you've never known.

First, because it represents release. On a visceral level that is impossible to replicate through any other human experience, being penetrated by a partner has the potential to undo everything you were taught about who you are. As a partner enters you for the first time, even with just a finger or a tongue, you will encounter fear, anxiety, stress, and uncertainty like you've never known. Then you'll adapt. You'll unclench. Your entire soul will relax alongside your body. In a moment, you will feel the pressure of masculine expectation—the pressure to be impenetrable, inviolable, invulnerable, stoic, a *real man*—relent. As your sphincter opens, your heart opens, too.

Being fucked or fingered for the first time is surreal because you'll realize that until the moment you were first penetrated, you did not truly know the fullness of human experience. You'll realize, *inside your body,* that there is not so much separating you and women. That the idea of strict gender polarity itself has always been something of a lie. And you will never again correlate being penetrated with being weak. You will only ever see vulnerability and openness for what they are: signs of immense strength and bravery.

What's more, you will find liberation from your doubt and your guilt. Because let's face it: penetration was one of the places where your empathy first began to die. For most of your life, since you became sexually active, you've been haunted by the fact that you have put yourself inside of your partners over and over again without knowing what it's like to have someone put themself inside of *you.*

Or worse, that thought hasn't even occurred to you. You've fucked your girlfriend for years without once wondering what it feels like on her end. You've penetrated your wife for years, knowing *next to nothing* about what she's going through. Though men rarely speak of it, the cognitive dissonance is foundational and astounding.

And it is warranted. Because if you've never had someone else inside you, you simply do not know what it's like. You are doing something *extremely* intimate to another human being that you have no knowledge of. In a world where you have no visceral understanding of what your partner is going through, it *should* be difficult to feel secure, shouldn't it?

It certainly was for me.

The first time I tried to top, the first time I tried to stick my penis inside of another human being, I hadn't actually bottomed: I hadn't had someone stick *their penis* inside of me, first.

It went like this: It was late at night and I was sleeping over at a friend's house. Unbeknownst to me, he'd been struggling with his sexuality. He's since come out as bisexual, but at the time, he was still piecing it together. At two A.M., as we were going to sleep, the dam of his curiosity finally burst. He asked me if he could suck my cock, and once the shock wore off, I was thrilled. *Of course he could.* Blow jobs were solidly within my comfort zone. I'd given and received oral before. I was excited.

Actually, "excited" is an understatement. The whole thing was a dream come true, a homoerotic sleepover fantasy come to life.

After a few minutes of clumsy (albeit exhilarating) head, he paused, looked me dead in the eye, and said: "I want you to fuck me, Jacob."

Which was when the anxiety set in. I'd never had anal sex with *anyone* before, as either a top or a bottom. This was "my virginity," and I didn't want to start by topping. I wanted to start by bottoming for someone I trusted, ideally in the context of a relationship of some kind, ideally with someone who'd had some experience with anal sex and could help teach me.

But here I was. He wanted *me* to fuck *him*—to steer the ship blindly for *us both*—and I had to make a choice. I told him I'd never done it before, but I was game to try.

What ensued was one of the more psychologically stressful experiences of my sexual existence. I had no idea what I was doing, and he didn't, either. He didn't have lube. He didn't know where his mom kept the Vaseline. We had to use *spit*.

I tried to do what I'd read online, which was to begin by fingering him and trying to help him relax. He was nervous and hadn't really explored his butt on his own before, so he was beyond tight, and it didn't look like he was having much fun. But he kept telling me to keep going. He wanted this. He wanted me to try.

I struggled to get hard. I was nervous and stoned and exhausted and existentially stressed and it was five A.M. or something heinous by the time this was finally happening. When I eventually managed to coax back an erection, I started to push inside of him.

That's when it hit me: I was *terrified.* In addition to never having been inside of someone else before, I'd never had anyone *inside of me.* I had no real way of knowing what this experience was like for him. I was pushing my cock into the literal and epistemological dark. Though I kept checking in with him and asking him if he was okay, I couldn't tell if he was being honest with me. Was he actually okay, or was he just saying that? I knew from friends who were girls that people often lied to their male partners—told them that they were okay during penetration when they were in pain. Said that it didn't hurt when it really did.

The moment my dick started entering his body, I had to face the stark reality that I did not know what he was going through.

I didn't last long. A few tentative, trepidatious strokes and I finished into the anxiously applied condom. The whole thing felt lackluster and sad. I knew this wasn't the experience he'd hoped for. It wasn't the experience I'd hoped for, either.

Afterward, I asked him repeatedly if he was okay. He reassured me that he was, but in the type of way where you know someone maybe isn't. As I tried and failed to go to sleep on the floor next to his bed—closeted queer experimentation doesn't afford the dignity of falling asleep *next to the person you've just had a life-changing experience with;* there's no cuddling allowed—the shame spiral hit. I hadn't had the firm, easily hard cock I'd wanted. I hadn't lasted long enough. I'd floundered. I'd failed in my duty as a man, an identity that still sort of mattered to me at the time. And the instant it was over, he'd kicked me out of his bed. No real intimacy, no aftercare for either of us. The moment his arousal had faded, his shame had ratcheted back into high gear.

His closeted ignominy shook me to the core. I felt like a failed experiment. That feeling stayed with me for years.

But laced in with the shame were other feelings that defined the experience: Doubt. Culpability. Anxiety. Fear. I felt guilty as hell. Not because I had any guilt about my sexuality or my desires but because I couldn't stop worrying that I might've hurt him somehow. He'd reassured me half a dozen times that I hadn't, but I still couldn't shake the feeling that I somehow had. Emotionally, at the very least.

And physically, I wasn't sure. If he'd been in pain, would he have told me? If I'd caused him injury with how sloppy and stressed and confused I'd been, would he really have shared that? I was ten thousand percent certain that he'd wanted me to penetrate him. Consent wasn't the question here. At no point had he told me to stop. I'd asked so many times that he'd gotten a little annoyed. He'd told me over and over again that he wanted this, that he wanted me to keep going.

But had I penetrated him *responsibly*? Should I have stopped anyway, even as he was telling me to keep going? Given the world we live in, where boys are socialized to tolerate extraordinary pain, could I really trust him to be honest with me about what was going on in his body? Two adolescents living under the dual tyrannies of rape culture and homophobia, were we able to truly communicate?

We should've stopped. I wasn't ready to be penetrating him—or, for that matter, anyone. I wish he would've told me it was okay to call it off halfway through. That there was nothing wrong with me if I wasn't enjoying it. And in spite of his verbal affirmations to the contrary, I think he needed me to stop, too. But we both felt so much existential pressure to keep going and prove ourselves that we didn't. I wanted him to have a good experience, to provide what I was told my male body was destined for.

Flailing in the throes of his nascent bisexuality, he wanted to have an experience good enough to help him overcome the shame he felt about who he was. I thought if I could fuck him well enough, maybe he could give me what I really needed too, something I'd never had before, which was *love*. Real, romantic love.

It didn't work out on either account.

The doubt stuck with me for years. I didn't try topping anyone again for a long time. In general, I'm more of a bottom, but that wasn't why. I simply couldn't risk the dread of failing to perform or having to wonder if I'd hurt someone with my dick.

A decade later, I called him and asked him about it, just to triple-check. He almost laughed at how worried I *still was.*

. . .

From that moment, I knew I wanted to experience being penetrated—wanted to learn to enjoy it—before I continued penetrating others.

I wanted to find someone to fuck *me.* Ideally, I wanted someone to love me and be my boyfriend first, *then* fuck me, but I went to school at a cruel university where everyone thought I was ugly and unfuckable because I was feminine, so I knew I'd likely have to settle for whatever I could get.

The first time I was penetrated, it confirmed all of my fears. I was traveling abroad, doing archival research in Johannesburg for my senior thesis, when I met the most gorgeous human being I have ever seen and he wanted to take me home. Across the ocean, continents away from what I was used to and in bed with a stunning stranger, I was *beyond* out of my depth.

I did the thing that both rape culture and gay culture—they are not *so* dissonant, you know—required of me: I pretended I knew what I was doing. I was twenty-one and embarrassed that I was "losing my virginity" so "late in life." I didn't want to kill the mood by telling him that back in America, at this stupid place called Duke, no one wanted to fuck me because I sometimes wore lipstick and didn't dress like a frat boy. He was the most beautiful person who'd ever wanted me: light-years outside of my league. In my dysmorphic mind, I was probably just a pity fuck for him. I couldn't be a pity fuck *with baggage,* a pity fuck whose *virginity he was taking.*

So I lied. I pretended that I'd already been fucked by a billion people and was a sexual expert. I did my best to fake it and act like I was totally comfortable. *If I tell him it's my first time,* I thought as he took off my underwear, *he'll freak out and not want me anymore.* I'd wanted this for so long. This brief summer sojourn felt like my only chance.

I tried to calm down and open myself to him, but it was far more difficult than I'd anticipated. Terrifying. I was momentarily convinced I was going to die. Or at least that my body would never work correctly again. For the first thirty seconds he was inside me, it was an outright crisis. He was "being gentle," but it still burned and ached and tore. I felt like I was being ripped open, because I kind of was. Done too swiftly and with insufficient lubrication, anal penetration causes fissures—literal tears along your sphincter. My body freaked out, but I was committed. I was going to make this work. I wasn't going to let him know I was in pain.

The pain eventually lifted, somewhat. Then the pleasure and pain began informing each other, switching back and forth, until my body acquiesced and it got a little easier. He came and I came, and like so many people's first times, it was simultaneously everything I'd ever wanted, the hottest thing I'd ever experienced, and one of the most terrifying things I'd ever done. Afterward, when I went to the bathroom to clean up, there was some blood. Not *a lot,* but enough to send shivers up my spine. *Was this okay? Was this part of the process? Was this just what losing your virginity was like?*

I have been penetrated a number of times since then. I have felt pain as the physical limits of my body were pushed. At times, it's been too much. At times, I've wanted it to stop but have been too embarrassed—or simply not known *how*—to say so. When you grew up a lonely faggot, when you spent most of your life feeling like an ugly tranny freak desperate for love and touch, consent isn't always a skill you're great with.

But over time, I learned. I learned how to confidently exercise my consent. How to tell people what I needed and bottom more manageably, with better communication and without much pain. I've learned to set boundaries and get the crescendo mostly right.

I still don't get it right every time. To this day, I don't have nearly as much sex as I would like. I'm still a fairly lonely faggot. But on the rare occasions when I can actually pull it off, I've learned to enjoy getting fucked.

And now that I've learned to enjoy it, penetrating others has become a hell of a lot less stressful, too. Now that I know what it takes, I can fuck someone without fear or anxiety that I'm hurting them. I know the signs. I know how to communicate and lighten the mood as we're warming up. I know how it's supposed to feel. I know what to look out for—how to be a compassionate, gentle, communicative top *well before* getting (upon request) faster, deeper, rougher, or more intense.

But I will never forget my first times, the anxiety and fear in both fucking and being fucked. Those experiences made me cautious, and rightfully so. With some distance, I'm grateful for those instances when things were difficult for me, when being penetrated by a partner was scary or unfamiliar or challenging or hurt, because those experiences inform *how I go about penetrating others.* They help me understand the full power my own body can have. They help me know, on the level of muscle memory, exactly how gentle and slow and communicative I must be as I'm getting to know someone.

And now—on the rare occasions when I get comfortable with someone and we're both enjoying ourselves—the pleasure is far greater. Because I don't have to be so afraid. Because I no longer have doubt. Because I'm no longer fucking in the epistemic dark. As I'm thrusting away, I know the pleasure reciprocally. I know approximately how good what I'm doing *to* them feels *for* them, that I'm doing it *the right way.* I know viscerally, inside my own body, that my pleasure is not at their expense but to their benefit. That, with good communication and proper buildup, I can go wild and it will only augment our mutual experience.

It is a type of knowledgeable, reciprocative sex I think everyone should aspire to. There is a fullness in the way queer people have sex that most straight people struggle to know. Queer sex is necessarily more empathetic, because most of us know both sides of the equation. When I have someone inside me, I know what it feels like on their end. When I am inside someone, I know what they're going through under or on top of me.

Which leads me to wonder: What do men who have never been penetrated *do* with all that anxiety and doubt? With the fear that you might be hurting someone you're having sex with? With the lack of firsthand knowledge about what the human being you're *inside of* is going through?

I think many of you just bury it. You kill off empathy. The doubt is untenable and uncomfortable and *weird,* so you brush it off or push it down as deep as you can. I think many men learn to have sex in a dissociative way, one where you pay little attention to your partner's cues. You make it your partner's responsibility to stop sex if it's hurting. If she isn't telling you it hurts, then it must not be.

Or worse, you eroticize the pain. You take it as a sign of sexual success. You normalize rough, aggressive sex and expect women to go along with it, whether it feels good for them or not. You allow cognitive dissonance to run its natural course and simply become the monster you suspected you might've been all along.

Many people settle for this type of painful sex because the social pressure to "take it" is so immense. Many people who have sex with men try to eroticize abuse or trick ourselves into thinking pain is a good thing, that sexual injury is a sign of success.

And don't get me wrong: I'm totally fine with rougher sex *if it's what you want* and *if it's free from coercion,* but those are massive ifs. I am a kinky motherfucker who enjoys pain in an erotic way. But when you're maybe causing internal injury, it's not hot anymore and we need to stop. Choke me, sure. But *correctly* and *only if I tell you to.*

All of this is why I find men's aversion to *being penetrated* fascinating. Oftentimes, I think it's an indictment of how they treat the people they penetrate. I'll bet the men who are most afraid of being penetrated are the ones who penetrate in the least responsible ways. They know that they're likely hurting their partners or being too rough, and they are terrified that this force may one day be redirected at them. These men walk around metaphorically clutching their butts, hoping they'll never have to take what they dish out. It's a sad existence.

Which, at last, brings me to the beating heart of the matter.

It's my belief that, without having been penetrated themselves, men are being spiritually trampled. It's not hard to understand why: the psychic weight of the thing is simply overwhelming.

As a man, you are told that you should *never* be penetrated, that being penetrated makes you weak, establishes you as less than, and leaves your masculinity in ruins. For most men, the idea of being penetrated is the worst thing they can possibly imagine. It represents the very death of their ego.

A man is someone who penetrates.

A woman is someone who is penetrated.

If I am ever penetrated, I am no longer a man.

Men often see being penetrated as an act of violence that, in their minds, is solely for women to endure. They are terrified of being penetratively sexually assaulted because it would permanently change how they see themselves and their place in the world. If you want to understand how deeply this fear pervades the masculine psyche, you can ask the men in your life a simple question: If you had to choose between being raped and being murdered, which would you pick? You'd be shocked how often the answer turns out to be murder. *Destroy my body. Burn my house to the ground. Just, please, leave my manhood intact.*

This ideology hurts male survivors of sexual assault most of all. Culturally speaking, male survivors of sexual assault are erased wholesale. Of course, not all assault involves penetration or is perpetrated by people capable of penetration, but the idea of a man being penetrated is often considered to be so shameful that men who *are* assaulted in that way end up feeling shame that they *allowed it to happen.* As if that's how sexual assault occurs. As if the primary issue is that they were "too weak" to fight off their aggressor. As if assault was somehow a test of their manhood, a test they failed.

The sociological data and qualitative studies on this front are mortifying. Even *boys* who are assaulted by full-grown adults feel they should've been able to stop it from happening. Male *children* often feel that their sexual assault or rape was some sort of fucked-up test of their strength or masculinity, a test they tell themselves they failed *because they were raped.* This ideology is prevalent among adult male survivors, too.

What are we to do for these survivors? What are we to do as a culture?

In general, we need to create a world where there is no shame for men who have experienced sexual assault. There should be no shame in being a survivor of rape, regardless of your gender identity. You did nothing to deserve it, and it was not your responsibility to fight it off. You are not broken by it. You are not less of a man. You are not less of a person. You are not less than, period, because of what happened to you. You may not feel like it yet, but you are still a whole person, a complete soul, *strong, worthy.*

Other than providing *far* greater resources and awareness for male survivors of sexual assault—therapy, funding, and support, something we've barely begun to do—one of the best ways to help male survivors is, paradoxically, to transform masculinity by destigmatizing penetration itself.

We need to create a world where there is no shame in being penetrated for anyone. Currently, a male survivor of sexual assault that involved penetration faces a miserable double-edged sword. Not only is he struggling to reclaim his sense of safety and trust, he's likely also struggling to reclaim *his identity as a man.*

So if you aren't motivated to destigmatize penetration for your own benefit, consider doing so for the benefit of *other men.* Because I guarantee this much: in a world where being a man and enjoying penetration are no longer mutually exclusive, men who've experienced sexual assault that involved penetration would face far less shame and stigma. The journey toward healing could be made that much easier.

But we can't stop there. We can't just *destigmatize* men being penetrated. It simply isn't enough.

We need to *celebrate penetration itself.* We must turn being penetrated from a mark of shame into a badge of honor.

Because trust me, the shame is still real. Men, especially heterosexual ones, who yearn to be penetrated or fantasize about it are often still overwhelmed with shame about their desire. People struggle with that shame for decades. And my question is: Why? What is shameful in being penetrated? What is shameful in wanting to have someone else's body (or a toy) inside your own? What is shameful in wanting to relinquish control for once? What is shameful in desiring intimacy, pleasure, love, and connection?

I want that shame to be shattered completely. I want all men at all levels of society exploring their holes and talking about it. I want fuck-boy influencers on TikTok talking about getting their asses eaten. I want Hollywood A-listers creating their own lines of prostate stimula-tors alongside their own brands of tequila. I want frat boys to openly compete for who can get pegged by the most sorority sisters in a semes-ter. I want this discussion to be boisterous, public, sexy, fun, and not just relegated to an episode or two of *Broad City*.

Until men can not only ask to be penetrated, but *openly discuss being penetrated and enjoying it,* misogyny will never die. So long as being penetrated is seen as a sign of weakness relegated solely to women, sex-ism will never fully be stamped out. If we strive for true gender equality, it's a conversation we cannot avoid. Being penetrated must be seen as a gender-neutral sign of strength. It must be a sexual activity available to all. We must stand in awe of *anyone*—men included—who is tough enough to get fucked, powerful enough to open up their body for an-other, and audacious enough to allow someone else in.

· · ·

Men—if any of you have made it this far in the chapter without burning this book—you need to ask yourselves: Do I really want to be one of those men who loves to eat but cannot cook? One of those guys who loves sports but can barely throw a ball? One of those dudes who starts a car company but can't fix a flat tire?

After all: Who appreciates a concert more, someone who just likes the band or someone who *plays guitar*? Who better appreciates a fine restaurant, someone who can or can't cook for themselves? Who grasps the mastery of an NBA game better: a random fan or someone who actually played ball? You can practice law as a full-time prosecutor or a full-time defense attorney, but you have to learn how *both sides* work before you can get licensed by the bar.

This is why I'm a firm believer that, on an existential level, every man would benefit from being penetrated by a partner a few times in his life. If you want to fuck, you should experience, at least in part, what it's like *to get fucked.* It changes you. Putting something up your butt won't magically unlock a complete understanding of misogyny or the female body, but it *can* help you grasp, in a visceral way that never leaves you, the gargantuan responsibility you're really taking on when you *put yourself inside of someone.*

This is in no way a perfect solution. I was born with a penis.* Being penetrated vaginally is something no male-bodied person can ever fully understand, myself included. Vaginal penetration comes with its own unique challenges—genito-pelvic pain/penetration disorder (GPPPD), vaginismus, and dyspareunia, among others—that cannot be replicated via exploring your own anal sphincter. But through exploring the penetration you *can* achieve, men can get at least a few steps closer to true empathy.

And, men, if you aren't sure whether or not you'll enjoy it, that's precisely the point.

You might not know how to enjoy penetration at first. But it's important to work through the confusion and disorientation and anxiety of being penetrated, *because that's precisely what you ask your partners to do.* Women and gays alike are asked to confront not only the prospect of a penis being shoved inside of us, but of learning to *enjoy it while it's happening.* And you can! There's just a learning, well, *curve.*

It's an experience men should know. We need to normalize it and encourage it and venerate it. That way, they can learn to respect limits through firsthand experience.

Men must confront this challenge. Think of it like a Tough Mudder or an ultramarathon or a boot camp, if that helps. Because until you confront that fear and anxiety, you can't find the joy and bliss and ecstasy on the other side.

The joy and bliss is much, much deeper than just having your prostate stimulated. It's existential. Being penetrated is a religious experience. The feeling of someone else momentarily taking over your body,

---

Womp womp.

of losing control and being at someone else's whim, is stunning. The release of control, in letting someone else be in charge, is healing and powerful and glorious.

It's ego death and vulnerability, on par with the most powerful psychedelic. It's about understanding both humanity and your own body on a different level. It's about reconceptualizing yourself, and allowing yourself to be small and vulnerable and cared for and safe. It's about unseaming your gender from tip to toe and rebuilding your masculinity from scratch.

Let your girlfriend *fuck you* for a change. Let her be inside *of you,* even if it's only once in a blue moon. See what it feels like to ride shotgun instead of driving all of the damn time.

Granted, not everyone loves it. Not everyone *likes* being penetrated or having something in their butt. Many gay men give bottoming a try and decide it's not really for them. You don't have to enjoy being penetrated or having your ass eaten or fingered or even stimulated. You are under no obligation.

But don't knock it before you try it. For the love of everything hole-y, give it a shot. Ride that roller coaster once. Get those strange limecolored *huevos y jamón* in your mouth, chew 'em a little, and *then* form an opinion. Pick up the fork and take a bite.

I dare you. Because we all know how that book ends, don't we?

P.S.

It is my belief that proctologists are doing humanity a gargantuan disservice. Frankly, they're violating their Hippocratic oath. They are doing harm by making men feel like they understand what it's like to be sexually penetrated. Before beginning a prostate exam, it's my opinion that proctologists should be legally required to give the following disclosure:

Hello Mr. [Patient Name Here],

Have you ever been sexually penetrated via your anus? No? Okay. Have you ever experienced pleasure from having a lover stimulate your prostate? No. All righty. Then it is my obligation to inform you that this exam will be uncomfortable. Not because it will hurt, but because, through your negligence, intransigence, and complete disinterest in your own ability to cum like a fucking horse, you have now created A Terrible Situation. The Terrible Situation being that I, a medical clinician, must now be the first experience you ever have getting your prostate touched in your entire life. In essence, I am giving you your first rectal handjob. But I will not be touching it with the goal of helping you cum. Which is awkward. You really should be able to enjoy this. ANYWHO.

Here are your options. We can either go through with this exam and have your first experience with prostate stimulation be a completely desexualized, annoying, not-at-all-hot-one, OR you can follow the official recommendation of the American Proctological Association and put off this appointment for two weeks, during which time, you will stick your own finger in your own butt while watching a hot video or have a lover stick their finger in your butt while making out. It doesn't matter who does it, just that it is done with the goal of helping you orgasm.

Give it a shot. Trust me, I'm a doctor.

Something like that.

Sixty-three percent
of young adult men
are currently single.

Fifty-two percent
of young men
are currently living
with their parents.

One in three
young men
reported that they'd had
no sex
in the past year.

IT'S BEEN A PRIVILEGE

When you drive from Los Angeles out into the desert, the highway does a magic trick for you. It doesn't always happen at the same point along the map. Sometimes she'll really make you wait. If you leave on the wrong day, or if there's an accident, or if you couldn't decide which sweater to bring and left the house twenty minutes later than you intended, you can find yourself in bumper-to-bumper traffic for *hours*. A wily magician replete with caprice, the highway does as she pleases. But no matter how bad the traffic, how hot the asphalt, or how infuriating the backup, the time comes, and she does her best illusion.

One moment, you're trapped behind an endless line of cars, squirming along the crushed freeway like so many ants. The next moment, you're sailing. Out of nowhere, the congestion lifts, the highway opens up, and adrenaline and hope course through your veins in equal parts as you freely accelerate. The exurban hellscape floats off, the buildings fall away, and it's open road. Just you and your engine. Thelma and Louise flying past cholla and creosote across the sand.

It was around that moment, when the road opened up and we started coasting away from the sunset at eighty miles per hour, that I began tearing up. I was riding shotgun with one of my friends in her camper van as we headed out past Joshua Tree to Quartzsite, Arizona, where we were going to buy crystals at the annual Desert Gardens International Rock, Gem, and Mineral Show.

And I was self-flagellating about—you guessed it—my career. Which, at the time, was in a pretty rough spot. After spending a year and a half back home in North Carolina contending with and then grieving my father's protracted death, I'd finally moved back to Los Angeles to start afresh in Hollywood. Coming back to a notoriously brutal industry when I was still actively grieving was not going particularly well.

"Sometimes I'm afraid that things will never stop being so hard for me," I said to my friend, trying to pretend that I wasn't about to cry. It was not an easy admission—until then, I'd played the fake-it-till-you-make-it card hard, staunchly committed to the precept that if I always *told* people things were going well, then they would finally *start to.*

I looked out the window at the fiery orange mountains in the distance, reflectors of the burning star setting at our backs. "Other people just have it so easy."

The engine hummed for a moment.

"Can I be honest with you, Jacob?" my friend asked.

"Sure," I muttered, lackluster. This friend is notorious for never taking any of my shit. A trait I love but sometimes find scary. Especially when I'm feeling vulnerable. "Why not."

She took her eyes off the road for a moment to look at me head-on.

"*No one* has it easy. Everyone suffers. Everyone is hurting all of the time. And the sooner you realize that and let go of your victim narrative, the sooner you'll be free."

That did it. Right on cue, we started fighting. And I *actually* started crying a little. Angry tears. Exasperated ones. *How could she say that to me? How could she dismiss my aching heart?* It felt cruel.

I racked my brain, trying to list every way that I, as a gender nonconforming person who the world doesn't consider beautiful enough to be a model or whatever, have been uniquely maligned. I rattled on about all of the opportunities I'd been denied, the slights I'd endured, the discrimination I'd borne, and how those things had completely scrambled my mental health and sense of purpose in the world. I tried my absolute darnedest to convince her that I *was* in fact a distinct sort of victim. That I was *uniquely* hurting. That I'd endured more and worse suffering than others. That other people got all sorts of good things I could never have and got them easily. But nothing I said seemed to break through. A true friend, she wouldn't relent or let me outmaneuver her.

"Everyone's hurting, Jacob," she said firmly. "No one lives a life free from pain."

Then she softened. "You *are* unique, of course. I adore you. You're special and individual, but not for having endured those things."

Half an hour of back-and-forth later, I just let her win. I didn't agree with her and thought she was being kind of an insensitive asshole, but she was sharing her camper van with me, had two very cute dogs, and I wanted to enjoy the trip. So, I half-assedly assented. I told her I understood, just to make the conversation stop.

She knew I was lying. But she also knew I was at the limits of my emotional and discursive capacity, so she relented. We changed the subject to labradorite.

It's taken me a long time to internalize what she said. I'm still in the process of doing so, to be honest. There are days when my heart isn't on board with the idea, but my brain seems to be mostly signed off. I may not always believe it, but I always know it to be true:

There is no such thing as living easily.

Struggle is inherent to being alive. As living beings, we have no choice but to metabolize. Which means we have to find food and put it in our mouths and chew it and digest it and poop it out, and none of that is easily done for pretty much anyone. To metabolize is to suffer. It is the human condition.

There is simply no such thing as an easy life. Which is why I find the current conversation about privilege to be, at best, ineffective. The (biologically essentialist) term "Male Privilege" has become the cultural equivalent of Wonder Bread. It's everywhere, mass-produced, generic, and barely has any nutritional value.

The words are thrown around on the internet like so many cheap beads at our feminist parade; they get the crowd going temporarily, it may *feel* powerful to throw them down to all the cheering people, but at the end of the day, they're plastic. Shiny on the surface, sure, but ultimately kinda trash. If we're not careful, they'll end up polluting the oceans and landfills of the world for generations.

When it comes to the conversation on gender, I think we should lovingly place the term "Male Privilege" into the recycling bin alongside

"Toxic Masculinity." We don't need to be rid of it so much as we need to melt it down, separate it into its component parts, and reconstitute it as something more useful.

I know I sound like a Men's Rights Activist right now, but humor me for a few pages.

I want us to really think about what we're saying—and, equally important, what we're *implying*—when we categorically name men as privileged. It's semantics, yes. But when it comes to identity and power, semantics have a nasty habit of fundamentally reshaping how we see ourselves and the world around us.

In my experience, "Male Privilege" most often functions as a generalization or a catchall. When we talk about Male Privilege, most of us aren't thinking about specific advantages so much as we're thinking about the vast, generic sense that men's lives are *better*. That they have *more*. More of what? We aren't always sure, but certainly *more of it*.

This, to me, is the first problem with the term. Most of the time, it's used vaguely. Unspecifically. Online and across discourse, we tell men that they need to "check their privilege," as if such a broad, harrowing instruction points them anywhere helpful. A man says something that seems sort of ignorant. We roll our eyes, mutter, "Male privilege strikes again," under our collective breath, and accomplish nothing.

Male Privilege has become a lazy attempt at an overgeneralized panacea. And I fear that this lack of specificity may be ruining us as a feminist movement. In the abstract, telling a man to "check his privilege" is about as useful as flippantly telling a fish to notice water. They'll just shrug their fishy shoulders and swim on their way.

Though it is burdensome, it's worth thinking through how it feels to men when we tell them in such an overgeneralized fashion that they are privileged. "But, Jacob," you may be thinking, "you are asking us to center the perspective of the oppressor instead of the perspective of the oppressed." And to that I say: Yes. I am asking us to center men's perspectives. If those are the perspectives we seek to transform, we must center them sometimes.

These days, the messages we disseminate about Male Privilege are as contradictory as they are baffling. We tell men that Male Privilege is a terrible, enviable, wonderful, amorphous thing they have. That it is great *for them,* but awful for the world. That no matter what they do, they have it inherently and are moral failures for having it, despite the fact that it's inescapable and not necessarily of their individual creation. And then we say that it isn't our job to educate them about it. We tell them that it's *their* job to fix it and understand what in the hell we meant when we said all that, because that emotional labor shouldn't be put on *us.*

It's a sphinx's riddle: disorienting, inconsistent, conceptually convoluted, and logically labyrinthine. Men have privileges that women don't have. We call them privileges, ostensibly, because they are good things to have: money, power, access, agency, et cetera. But the moment these become *male* privileges, they are somehow now bad to have? And men are supposed to feel immoral for having them?

If we were to parent our children in this way, they would lose their minds. Little Timmy gets thirty minutes of TV privileges each night, but the moment he starts watching, we glare passive-aggressively at him and tell him he is terrible for doing so. Give him a cookie, then chastise him for eating it.

In the context of gender, the invitation to "check your privilege" is a trite invitation to feel guilty and miserable about living your life. Or, at least, I imagine that's how many men must feel. Get a good job and do it well but feel terrible about it. Buy a house but feel guilty for living in it. Eat a nice dinner but don't enjoy it. Have sex but know that that sex is occurring against the backdrop of centuries of misogyny and you are horrible.

And so men shut down and walk away. They stopped listening to us ages ago, because the imperative to feel guilty about enjoying your life—or, as one male Princeton undergraduate put it in an op-ed for *Time,* "realize that nothing you have accomplished is real"—is a ridiculous thing to ask of anyone.

Most of the time, especially online, we don't take the time to explain what we mean when we say "Male Privilege." And truthfully? I think that's because we haven't taken the time to sufficiently examine what we mean by it ourselves. If we took a moment to be as reflective about our own language as we ask men to be about their privilege, I think we'd realize that, at least when it comes to gender, the language of privilege is inherently flawed.

That's because we shouldn't be calling half of these so-called advantages *privileges* in the first place. I honestly don't know why that nomenclature caught on. It sounds like we are jealous of men and the lives they lead.

I want to be very clear: I am not jealous of most men, and I don't think you should be, either. In fact, I am so not jealous, I abandoned being one.

I do not envy the lives that men often lead. I do not envy the ways they have been taught to wield power and violence, the ways they have emotionally shut themselves down, or the hobbies (guns, beer, sports, etc.) they've developed in order to cope. Yes, men get good things as part of participating in patriarchy—money, power, and agency, to name a few—but those things are not given to men in a vacuum. Men must earn the "good parts" of Male Privilege by participating in the parts that are bad. The system of Male Privilege is nothing more than a deal with the devil. A sparkly chance to sign away your very soul.

Take Jeff Bezos, for example. I am not jealous of *that* fucking dude at all. I don't want his life for one second. To become the literal dragon in the fable? No, thank you. Being the CEO of Amazon sounds like the worst job in the entire world. Sure, he can buy a solid diamond vase and a Birkin made out of alien skin, but he still has to be *the CEO of Amazon*. He oppresses and exploits workers for a living.

You're thinking, "Yeah, Jacob, but that's Jeff Bezos we're talking about here. That's a little extreme, dontcha think?" Fine—take, for example, then, the frat boys I went to college with at Duke. Am I envious of them? Do I consider them to be "privileged"? No! Is it a privilege to be compelled to wear salmon shorts and boat shoes until you die? Is it a privilege to be forced to chug Natty Light? Is it a privilege to have to go to terrible parties where the floor is sticky and everyone smells kinda bad and you have to listen to the worst EDM the world has to offer on repeat for four hours until you drunkenly pass out? Is it a privilege to be hazed, just so you can get a gig as an analyst at Goldman Sachs, one of the worst, most psychologically abusive jobs that white-collar capitalism has to offer? Is it a privilege to participate in a sexual culture that demands you *fuck* and *get bitches* and dissociate from your own body and mind in order to perform disconnected, miserable sex that's completely lacking in empathy, human connection, or anything truly hot? Is it a privilege to be surrounded by "brothers," some of whom are *rapists*? None of these things are privileges. They're all *terrible.*

What in the world do we have to be jealous of?

There are times when I feel like our entire feminist movement is just us being a little sister, watching our older brother hog the video game console, fighting for him to share the controller, when we live smack dab in the middle of the most beautiful forest in the world. Like we are competing to stare at a fake, made-up world on a screen when we could go play *outside,* in the real world, in the glorious, babbling creek that runs immediately up to our house.

But instead, we've hyperfocused on our brother's video game "privileges," lost in the simulated environments, staring at the pixels endlessly, with envy, wishing that we could participate in their artificial magic. And the more we tell our brother how unfair his video game privileges are to us, the more we chastise him for hogging the controller, the more desirable he feels it to be. The more we glare at him, the harder he holds on to that little plastic object, the more deeply he peers into the screen, and the more completely he is entranced by that counterfeit world.

We tell men that they are privileged because they get to run the world with an iron fist and do violence and decide which wars happen when and which people will be murdered in a drone strike and which populations will be wiped out by genocide and which trees will be cut down and which bombs will be detonated and which mountains will be leveled and which habitats will be destroyed and which animals will go extinct and which people will be raped and which workers will starve and which rockets will be built to escape the hellhole they've made of this planet. And my question is: *Why?*

Why do we call these things privileges if we do not envy them? What kind of world are we aspiring to when we do so? Do we want more Karoline Leavitts and Betsy DeVoses and girlbosses and Elizabeth Holmeses? Do we need more women hoarding more wealth? More women enacting violence? More Condoleezza Rices blowing up brown people and Hillary Clintons voting for the Iraq War? Do we need another Queen Elizabeth, trying and failing to keep monarchy relevant and holding the entire racist colonial project together?

The answer is no.

When we use the framework of privilege in the context of gender, I'm afraid that we get what we deserve. A world where a more diverse array of people get to be awful and vile. A Met Gala bursting with gender diversity as the world burns and becomes uninhabitable. We do not want that world. We do not want a world where women and trans people are equally "privileged" in that sense, i.e., *allowed to be equally depraved.*

And so, we must shift our language.

We should stop calling men privileged, because men are *not* privileged. Men are mostly just cursed.

They are lost boys clinically addicted to violence and the counterfeit world they've built. Unable to socialize, unable to go outside, unable to put down the controller, unable to sit at the dinner table for five minutes without jonesing, unable to pee without worrying that they're falling behind, they are spiritually at sea. Have you ever known a young person who was addicted to video games? It is abject misery. You have no control over your mind anymore. It fries your neural pathways, ruins your dopamine receptors, and can be every bit as disruptive and life-wrecking as drug addiction.

Here's what I'd posit: If our brother is addicted to video games and ruining our family and our entire home because of it, we do not disabuse him of his addiction by demanding equal video game "privileges." We do not help him recover by talking endlessly about how unfair it is that we don't get to have the controller, too. The more we tell him how lucky he is to have the controller, the worse things get.

No. We win by doing the opposite. We tell him that his supposed privilege—his capacity to wield the controller—is empty. We tell him that his obsession with controlling the video game has made him violent and awful to be around. We focus not on getting the controller for ourselves, but on unplugging the entire console, smashing it to pieces, and throwing it into the trash. We destroy the thing he's addicted to, take it from him by force if necessary, and then make him learn the joy of finding a salamander under a rock in the creek. *That's* how we win.

We cannot do so with the language of "Male Privilege." For our own efficacy, moral clarity, and best interests, we have to stop using that term. Anytime we're tempted to tritely talk about Male Privilege, I invite us to pause and take a brief moment to dig more deeply. Because odds are, what we actually want to talk about is *the violence, greed, and neglect of men.* Or, conversely, *the fundamental human rights that we all deserve.*

As didactic as it may seem, let's practice this reframing together by examining some of the more common areas in which we position Male Privilege.

There is no such thing as Male Privilege when it comes to sex. The ability for *only your pleasure* to matter is not a privilege. We are not jealous that many men center only their orgasms. We do not want a world where we, too, only prioritize our orgasms and completely disregard those of our partners. We do not want to become so self-centered and awful that we do not care about our partners' pleasure.

In the context of sex, we do not need men to "check their privilege," because they don't have it and we shouldn't be jealous of how they (often) fuck. If anything, we should feel sorry for them, because they can never know the joy of good sex until they unlearn their selfishness. They will never know the absolute bliss of watching their partner melt into waves of authentic pleasure until they do. We don't need men to "check their privilege"; we need them to stop being neglectful lovers and find the erotic joy in mutual orgasm and providing pleasure. And until they do, we should pity them, not talk about their so-called privilege. There is no Male Privilege when it comes to sex—only a sad existence, a sex life half-lived.

The same is true for capitalism and money. There is no such thing as Male Privilege when it comes to capitalism. The ability to be an oil executive is not a privilege. We are not jealous that men get to run awful companies that pillage our natural resources, poison our planet, and make it less habitable and beautiful for future generations. Ruining the planet for your children is not a privilege, even if you get a yacht in exchange. Spilling millions of gallons of thick, black gunk into the ocean and destroying entire ecosystems is not a privilege, even if it buys you a Maserati. Fighting to survive in a corporate ecosystem predicated on backstabbing, ruthlessness, and low-grade sociopathy is not a privilege, even if you get a summer house. Lord knows you won't get any time to actually enjoy it.

And if you think that women are somehow immune from perpetuating this type of global violence via the corporate sphere—frankly, via any sphere—I hate to break it to you, but you might have some internalized misogyny worth exploring. The idea that women are always kind and free from cruelty is, in and of itself, based in misogyny and the belief that women have an "inherent nature" that is both gentle and docile. Women are not "inherently good" where men are "inherently bad." Women are every bit as tough as men, and with that toughness comes the capability to enact similar violence with equal gusto. Just ask Regina George. Or Margaret Thatcher's ghost.

Which is why I'm concerned. Are we really out here watching *Succession* and thinking, "That Kendall Roy sure is having *fun*. I wish I had the *privilege* of choking out *my* brother in the boardroom and then losing the family company anyway." Every single character in *Succession* is miserable. So why in the world would we talk about men's dominance of the corporate sphere as a "privilege"? Like, congratulations, dude: you get to emcee *The Hunger Games*! Bravo, hombre: you get to murder the very last Siberian tiger. Felicitations, stud: you get to deprive people of, like, food? Sweet, man: you get to be a cop, shoot civilians, and be haunted by the specters of the innocent people you've killed for the rest of your days.

We should not be jealous of men's dominance of the corporate world or their monopoly on violence. We should merely be furious that they have channeled their trauma and lack of purpose into destroying the rest of us. We should be enraged by how senseless their greed is for them, and how gut-wrenchingly violent their greed is for the rest of us. We don't ever need a woman CEO of Chevron; we just need to Luigi the *current* CEO of Chevron and go on our merry way.* There is no Male Privilege when it comes to running Corporate America—only misery, neglect, and a sad existence for the men who are doomed to do so.

And for the *beneficial parts* of men's privilege—for example, the fact that men are more likely to have their medical concerns taken seriously by doctors (who are still disproportionately men themselves) or the fact that men are, on average, more likely to be paid a living wage—we need to abandon the language of privilege most of all. Because first off, most men *do not have these things.* Globally, most men do not have access to adequate medical care or a living wage, either.

Capitalism has a penchant for taking those things from almost everyone. As I saw one male TikTok commenter put it, "They only wanna be equal to rich men in the C-suite, never working men in the sewer." That took my breath away. When's the last time you talked about Male Privilege without erasing the type of men who work hard labor fixing sewer systems for poverty wages for their entire lives? For me personally, the shameful answer, up until this moment, was *Never.*

Secondly, it is not a "privilege" to have bodily autonomy or control of your reproductive health. It is not a "privilege" to be safe walking in the street. It is not a "privilege" for your doctor to *listen to* you and provide adequate medical care. It is not a "privilege" to be paid fairly for a day's work. It is not a "privilege" to be listened to by those around you and given credit for your ideas. Those things are not privileges; they are *God-ordained rights.* And it behooves us to speak of them in those terms only.

When we call it a "privilege" to not be *sexually assaulted* or to have

---

*At my attorney's insistence, I should clarify that this is "a joke."

legal sovereignty over our bodies and reproductive health or to not be *economically exploited,* we make it seem like those things are somehow "extras," "bonus packages" added onto our basic humanity. They are not extras. They are basic humanity itself. Talking about bodily autonomy as a privilege that men (sometimes) have suggests that we resent men for (sometimes) having it.

I do not resent (wealthy) men for (sometimes) having bodily autonomy. I want every single person on the planet to have bodily autonomy. Bodily autonomy is a human right. Period.

But when we place such fundamental rights as bodily autonomy, consent, housing, healthcare, or access to food under the umbrella of "Male Privilege," it makes it seem like we're competing under capitalism for these things. Like they are things men have somehow accrued to our detriment.

A rights-based framework—rather than a privilege-based framework—ensures that we are speaking with far greater moral clarity. We are not speaking about what *we* lack that some men (sometimes, often rarely) have; we are speaking about the *rights* we all deserve. We are being clear that, as a feminist movement, we have no interest in a mutually exclusive game. That we have no interest in *taking privileges* from men, only in *securing fundamental rights* for ourselves, too. No matter how you slice it, deeming something a "privilege" etymologically conjures a competitive and mutually exclusive quest for power. Deeming something a "right" brings forth the opposite: a quest for collective care, mutual aid, and a basic quality of life for all.

Boiling this all down to one extreme, the moment we start discussing "food privileges" instead of "the right to eat," we have all lost.

Lastly, my principal anxiety about the language of privilege is this: When we call men "privileged," I'm afraid we're setting them further apart from healing their trauma and identifying with it. When we reductively say that men are privileged and women are not, I'm concerned we're implying that men's lives are easy and women's lives are not, that men are doing well and women are doing poorly, that men are okay and women are not okay.

I find this particularly dangerous because, as of now, I am completely desperate for men to understand how very *not okay* they are, and in my estimation, that task is incommensurate with the far less important task of "calling out Male Privilege."

I fear that every time we tell a young man he is privileged, we place him one step further away from identifying his own, very human brokenness. I'm worried that we're creating a generation of young men who are *even worse* at unearthing their pain and trauma than their fathers. I'm terrified that we are raising a generation of young men who believe us when we say that it is a privilege to sit upon a blood-soaked throne.

As my friend so aptly reminded me during our drive through the desert, there is no such thing as an easy life. Everybody suffers. Everyone experiences pain. Men included. It is an awful truth to accept—one that, on its face, feels like it is erasing the unique struggles women, gender nonconforming people, and trans people have endured for centuries. But we must move beyond that feeling into a position of greater moral clarity if our movements are to succeed. We must not have a scarcity mindset when it comes to acknowledging human suffering. We must welcome the acknowledgment of all human suffering with open arms. And the sooner we can adopt language that emphasizes that fact, that helps men understand their suffering and hold it sacred, the better.

P.S.

As something of an afterthought, I personally find the "Male" part of "Male Privilege" to be especially stupid. At the very least, we need to say "Man Privilege," because there is little inherent privilege in having a male body unless you also *identify as a man and are treated as one.* Take it from me, someone with a penis 'n' balls. The moment you start wearing lipstick and nail polish and dresses *on top of your penis and balls,* all of a sudden lots of strangers on the street want to stab you.

P.P.S.

The language of Male Privilege also doesn't stand up particularly well when you add an intersectional analysis. Wealthy White American Women, for example, complaining about "Male Privilege" sound pretty dumb. You're telling me that you, a white lady millionaire in Minnesota, believe that every male-bodied person on planet Earth is more privileged than you are? That an impoverished man in war-torn South Sudan has "more privilege" than you? That some guy working in the mine that provided lithium for the battery in your Tesla is somehow doing better? At a bare minimum, we need to start holding people accountable for saying what they mean. If you are a Wealthy White American Woman, for example, you should be able to talk about Male Privilege only if you add the modifiers "Wealthy," "White," and "American." Please stop implying that all men are structurally above you when that's a bald-faced lie. Men of color exist. Men in the Global South exist. Poor men exist. Class consciousness matters. And because of the colonial, imperial, capitalist, racist bullshit that you *directly and materially benefit from,* their lives are mostly filled with struggle. If you're going to profit off their labor and degradation, the least you can do is acknowledge that *they exist* when discussing who has "more privilege" than you. *God.*

Only twenty-one percent
of men
reported receiving
emotional support
from a friend
within the past week,
as compared to
forty-one percent
of women.

Only twenty-five percent
of men
have told a friend
they loved them
within the past week,
as compared to
fifty percent
of women.

TEETH

2017 was a hell of a year.

I began the year driving my car across the country to move to Los Angeles. I'd scored a coveted job as the Director's Assistant on season 4 of the Emmy Award–winning Amazon series *Transparent*, and seemingly overnight, my world had changed. It took four days on I-40, but at the other end of that ribbon of highway, my future lay in wait. One moment, I was a writer in New York praying to *ever* work in television; the next, I found myself at the hub of queer and trans power in Hollywood.

Transparent was historic in many senses. Not only was it the first time a major television series centered a trans protagonist; it was also one of the first times that trans people got some semblance of control, power, or money *behind* the scenes. The show became a pipeline for dozens of trans and queer artists, myself included, to get our first real credits in the business. For many of us, *Transparent* was the first rung on a ladder that led to vital, enduring careers. Most people who dream of working in Hollywood never get permission to climb the ladder *at all*; I cannot overstate how important it was to gain access to that first metaphorical rung. An association with *Transparent*, if only as an assistant, was dynamite. I used it to blow open door after door.

I wasn't the only one. If anything, I was a latecomer. Each successive season before me, the show's ranks had been filled with more trans and nonbinary artists. It was the first show in Hollywood history that seemed to care about us, where the showrunner bothered to prioritize hiring trans people and giving trans artists a break. *Transparent* wasn't just the first show that centered the story of a transgender woman— albeit a transgender woman portrayed by Jeffrey Tambor, a cisgender man—it was also the first show that cared about hiring trans directors, actors, producers, writers, assistants, costumers, grips, camera opera- tors, gaffers, sound engineers, editors, post-production supervisors, musicians, and much more.

As a result, the sense of community on the show was bar none. It was a place where, as a gender nonconforming person, I felt celebrated. Showing up to work in a dress took, like, *no* energy. I had no fear about the professional repercussions of my gender expression—if anything, my identity as a nonbinary person was considered an asset, one that enriched the community and artistic integrity of the show. There were challenges, sure. As a television show operating under the punishing strictures of entertainment capital, it was far from perfect. There was still an iron-clad hierarchy and creative disputes galore. But at the time, it was indisputably the best thing trans people had ever gotten in the history of entertainment.

Plus, I loved Maura Pfefferman, the show's main character.

There's a moment in the *Transparent* pilot, before Maura has begun any sort of medical transition and is still presenting to her family as a man, where she goes off to her bedroom, changes out of her masculine clothing, dons a floral-print caftan, flops into bed to read, and lets her hair down.

The shot is framed with grace. Maura is gently and gorgeously lit as she reclines in bed. The camera wafts over her with care and compas- sion. The direction makes it clear: this person is not a freak. This older trans woman is someone to revere, to love. She is your family. She is your friend. There are no invasive close-ups of her breasts, hairy legs, or the still-untamed follicles on her face. There isn't anything voyeuristic about it at all. She's a sixty-something woman reading in bed after a disastrous dinner with her selfish idiot children.

I loved Maura because she represented a different type of trans woman: one who wasn't patently glamorous or particularly sophisti-

cated, one who wasn't trying her absolute hardest to be the most beautiful, passing woman she could be. One who'd accepted her unwieldy
body in the radical sort of way I hoped to. I loved her for all of the ways
she failed to be an "ideal woman." It felt rebellious, letting an older
woman be the first major trans character to anchor a series.

In today's culture, where almost all the trans women I'm given to
look up to are rail thin, hairless, blemish-free, and discovered on Tik-
Tok or the runway, Maura still feels radical. I looked at Maura and
thought: *Finally, a trans character who looks like an honest to God person. A human being. Someone who isn't a plastic Barbie doll. Someone
who is okay with the fact that she "looks a little trans."*

I looked at Maura and thought: *That's what I'm going to look like
when I'm old.*

Which made what came next all the more devastating.

In the fall of 2017, just as the show's writers were gearing up to out-
line season 5, all hell broke loose. In the wake of Harvey Weinstein's
serial abuse coming to light and the #MeToo movement beginning in
earnest, two trans women from *Transparent*—incredible artists who I
adore and venerate to this day—came forward and shared that they had
endured sexual harassment at the hands of Jeffrey Tambor, the star of
the show.

That was all it took. It unfurled exactly as you would assume: a course
of predictable events set in motion by corporate, legal, and media forces
outside anyone's individual control. Jeffrey denied the allegations, and
the writers paused their work. A few months later, it was announced
that Jeffrey had been fired and the show would no longer be returning
for another full season.

It was horrendous for so many reasons.

On a personal level, it felt like Jeffrey had killed Maura—a fictional
woman, sure, but one who meant everything to many of us at the time.
In a world where flesh-and-blood transgender women are often abruptly
killed off, seeing the character of Maura be destroyed by the indiscretions of a cisgender man was a knife to the heart. Her demise ached. It
burned. Our show, one that was supposed to imagine a fundamentally

different future for trans people, had ended with yet another trans woman being unsanctimoniously discarded because of a man's violence.

But it cut deeper than that, because when the show disbanded, so too did our careers and sense of community. For trans artists on the show, people who were otherwise structurally excluded from most rooms in Hollywood, the setback was particularly painful. We had one safe home in town. One set where *we* could feel like the center, for once. The moment Jeffrey's indiscretions came to light, Amazon ripped that away and offered nothing in exchange. No one helped us find jobs on other shows. Trans Hollywood orphans, we were mostly left to fend for ourselves.

From the outside, I'm sure it seemed like justice was served. The allegations were taken seriously. Jeffrey rightfully lost his job. But so did the rest of us. So did I. I'd left salaried employment with benefits and moved across the country to work on this show, and now it was cooked. If I hadn't lucked out and sold my first book a few months *before* the allegations came to light, I would've been immediately destitute.

In the end, hundreds of trans people were punished alongside Jeffrey. Everyone had to find new work. For years, the women who Jeffrey harassed never received an acknowledgment, settlement, or real apology. There was little recompense or healing for anyone involved. And the entire trans community was made to feel embarrassed and ashamed, because once again, something we loved had been publicly taken from us. Once again, we were powerless to stop that.

A few months after it all transpired, Van Barnes, one of the women who came forward about Jeffrey, sat down for an interview on *Megyn Kelly Today*. It serves as a haunting coda to the whole thing. Toward the end of the interview, Megyn asks Van, "Do you feel like it was handled to your satisfaction?"

Van's response is both telling and brave. "Partially," she says. "Him being fired is just in a male-driven Hollywood. He brought this on himself. *But they haven't completed the whole process of helping me stand back up on my feet.*"

Hearing that, something seems to change in Megyn. She interrupts

Van and says, less as a television journalist and more as a woman commiserating: "That's one piece of it that *never* gets completed."

"Well, maybe we can change things going forward. Y'know?" Van responds, hopeful. "I'm speaking up for the next victim."

But Megyn isn't satisfied with that optimism. As a survivor of abuse and harassment under the cruel tenure of Roger Ailes, she drives it home herself.

"It's a shame for many reasons," Megyn says, "including that this show has been a vehicle, a lens on what it means to be transgender. It employs a lot of transgender people. And now he's been fired and that does not work to the advantage of those employees.

"It took guts to come forward," she continues, solemn and sincere, clearly not just talking about Van's experience or *Transparent* anymore. "And I hope you do find another job. *Too often, these women who complain do not. It's wrong.*"

By the end of that year, I was beside myself. As the rest of the world was celebrating #MeToo and sporting black at the Oscars, I was mourning the demise of an entire community of trans artists.

We'd wanted to punish bad men for what they'd done.

But, like so much wildfire, our punishment proved extremely difficult to contain.

. . .

There is no point denying it: Men have enacted unconscionable violence. They have hurt us. They have hurt one another. They have hurt themselves. Everywhere we look, we face wounds.

As a feminist movement, we seek to hold violent men accountable. We want men to answer for the myriad harms they have caused. We cry out for justice. We demand it. And we are right to do so. Justice is, perhaps, the highest ideal any movement could aspire toward.

But demanding justice is a useless endeavor if we have not first defined what we mean by it. Justice according to whom? Through what means? Under what system? Justice *how*?

The elephant in the contemporary feminist room is that the work of defining justice remains largely undone, and in that vacuum, violence, retribution, and hypocrisy have taken root.

It is my belief that over the next century, the primary work of the feminist movement will be to overhaul and redefine justice itself. As it stands, we do not have a broadly understood concept of "feminist justice" or a shared rubric for holding men accountable while healing them and ourselves. We have not adequately differentiated how *our justice* differs from theirs. We have not asked hard enough questions or allocated the requisite time and resources to take their (failed) concept of justice apart and build a new or improved model. We are hungry for justice but have neglected to specify *what we want to eat* or learned *how to cook it.*

We are not procrastinating the task because we are lazy. We are procrastinating because, at the heart of the thing, we do not yet agree. Our trauma and pain interfere at almost every turn, clouding our judgment and making strategic thinking extremely challenging. There are chasms in both our movement and our hearts, chasms driven primarily by where we each find ourselves along the continuum of healing and spiritual development.

Nothing places these differences in starker relief than #MeToo. It was the single greatest moment in contemporary American history where we as a feminist movement had the chance to model for the world what justice means to us. In my eyes, we failed at that task.

As someone who worked in entertainment at the time, I can tell you firsthand that #MeToo's "justice" was sloppy, inconsistent, uncaring, and punitive in the extreme. There was little consideration given to the process of justice or the complex ramifications of rooting out powerful men. Almost zero care was given to the hundreds of bystanders and innocent people whose livelihoods were dependent on each abusive man we ousted.

#MeToo's apparatus of justice functioned less as a juridical process and more as an indiscriminate purge. Whole ships were sunk haphazardly; entire crews drowned because of something that happened in the captain's quarters. Crusaders plowed down fields of people, simply to hit one target.

It's as difficult as it is imperative to acknowledge that during the #MeToo phenomenon, there were two groups of people who caused harm. There were the abusive men who did abominable things. And then there was us: feminists who, in the process of punishing those bad men, inadvertently hurt a lot of innocent people, too.

I understand what we were *trying* to do: we were trying to show our strength. The common view, or certainly a plurality one in popular feminist discourse, is that our movement should have teeth.

In the case of #MeToo, we wanted a movement that was tough, effective, powerful, and commanded attention. We were tired of gnashing our incisors and wanted to *use them*. We wanted to bite back. For our abusers to feel it, for once: the feeling of being turned from a human being into meat, then devoured. A taste of their own medicine.

Because let's be clear: for far too long, women and gender nonconforming people have been hunted. We were the prey. They were the apex predators, stalking us across the landscape, cornering us where they could. They rarely hesitated; for centuries, they sunk their canines into our necks when given the chance.

It was time for those dynamics to shift, we told ourselves, for those tables to turn. Their time was up, and it was our turn to hunt. We wanted to feel *their* cartilage grind between our molars. Taste *their* blood. In a doomed attempt to reclaim our power, many of us wanted to become predators ourselves.

This was the undercurrent that characterized the #MeToo movement. This is the energy that pervades a not-insubstantial part of contemporary feminist discourse, especially online. We will hunt the bad men. We will swarm on social media and across the internet and throughout culture. We will find them and punish them. It is their turn to feel pain and our turn to inflict it.

This, we are told, is balance. This, some hold, is justice. This, it's often said, is only fair.

But we go further than that. We say it isn't just *fair* to punish men, it is *radical* and *good*. We tell ourselves that, as women and femmes and trans folks, we are at our *most* powerful and self-actualized when we are punishing men. We must not give in to our disposition for mercy. We must not give in to hesitation. We must not go soft. Attack first, think later.

Many people within the #MeToo movement (and across feminist discourse to this day) enjoyed being cruel. We got a kick out of it. We had yet to heal from the myriad traumas of growing up in a misogynistic world, and so attempted to find healing through punishment: through ruining men and incarcerating them and ostracizing them and taking them down. We focused on continuing, rather than disrupting, the cycle of abuse. We felt that given the violence and subjugation we'd endured, it was only right for us to get a turn.

I'm here to say that this approach to men is, in fact, the least radical position one can take. There is a way to be tough without violence. We have higher angels and greater virtues than our desire for retribution.

When we punish bad men, I fear we become them. We become the very monster we loathe. We become the villain we abhor.

· · ·

For me, nothing illustrates our failures more viscerally than what has happened to Harvey Weinstein. In researching his fate for this essay, I came across one detail I can't get out of my mind.

Harvey Weinstein's teeth are rotting. They're falling out.

As his health has declined in the American prison system—which *of course* it has, the man is in his *seventies*—his teeth have decayed to the point that he filed an emergency plea with the court in the lead-up to his Los Angeles rape trial. Apparently, he'd already lost some teeth. Three of his front teeth were gone, allowed by prison officials to simply rot. Many of the rest of his teeth were facing the same fate. His molars were turning to mush in the back of his mouth, riddled with cavities and decay.

When Harvey went to the prison dentist in Los Angeles to ask for help, he was given two options—the *standard options* for any American prisoner: he could either have his molars ripped out and never replaced, or he could continue to let them molder where they sat. Alongside his attorneys, he pleaded with the court to allow him to go to a private dentist outside the prison, a dentist who could salvage his existing teeth or, if they had to be pulled, provide the necessary dental surgery required to give him implants. You know, so he can *comfortably chew food.*

He didn't ask the government to pay for his procedure. He offered to pay for the entire cost of a private dental visit, including transportation to and from the doctor.

When he appeared before the court, he told the judge, "I'm in pain every day. I have cavities and I can't eat because I'm missing teeth. This situation is an emergency. I will pay for the dentist. It will be one trip and one trip only."

In large part, the media and the public trivialized his request.

Convicted rapist whines about teeth.

Absolute monster Harvey Weinstein has the audacity to want to chew food after what he's done.

Manipulative, heartless human is using the fact that his teeth are rotting to get attention and sympathy from a jury.

That type of thing.

But the headlines could just as easily have read:

Seventy-year-old man begs prison officials for the right to keep his teeth.

Or: *Facing the inability to eat, Los Angeles prisoner appeals for better medical care.*

Or: *Harvey Weinstein's teeth are falling out: What does that mean for the rest of America's two million prisoners?*

It is difficult to extend empathy to someone who all of us consider to be so awful, but in our quest for a more just world, I believe we should try. And in this case, I don't think it's so hard to do.

Have you ever had a bad toothache? Have you ever seen someone in excruciating dental pain? Have you or any of your loved ones ever been in so much dental pain you could not eat?

I've witnessed that. After my father had a traumatic bicycle accident where half of his face was bashed in by a rock, I remember watching him struggle to eat because of the pain. I remember how he'd have to take all of his favorite foods, cut them up into tiny little pieces, and chew through the pain in order to simply have family dinner with us. I remember how hard he worked to mask his pain as he ate, pain that worsened until the day he died. I remember how dehumanizing and terrible that felt, how *cruel*. During the course of a terrible death, the memory of my father struggling to eat is right up there with finding him downing Valium in the bathroom on the night that he overdosed.

Protracted dental pain is misery. And when protracted dental pain is forced upon you by prison officials who refuse to give you humane treatment, it is torture. Under the Geneva Convention, I'm pretty sure it qualifies. It is most certainly cruel and unusual punishment. It is entirely unconstitutional; in so much as the Constitution even *has* meaning these days.

As his teeth rot, his ability to eat is taken from him, and his pain goes untreated, Harvey Weinstein is being tortured. Through the systemic neglect and cruelty of the American prison system, he will likely be tortured in one form or another until the day he dies.

Is this our concept of justice? Are we to believe that this is *fair*? He hurt hundreds of people, so now we're pulling out his teeth, via decay and neglect, in slow motion, one by one? *That's* our feminist justice?

The American judicial system provided us only two options: either Harvey goes free, or he is condemned to fester in an American prison. Which would we like? Which of those two options feels more like healing to us? Which of these two options brings us peace?

I've slowly come to an understanding that the answer is neither. Neither of those options are justice. Neither of those options heal anyone, not really. Torturing Harvey Weinstein is not justice. Incarcerating people is not justice. We need something else entirely.

I do not believe that Harvey Weinstein should be in prison, because I do not believe that *anyone* should be. I'm a prison abolitionist. I do not believe that prisons should exist. House arrest or some other form of less punitive supervision? As an interim measure for murderers and violent offenders, sure. Actual rehabilitation, restorative processes, survivor-driven community accountability, and compassionate mental health treatment for perpetrators? Absolutely. Programs where the structural causes of violence (poverty, trauma, abuse, etc.) are obviated to the point that we barely *have* crime anymore? Yes, God. But *prison*? As it currently exists in the United States of America in the twenty-first century? Nope.

And there is little you can say or do that would convince me otherwise. I don't care how many people you murder or how many people you hurt or how much suffering you cause, prison is never helpful because it never undoes the suffering of those you hurt. All it does is cause more suffering and lead to more violence. The world has treated us terribly, someone we love was killed, and the only option for justice that's presented to us is to *inflict more misery*? As if that will heal us. As if that will set us free. As if that will bring back our loved ones or undo our trauma or restore our dignity.

The reality that none of us want to face is that Harvey Weinstein is a litmus test of our feminist ability to navigate, resist, and transform American "Justice." One that, in my estimation, we have failed. If Harvey, one of the richest, most powerful people currently in American prison, with his army of attorneys and connections and substantial financial resources, cannot so much as *keep his teeth,* how do you think the rest of the prisoners are doing? American prisoners are suffering from neglect. American prisoners are enduring abuse. American prisoners have been condemned to a life of structural violence, one that strips them of their most basic human dignity. American prisons are factories of cruelty. They take people whose lives have already been marred by violence—many of whom are survivors *themselves*—and ensure that they never recover. They ensure that rehabilitation remains a pipe dream. They ensure, via their neglect, sadism, and inhuman contempt, that we will always live in a violent world. Prisons don't prevent crime; they create it. They don't protect us from violence; they further it.

The reality that no one in Hollywood, at Time's Up, in the media, or seemingly anywhere else wants to contend with is that when we cheered for Harvey Weinstein to rot in prison, we cheered for prisons themselves. When we cheered for a wealthy white man to be incarcerated, we cheered for the millions of Black and brown people who are wrongfully incarcerated to remain so. When we asked a court to ensure that "justice was served" by sending a man like Harvey Weinstein to prison, we were participating in a lie. We reinforced the misguided notion that justice can *ever* be served by condemning a person to incarceration. When we celebrated Harvey's conviction, we celebrated conviction itself.

I don't want to celebrate prisons. I don't want to celebrate Black and brown people being ripped from their families and kept under conditions many legal scholars assert are tantamount to slavery. I don't want to celebrate poor people of any race or ethnicity being locked away and subjected to brutality without the means to properly defend themselves. I don't want to celebrate anyone being incarcerated, Harvey Weinstein included, because neither American prisons nor American "Justice" are worthy of celebration whatsoever.

This is the failure of what many call Carceral Feminism but what might just as easily be labeled *Cruel Feminism*. As elucidated by University of Southern California law professor Aya Gruber:

> "Carceral feminism" describes mainstream American feminists' support for and reliance on the police and prison system as a tool of liberation. Attributing gender inequality to individual male abusers, feminists have found great success in expanding criminal laws, increasing arrests and prosecutions, making it easier for prosecutors to gain convictions, and subjecting individuals to long—and therefore "meaningful"—prison sentences. When feminists embrace individualistic criminal punishment, they relieve the state and society of the responsibility to create the structures and provide the support that prevents gender violence in the first place. Conventional accounts of mass incarceration fail to recognize the significant role carceral feminism played in building the American penal state and

elevating the United States to the condemnable status of most carceral nation on earth.

Simply put: carceral feminism functions from the logic that, as feminists, we can punish our way toward a brighter future. That by turning to state violence for solutions, we can build a safer world. That by enacting violence upon those who have enacted violence upon us, we will find healing.

At certain moments, it felt like the #MeToo movement got swept up in this. The goal of the movement increasingly became about identifying and punishing bad men.

It was hard to watch anger and a desire for punishment guide the conversation. To be told that it is *radical* to want to brutalize someone back. To be told that we are *good, powerful feminists* if we call for incarceration and further violence.

I want to be clear: there is no place in feminism, anti-racism, or trans/queer liberation for prisons. There is no feminist way to send someone to jail. In my view, there is no version of transformative feminism that includes prison sentences at all.

There is only ever room for restoration. Restorative justice—that overused and rarely enacted ideal—is the way forward, and the great failure of the #MeToo and Time's Up movements was that they barely considered that. Instead of calling for a fundamental rebuilding of how we understand justice, we called for more funds to file more court cases to incarcerate and punish more men.

What's most upsetting to me about this process is that it was cruel toward survivors. If we tell a survivor of any violence—especially sexual violence—that they are going to find healing or peace in an American court of law, we're mostly lying to them. What we're actually doing is setting them up for a retraumatizing trial with very little payoff, *if the case even goes to trial at all.* Even though he was found guilty, I imagine Harvey's trial was still harrowing for the survivors who had to testify. Enduring cross-examination from a defense attorney—where your character, reputation, and story are subjected to totalizing scrutiny and assault—is the last thing any survivor needs. And now that the New York State Court of Appeals has overturned Harvey's initial conviction on procedural grounds, his survivors will likely have to do it all. Over. Again.

We set survivors up.

And we tell them the lie that sending their perpetrator to prison will be justice served. We reinforce that notion over and over again. Which is ironic because most perpetrators are found not guilty, if charges are pressed in the first place. Harvey being found guilty is a *massive* exception to the rule. We ask survivors to testify and rip open their wounds afresh in front of the police, a judge, the media, and the world, and then most of the time, their perpetrator isn't even found responsible. This is by design.

We could design a justice system and judicial processes that don't treat survivors this way. The primary task of the #MeToo and Time's Up movements could've been to do so. We could've directed our attention toward reengineering and reimagining the justice process itself, used the momentum and momentary power we had to claim what has always been true: survivors of sexual violence—and, for that matter, survivors of *any* violence—are abused afresh by American courts. We could've used Harvey's trial as an opportunity to call for a fundamentally different type of justice and as a moment to name, for the world to hear, that a restorative justice approach is the only approach we will accept.

But we didn't. The attorneys—the people often least capable of seeing beyond and outside the confines of the abusive American "Justice" system, the people who've spent their lives *training* within it, perfecting its protocols and rules—took over and told survivors that sending Harvey to prison for the rest of his life would bring them peace. We should throw all of our funds toward *that*.

Technically, we won. We won the case. Harvey was found guilty not just in New York but in Los Angeles. Even with his New York conviction being overturned and a retrial on the horizon, he is likely going to die in jail. And at the time of his conviction, pundit upon pundit stated how happy they were that he would spend the rest of his life in prison. That this was him getting what he deserved. And we cheered as they said this, not yet able to acknowledge the fact that prison is never justice, that, spiritually speaking, this punitive response to trauma ultimately hurts *us* as much as it hurts our perpetrators.

I'm afraid we have a bad case of Mariska Hargitay Syndrome. We have watched too many episodes of *Law & Order: Special Victims Unit*. We have seen too many scripted narratives about court cases where justice is served. Hollywood has told story after story about "ethical prosecutors" and "good cops" and "dedicated detectives" and "impartial judges." We have venerated these fictional narratives because the stories about what actually happens in an American courtroom are rarely satisfying to watch. If we made a *real* anthology series about people coming forward to face their rapists in America, it would be four seasons of cops refusing to press charges in the first place.

As a feminist movement, our focus is every bit as myopic as Dick Wolf's. We direct seemingly all of our attention on attaining a guilty verdict. We focus the preponderance of our effort on getting to trial and "winning" incarceration. Then we CUT TO BLACK.

We rarely talk about what happens after that, after the guilty verdict is rendered and the perpetrator is locked away. The media considers the story done, the cameras are turned off, and the episode is over. Justice has been served. The story has come to a close.

But it hasn't.

Because now another human being has to spend the rest of their life in prison, alongside two million predominantly Black and brown men, writhing in pain, unable to eat as their collective teeth fall out.

· · ·

Justice contains multitudes. It is a cornucopia, holding within its vast horn an abundance of concepts, desires, and options. Most of it will nourish us; but hidden among what is nourishing, there is poison fruit. As a feminist movement, it's our job to go through and choose what we want for ourselves. We must carefully root around in the basket and delineate what will nourish us from what may kill us.

When we demand justice, we are asking for some combination of acknowledgment, culpability, apology, consequence, restitution, prevention, transformation, punishment, and retribution. The system of American "Justice"—and most court processes and systems throughout the world—contain a measure of each.

When we press charges against a man who assaulted us, we may receive an acknowledgment of what he did, a formal designation of culpability/guilt from the court, and an apology of some kind from him at the time of sentencing. If it's a civil case, we can receive financial restitution, and he will face some form of consequences as the perpetrator. If it's a criminal case, we don't receive restitution, but we get to see punishment doled out in the form of a jail sentence; therefore, retribution is done.

What we rarely receive is what we want most of all: the prevention of further harm and transformation of the culture and world that hurt us. Punishing and incarcerating perpetrators means they mostly do not transform. Recidivism is the expected outcome of American incarceration. In an American prison, there are few resources for perpetrators to heal or transform. Instead, they are forced further down the pipeline of violence and harm. American prisoners are released back into the world more destitute, more spiritually (and literally) impoverished, and more likely to hurt other people. If we pursue "justice" via an American court, even *if* our perpetrators are found guilty, we will not see prevention of further crime. We likely will not see transformation of either our perpetrators or the world that created them.

And if a perpetrator is found *not* guilty, we will receive worse than nothing. We will be forced to live in a world where we have not only been assaulted but have been formally and publicly deemed liars. We said he was guilty. We tried to hold him accountable for what he did to us. And then a jury of our peers and a judge decided that we made the whole thing up. This is the outcome for most people who try to hold perpetrators accountable in a court of law.

It is time for us to clear up any doubt about what we mean when we say "justice."

It begins by swearing off retribution and punishment altogether. We've gotta take those two options off the table. We are interested in stopping men from enacting violence, but containing further violence does not require punishment.

As a very rudimentary, far-from-perfect-but-immediately-actionable starting place, it could be as simple as differentiating between house arrest and prison. What is accomplished by imprisoning someone that cannot be accomplished through house arrest? Sure, house arrest isn't as *punishing* as a prison sentence, but that's precisely the point. If we are truly feminists, we do not need to punish people who have committed crimes; we merely need to prevent future harm (and, if we are feeling particularly brave and transformative, address the social conditions that lead people to inflict harm in the first place). House arrest, though still an imperfect type of confinement, could ensure that no one in your community—neither survivors nor anyone else—would have to confront a perpetrator of rape "on the street." Someone could be kept accountable and prevented from hurting others without forcing them to rot in a prison cell. And they could earn back their mobility and community status over the course of years and decades, sans incarceration, retribution, or torture.[*]

Is that so hard to imagine? A world where, as a feminist movement, we work to abolish prisons and fortify a different system altogether? Would it have been so impossible to gather the star power behind the #MeToo movement and declare that our moment *for* justice requires transforming what we mean *by* justice? Can we imagine a world where we empower the best in survivors and remove incarceration in an American prison from the table? Can we envision a world where, at the

---

[*]If you would like to know more about prison abolition and the myriad possibilities available to us, I recommend reading Angela Davis's *Are Prisons Obsolete?* (Seven Stories Press, 2003), Ruth Wilson Gilmore's *Abolition Geography: Essays Towards Liberation* (Verso Books, 2022), and Aya Gruber's *The Feminist War on Crime* (University of California Press, 2020).

beginning of Harvey Weinstein's trial, the women pressing charges released an op-ed in *The New York Times* declaring that they would not seek a prison sentence and were instead seeking financial restitution and house arrest? Can we dream of a world in which we extend radical mercy toward men who perpetrate rape and assault, predominantly as a way of retaining our moral superiority and our own souls?

I may be naïve, but I don't find such a world so difficult to imagine. We can knock powerful, abusive men off their pedestals without *torturing* them. I don't like living in a world where Harvey Weinstein is being abused by some prison warden on our feminist behalf. I would prefer to live in a world where, instead, all of Harvey's money is given to survivors and he is compelled to spend the rest of his days under house arrest in a meh one-bedroom apartment somewhere in L.A., allowed out into the world to perform community service, go to doctor's appointments, attend worship services, see his family, and receive therapy. I want a world where Harvey's fate can stand as a symbol of our feminist compassion, strength, and moral superiority.

Instead, Harvey's fate—to be neglected in an American prison and subsequently die there—exists as a mark of shame.

If we want a world free from violent men, we must first free ourselves from the idea of carceral justice. If we want to create a system where both survivors and the world can heal *through* the process of seeking justice, we must boldly declare the truth:

When it comes to Bad Men, there's a difference between desiring culpability and desiring punishment. One heals us. The other rips us all to shreds.

Ninety-three percent
of inmates
in federal prison
are men.

In America,
one in every 112 men
is behind bars.

THE BUNKER

When it comes to identity and our sense of self, metaphors matter more than we give them credit for. Ask any queer or trans person you know. For almost all of us, the metaphor of "The Closet" shapes our self-understanding from the moment we realize we are different.

There's a glorious efficiency to the thing. When I was first coming to terms with my sexuality as an adolescent, the path was made astonishingly clear. I learned what "the closet" was in the same breath as I learned about *being gay*. The metaphor didn't miss a beat. It was an idiot-proof path forward, a flow chart with very little room for error.

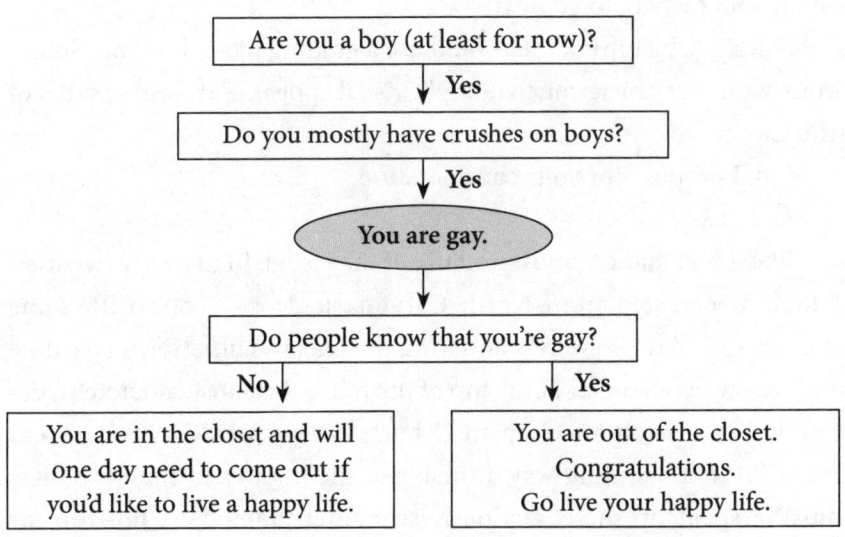

The idea of coming out of the closet was instilled concurrently with my newfound identity as a queer person. And it took the guesswork out of the equation. When it dawned on me that I was in fact gay, I never really wondered, *What do I do with this information?* I never scratched my head, unsure about where to go next. I didn't have to sit in the existential dread that comes with ambiguity. From the moment I realized I was gay, I knew, at least in part, what the future would hold.

I knew that I would one day come out. I would one day open up the heteronormative chamber I'd been sealed in and show the world my true colors. I would make my way past the coats and shirts and ties and blazers, grab for the metaphorical doorknob, and enter the room. I would reveal who I really was to the world, and though it would be scary, it would set me free.

I'm not sure what I would've done with myself if I hadn't had the metaphor of the closet to guide my next steps and help me conceptualize where to go next. The fear and anxiety of not knowing where to go would've probably eaten me alive.

But I never had to answer that question.

Through the power of a single metaphor, I was set on a course toward freedom, self-actualization, joy, and late-night sequins. I was freed from doubt about where to go next.

Which is why I think men could use a guiding metaphor, too. Something with every bit as much oomph, visual appeal, and clarity as that of The Closet.

Men, I propose for your consideration:

The Bunker.

I like it first and foremost because of the visual. In my early twenties, I took a road trip from North Carolina to Nova Scotia with some friends. One day, we were wandering the craggy, cliff-strewn coastline and we saw it: a bunker at the top of the hill. A brutalist concrete structure built to watch for German U-boats during World War II, it was beautiful in a haunting way. I imagined the hours and hours soldiers must've spent up there, anxiously searching the endless horizon for threats that, by and large, never materialized. I thought about how cold and miserable they must've been as the wind whipped up the cliffs and through the many openings in the concrete. I thought about how agonizing it must've felt to be sealed off from such a beautiful landscape by thick concrete walls. As you stand in one of these old Nova Scotian bunkers, the cliffs and sea beyond start to seem more like a projection on a very wide screen. You are just so *separate* from what's around you—the world framed in an uncanny, drastic way—it almost feels like you aren't even *there*.

The Bunker is the metaphorical space where men huddle together with their guns and rations, fearful, watchful, and scared of being hurt. It is the thick, brutalist, identitarian structure that men are confined to from a very young age. It is the concrete that, if they aren't careful, will be their tomb. It is cold. There is little comfort there, except a perfunctory sense of safety.

But the bunker is also a lie. Because so long as you are in a bunker, there is no such thing as safety. You may be safe from attack, but the idea of attack is always just outside. Ever present. A logical fallacy. Surely the outside world must be dangerous, or else why would this bunker exist? At a certain point, living under fear of attack is scarcely different from *being* under attack.

You stay there, miserable, malnourished, devoid of sunlight, eating terrible-tasting dehydrated rations, and do your best to convince yourself that this is life. That this is what you must do to stay alive. That this is what you must do to be safe. That the war is always, always just outside, right on your doorstep.

There's a psychological term for this type of thinking. Sociologists refer to it as *siege mentality*. It's a tactic most often used by authoritarian regimes—think North Korea, Nazi Germany, Russia, Israel, or, increasingly, the United States. Convince everyone that they are perpetually under attack and what do you receive in return? Perpetual obedience. Convince everyone that they are under siege and they will do whatever you want. Kill a mother in Gaza? Sure. Report your neighbor to the KGB? Absolutely. Starve out people you don't like? Why not. The moment someone starts trying to convince you that you're under attack from all sides, they're likely trying to manipulate you into doing something abominable—either to others *or to yourself.* Siege mentality is a psychological tool responsible for some of the greatest atrocities in human history, many of which are still ongoing.

As a spiritual description, I think this increasingly captures the nature of contemporary manhood. It is the demand to always be ready for conflict, to always have your guard up, to always be prepared for war. You go to the gym to keep your muscles big because you *never know when you might need to use them.* You keep a rifle under your bed and a second rifle in your truck, because *you never know when the attack is coming.* You don't let anyone new in because they could hurt you. All strangers are a threat. *Nonbinary people and trans people and women are coming for you and your children and your entire way of life!* proclaim vile right-wingers, attempting to scare you into submission. *Dangerous outsiders and immigrants are trying to take everything you have!*

Here's where the beauty begins, because it's so simple. The moment you accept that you are, in fact, in a bunker—the moment you recognize that you've fallen prey to a siege mentality—you've also accepted that there is only one thing to do: escape it.

Everything is waiting for you outside. Trees. Nature. Birds. Sunsets. Joy. Dancing. Other people. Food. *Proper* food. Fresh-baked croissants. Coffee. Burbling streams. Seashells. Everything.

You can't begin to live fully until you escape. Your real life only begins the day you flee.

In the same way that no queer or trans person can be happy until they come out of the closet, no man can be happy until he *escapes the bunker.*

And what does *that* mean? It means leaving behind the idea that the world outside is hostile. It means leaving behind the idea that life is nothing more than perpetual war. It means leaving behind the idea that you must be strong, that you are going to spend your entire life *defending* your life from others who want to take it. It means letting go of the idea that others are necessarily bad. That women and gender noncon- forming people and queer people and people of different religions and races and ethnicities are adversaries trying to steal what you have. That anything outside what you've been taught is dangerous and out to get you.

And it means leaving behind the people who trapped you. You may have to leave behind your father. You may have to leave behind your grandfather. You will certainly have to leave behind that one awful uncle who berated you when you expressed gentleness as a child.

At some point, your desire *for freedom* must overtake everything. You must flee the bunker with whoever is willing to go with you, and compassionately leave the others behind. You may not even be able to say goodbye. Men who are in the bunker with you may try to trap you there, confine you, or abuse you into staying. But you can't listen to them. You can't let them stop you. Sneak out in the dead of night with nothing but the clothes on your back, if you need.

Escape is not without risks. Like coming out of the closet, escaping the bunker is a gargantuan risk. At first it will be terrifying. You will have no idea what to do with yourself. You will leave behind the life you've known in pursuit of a mere promise: that a life lived in a bunker is no life at all. You will have no immediate guarantees of safety or ease on the other side. Those things may take years to find.

But you will find warmth again. You will find food. It may take a while, but you will find community. And you will find care. Bit by bit, piece by piece, you will build a life differently, on your own terms, of your own volition, by your own design. You will build, for the first time, a life of true freedom and agency. At long last, you will find liberation from who you were told you had to be simply because you were born with a penis. You will figure out what it means to be your own *person*, above what it means to be your own *man*.

We're all cheering for you. After you escape, we will be there on the other side, waiting to feed you and clothe you and help you build yourself back up. We will be there to help you heal. That is a promise.

But it all begins with your escape, with blindly fleeing into the dark night. Bravely, foolishly, but *finally* as the hero of your own story.

Want to become a happy queer person? The path forward is clear. You must come out of the closet.

Want to become a happy man? The path forward is now equally clear. You must escape the bunker.

Addendum: Some Sample Bunker Busting

A common misconception about coming out of the closet is that it's a one-and-done affair. That you come out a single time and then never have to do it again.

It doesn't really work like that. Coming out is an iterative process, one that occurs throughout various moments in your queer life. There are big coming out milestones—telling your parents or siblings is arguably the most common—but there are also small ways that coming out occurs in daily life. For queer women, it can be as simple as correcting a new acquaintance when they ask if you have a boyfriend. Simply responding, "I don't have a girlfriend right now, but lord knows I'm trying," becomes a form of coming out. If you're trans, it can be as simple as showing someone a childhood photo—a picture of you from before you transitioned—or saying something cheeky like "back when I was a boy" as you stand before someone in a cute dress. *Presto!* You've come out.

Escaping the bunker is no different. There are huge, large-scale ways for men to escape the expectations placed on them. But there are also subtle, smaller versions of the thing.

And because we're building this concept together from the ground up, I think it's helpful if I take a moment to spell out—in ways both large and small—what escaping the bunker can look like in practice. *Escaping the Bunker for Idiots,* if you will. A brief guide for you and/or the men in your life.

Large-Scale Bunker Busting:

- Your father is a professional football player, and he has been putting you in football training camps every summer since you were five. But you're thirteen now, and you know that you actually want to be an engineer, not a football player, when you grow up. Tell your father you aren't going to football camp this year. If he sends you anyway, run away from camp or get in a *ton* of trouble while you're there or just refuse to do any of the stuff they tell you to until they kick you out. This is escaping the bunker.

- You're fifteen and grew up in a military family. For your entire life, your father has been pressuring you to enlist in the marines when you graduate high school. Sit him down over a nice relaxing cup of chamomile. Tell him you ain't doing that. You've escaped.

- You're an adult now, and your cousin is abusive. He regularly hits his wife and his children. In your family, this has become normalized. Take him out for a nice dinner, buy him a big ol' bloody steak, just the way he likes it. When dessert comes and he's all bloated and sleepy, tell him that his abuse is not acceptable, that you're watching him, and that his children and wife (who have agreed to this plan in advance) are going to stay with you for a bit while he goes to an intensive, in-patient anger-management program. If he refuses, tell him you have a family attorney on retainer and will be providing his wife and children refuge at your home while they work on separating from him legally.

- Your father is mourning the death of your mother, but he's unable to access his grief and won't seek help. Instead, he's drinking. He's spiraling into alcoholism, fast. Sit him down, tell him he needs help. Take him to a meeting and some grief counseling. Do not allow him to escape talking about his feelings. Insist on asking him how his grieving process is going each time you speak. Ask a billion questions until he stops giving one-word answers. If he protests this, tell him you need him to work through his grief and feel it in order for you to have a healthy, safe relationship. Badger the living hell out of him until he starts sharing.

- No matter how old you are, if you are living with an abusive man who is hurting you, run away as soon as you are able. Protect yourself. Find a relative or a friend's family to stay with, permanently if necessary. Do not hide his abuse for him. Make it known.

- At any age, at any point in your life, sit down with your family at Christmas dinner and say to your parents, "I am not the man you want me to be, and I am no longer going to try. I am going to be my own person. The way you raised me, the ways in which you tried to make a man of me, hurt me more than you know." Then ask them to pass the eggnog.

- Similarly, you can sit down with your family at *your birthday dinner* and ask them why they thought it was okay for them to abuse you, emotionally or physically, as a child. A birthday dinner is the perfect trap. They'll never see it coming. Bring up specific memories of times when your parents tried to tell you to be a man, moments when they hit you if you didn't comply, or didn't listen to you when you protested, or shut you down, or shamed you for having emotions.

- If you are having a child and you work in a job that does not offer equal parental leave for men, call HR and tell them they need to fix that. Demand that they increase the maximum parental leave for male parents, and then *actually take the maximum*. Y'know. So you can raise your fucking child. It will set an example for every single man you work with: taking time off to raise your children is important, worth doing, and should not have to fundamentally disrupt your career. The more power you have at your company, the greater impact this will have.

- While you're at it, use every single one of your vacation and sick days, *always*. Ignore the socialization that told you a man is worthy only if he works himself to the bone. Relax. Take glorious vacations and brag loudly about them at the water cooler.

- Also consider starting or joining a union. Labor unions are pivotal tools where people band together in order to resist the imperative that they ruin their lives and bodies for corporate profit. They are important for everyone, regardless of gender, but for you they can represent a leap out of the bunker. Men are told that the more they work, the more manly they are. Men are also told that asking for a break or less work is somehow akin to weakness. Ew. Start a union and save yourself.

- If your extended family is big on hunting and a boy in your family doesn't want to shoot a deer, tell the rest of the family that they have to respect his decision and fuck off. Be bold about it. If a boy in your family *does* want to go hunting, be sure you have a long conversation with him about the sacredness of all life, about respecting the ecosystem, and about hunting responsibly.

- Get arrested protesting against police brutality in your local area. Or get arrested protesting against war. Get arrested protesting the violence of men. Let people know where you stand on men murdering for capital, pride, and/or sport.

- Tell your father that you will not permit his grandchildren to visit him unless he removes all guns from the house or securely locks them in a safe. He's welcome to visit them at *your house,* but you will not place your children in a home filled with accessible firearms.

- Or tell your father that you cannot have a relationship with him until he goes to therapy. That he has hurt you deeply, that you need to take a break, and that he needs to spend some time working on himself.

- *Et cetera.*

Bunker-Busting Light:

- Your little brother wants to take dance classes, but your father forbids it. Lie to your father. Drive your little brother to dance classes after school and tell your dad that you're taking him to the library or to sportsball or whatever. Keep this up as long as possible until your little brother is really talented and can go full Billy Elliot on your dad's ass.

- Your sister wants to cut her hair short, but your father and mother won't permit it. Wouldn't it be a shame if you took her to Great Clips anyway? Or, if money is tight, just grabbed the scissors in the kitchen and did it for her yourself? Watch a YouTube tutorial first, though.

- You are a sixteen-year-old and your friends are being misogynistic. Don't let them get away with it. Ask them to explain themselves. Make them sweat. The best way to ruin a misogynistic joke is to pretend that you don't understand why it's funny and ask someone to *explain it.* If your friends don't stop making misogynistic jokes, ask them to tell the joke again in front of their mom. Y'know, cause it was *so funny.* That'll shut 'em up.

- Hug your father. Like, actually hug him. None of that machismo "pat on the back" bullshit. A real, genuine, big squeeze that you hold for five seconds or more. Count it out. If he gets uncomfortable, good. He needs to learn to sit with that. You're his *child.* Unless he has sensory processing issues, he should be able to be held by you. *You're his child.*

- Cry as much as you want. Cry in public. Cry at dinner. Cry both in the airport and on the plane. Cry on the phone. Cry at everyone you can, whenever you get the urge. Just fucking weep. It's astonishingly effective. Blows the bunker door wide open.

- Show up for your guy friends like girls show up for each other in the movies. If your bestie's girlfriend breaks up with him, turn up on his doorstep with Ben & Jerry's, some Coors Light, or a nice IPA (I don't care) and a list of seventeen reasons why he's the best.

- Paint your nails bright pink. You'll destroy the bunker *and* look sexy in one blow. Everyone looks amazing with hot-pink nails.

- If you're feeling shy, you can also paint them black.

- Dark purple looks nice, too.

- Dress up as a woman for Halloween, but actually enjoy it. Like, be a hot girl. Have a grand old time and twirl in that tutu or whatever and explore your gender and let everyone see how much fun you're having and how much you're enjoying yourself, then question their own relationship with masculinity.

- Start a rumor that you're bisexual. Kiss your gay friend for fun in front of the entire school (if he's down for it, of course). Dance with him at prom. And if you happen to actually enjoy kissing him or dancing with him, that's great, too. Maybe you'll get yourself your first boyfriend. Either way, you'll mess with everyone and it'll be fantastic.

- Tell your mom and dad you're going to be a vegetarian for the month of December. Decline meat in their presence. You will be shocked how angry they get.

- Let your wrists hang limp. It's fun.

- Cross your legs the girlie way. Do so with confidence and poise. Like a *sophisticated artist.*

- Grow your hair out as long as you want. Revel in how glorious it is. You are a lion, and this is your mane. Sit in a sunlit field and braid it.

- In general, take a moment to look in the mirror and let yourself feel cute and pretty and handsome. Allow yourself permission to luxuriate in your own image. Men do not do this often enough (dysmorphically flexing at yourself in the mirror at the gym doesn't count).

- Fearlessly walk into the women's section of any store you'd like. Pick out a top you think is cute. Try it on in the store. Fuck the haters. It's a *garment*. You have every right to try it on and see how it feels. This is *America*, goddamnit.

- Wear short shorts. Or a crop top. Or if you're feeling bold, wear a dress for fun. Why not?

- The next time you're walking down the street, twirl. Even one twirl is enough to do the trick.

- Or you can skip. Or sashay. Or strut. Travolta that motherfucking sidewalk. "Travolta" is a verb now.

- Comment like a girl on your friends' Instagram posts: "Omg wife me!" "You are SOOOO HANDSOME." "Babe alert!!!!" "I'm so gay for you dude."

- Tell your friends you love them in a gay way. It's arguably the superior way to love.

- Notice the fact that your friend Ian actually has, like, really pretty eyes. Then tell him and watch him blush.

- Carry your child around in public a lot. Be all cute with your kid. Be a good, invested dad in front of everyone you can—it shouldn't be radical, but it is.

- Play dress-up with your four-year-old daughter. Let her do your makeup.

- Play dress-up with your four-year-old son. Let him do your makeup, too.

- Buy your effeminate nephew a Barbie for Christmas. Give it to him proudly, *in front of* your shitty brother-in-law.

- Give your neighbor's son a twirling fairy doll for his birthday. Those things are fun, period. (Watch out for fireplaces though. We've all seen the video.)

- The next time a "girlie" pop song plays, dance *with enthusiasm.* Go for it, babe. The stupider you look, the more good it will do your soul.

- Enjoy your life *exuberantly* and with *a general silliness.* Men aren't supposed to do that, apparently?

Congratulations! Your life has temporarily become a giant gender-stereotype-themed escape room. Normally you have to pay for that type of thing. But you're a man and live in a gender policing hellscape, so you get it for free. Patriarchy strikes again, or whatever.

Men are
seven times
more likely
than women
to use a firearm
when ending
their own lives.

MONSTER TALK

My father was killed in a cycling accident. That man loved his bicycle. Most weekend mornings, spring through fall, he'd meet up with a group of friends and they'd bike fifty miles for fun. Endorphins are a hell of a drug. I only sort of got it.

Usually, they rode in a large group. But occasionally, toward the end of the ride, my dad would peel off and bike the last two or three miles home on his own.

One Sunday, he was biking alone, a mile or so from our house, when a large car tried to pass him on a narrow two-lane road. He moved as far to the edge of the road as he could, but it was curvy, and he couldn't see ahead very well. Next thing he knew, the razor-thin shoulder of the road dropped out from under him, and his front wheel slammed into a pothole at thirty-five miles per hour. The bike stopped. My father did not. He was thrown over the handlebars of his bike, hurled through the air momentarily, then face-planted straight into a rock.

He didn't die right away, or even quickly. For the time being, he blacked out. The helmet took most of the blow. His face took the remainder, as well as a few portions of his skull and his neck. As chance would have it, the woman in the next car to pass him was a trauma nurse. She pulled over, stopped traffic, and triaged until the ambulance could arrive. Without her, I imagine my father might've died then and there. Thankfully, my father didn't remember any of this.

There are days when I am grateful that his helmet did its job so well and that nurse was there. He did not die in the crash, not *really*. He messed up bones, tore up large parts of his cheeks and face, and fucked up a few teeth, but he did not die.

Instead, he died slowly over the three years that followed. While his bones and soft tissues managed to heal, the nerves in his face did not. What ensued was the most harrowing, misery-filled death I can imagine: a slow, agonizing, years-long death at the hands of a neurological pain disorder that clustered around his trigeminal nerve—the most sensitive nerve in the human body. You know how you can feel the wind on your face more subtly than anywhere else? That one.

He spent years fighting the pain. Praying it would get better. Praying his face would stop hurting. But it never relented, not once. Toward the end of his life, three years and three failed brain surgeries later, he would have attacks of phantom pain so intense he'd pass out. He'd writhe. He'd tense up so completely, he'd stop breathing, approaching the edge of a heart attack or a stroke or aspiration on his own spit. In the heart of the COVID lockdown, my mom and I were powerless to stop it. For six months of my life, I had to watch my father endure a phantom knife entering his skull, at random intervals, two or three times a day. The doctors threw up their hands in confusion. It was misery. In the final equation, my father had to overdose. It was either that or he'd have to surrender himself to dying from raw pain, from his nervous system peeling itself apart, millimeter by excruciating millimeter.

There were many days when we all—my father included—wished his helmet hadn't done its job so well. That the nurse hadn't arrived on the scene so quickly. An instant death would've been far more compassionate. Now that he's been dead a few years, I can finally say such things.

Witnessing my father's agonizing death, a death by neurological torture, is the worst thing I have ever endured. It blows everything else out of the water by a mile. The scale of the trauma is so colossal I still struggle to contend with it. I doubt I will ever fully make peace with what happened. To this day, when I watch someone's face tense up in pain or twitch, I have to go to a separate room to stop the flashbacks. Sometimes a PTSD diagnosis is so redundant you don't even bother.

The full story of his accident, suffering, and death is not one I can tell in these pages.

But I want to share one facet of the experience, a facet that's continually come to mind as I've been contemplating the violence, anger, and hostility men have directed at me over the course of my genderfucked life.

And it is this: after my father's accident and subsequent death, I began to hate anyone I saw on a bicycle.

It's completely irrational, I know. But that's because it is a trauma response. And trauma does not always operate with logic or rationality. Trauma feels like a blender, pulverizing your brain and liquefying it into gruel. Trauma can rewire your brain so powerfully, your thoughts no longer fully make sense, even to you. The wires seem crossed forever. You think blue and see orange. You say yes when you mean no. You lash out when you meant to give a hug. Trauma gets your brain all fucked.

My brain is no exception. No matter how much therapy one does, no matter how many healing psychedelic trips one attempts, no one is exempt from the way trauma affects the mind.

I want to illustrate for you what these thoughts are like, to give you a small glimpse into my trauma-addled psyche. Fair warning: it is neither pretty nor flattering. It doesn't make me look good.

The other day, I was driving down Santa Monica Boulevard eastbound at rush hour when I saw a cyclist up ahead of me. My heart started racing. My blood boiled as panic and anger and grief geysered their way to the surface.

And all of a sudden, as if by mental reflex, all I could think was:

> Fuck you, you stupid fuck. I hope you die an excruciating death, too. And believe me, you will. It may not be today, it may not be tomorrow, it may not be the day after that, but one of these days soon, you will lose the war you are foolishly waging with cars. You will lose badly. You will be crushed and mangled by two tons of metal hurtling your way. If you're lucky, you'll die on impact

or the tires will snap your neck or shatter your skull or demolish your rib cage and all of your vital organs as they run you over. If you're unlucky, you'll survive. Then you and everyone you love will get to enjoy rehabilitating your brutalized body, which will never be the same. You might be paralyzed, or lose a limb, or never be able to talk again from the head trauma. Whatever it is, it won't be pretty. You and everyone you love will regret it for the rest of your life. You may have to end your own life, like my father did.

And you think that everyone who knows you and loves you will be sympathetic. You think that they'll consider your accident as a horrific error by the driver. You think they'll blame the driver who hit you or ran you off the road, into a ditch. But I got bad news for you, you psychopathic, risk-seeking idiot of a cyclist: they will all secretly blame you. They will hate you for putting them through that. They will hate you for your hubris. On your deathbed, they will look down at you and think, "If only they hadn't been so fucking stupid. Why did they put themself in harm's way like that? Why didn't they love us enough to keep themself safe? Why did they pursue a hobby that is tantamount to self-harm? Why in the world did they think they could wage a war with automobiles and *win*?" David and Goliath is a myth—a biblical allegory—not actual advice.

And then, for a moment, a different thought hits me, one that I never listen to, but one that comes up in my mind. Again, not pretty stuff.

Just run them over. How dare they do this to the people they love? How dare they do this to you? Run them over like someone ran over your father. Teach everyone a lesson: people who are idiotic enough to ride a bicycle alone down car-crowded roads need to be taught. If you run over this person, you can teach them.

Maybe if someone had gotten run over near your house in the

years leading up to your dad's accident, he wouldn't've been so stupid. Maybe he could've been spared if someone else had been the example. If someone had done you the courtesy of running over a cyclist in your neighborhood, maybe that would've been enough of a warning to your father. Maybe you wouldn't have had to lose him.

Which is why you should run this person over right now. You should hurt them so they stop. They are putting themself and everyone else at risk. They are terrifying you and retraumatizing you and now all you can think about is your father crying out for his mother, begging to die as he writhes in that hospital bed and the nurses do nothing.

"Just let me go be with my mom," he begged the nurses, tears of terror streaming down his cheeks. "Mom, I'm coming. Mom, please. Please let me di—uugghhhgughgpfttttchhhh."

(This is the sound of him choking on his own spit. I don't know the proper onomatopoeia. How do you transliterate the sound of your father being waterboarded by his own panicked body?)

Am I proud that I think these things? No.

Do I enjoy thinking this way? Also, no.

Would I ever, in a million years, actually listen to these thoughts as I'm driving a vehicle? Never.

Am I ashamed and horrified and crying as I commit these words to the page? Of course.

But these thoughts are there. They torture me each time my brain lights up with them. And every time I pass a bicyclist on the road, I have to confront the trauma afresh. I see a bicyclist and all I can think about is my father's face, contorted with inhuman, CIA-torture-grade pain. I see someone on a bicycle on the road and all I can think about is the fact that my father will never be able to hold my hand or scratch my back again, that he was taken from me twenty years too soon. That he will never read this book or any other book I write. I will never know the sound of his voice again, hear the love in it, because he was foolish enough to wage a war he couldn't win. It's brutal.

It makes driving hell.

. . .

Before we continue, take a breath here. Trust me, you need it. It's the home stretch.

And if you have the capacity, say a little prayer for my dad.

. . .

Even under the most seemingly irrational trauma responses, there is a logic of some kind. And for the sake of shifting our approach to men and their trauma responses, I want us to investigate the logic behind my own.

What's fascinating to me is that in my trauma-muddled mind, I have only formed a hatred of cyclists. It's to the degree that being a cyclist mostly disqualifies you from being my friend. I used to have a few friends who rode bikes. I have put distance between myself and them. I struggle to care for anyone who rides a bike anymore. If you ride your bike on anything but bike paths or bike lanes, know that you are already sort of dead to me. I can't lose someone to a bike ever again.

I have not, however, formed an equally strong hatred *of cars* or of *aggressive drivers.*

I think it's in part because *I* am an aggressive driver. I zoom through lanes like an asshole. I have road-rage issues. I don't stop at yellow lights. They put speed bumps in my mom's neighborhood and I regularly weave onto the wrong side of the road to get around them. You can condemn me if you like. But before you do, live and drive in central Los Angeles for seven years, first.

I have trouble being angry at the person who ran my father off the road because I see part of myself in them. In the past, before my father's accident, I passed bikers a bit too eagerly and perhaps a bit too close.

When a solo cyclist is on a two-lane road slowing traffic down to a halt and causing a huge clog in our municipal arteries, I often erupt in anger and frustration.

Trying to face the ways in which my own behavior as a driver was implicated in creating my father's accident is enough to undo me completely. If I sat with that thought for too long, I might never recover.

My mind and my trauma response intervenes to protect me from all that. I cannot blame the driver without facing my own (far more abstract but still very real) culpability. And so I don't. My subconscious shuts that door for me in advance. *The problem is not with the driver*, my mind whispers to me. *Like you, they were using the road in the normal, socially acceptable way. It was with your father, who was fundamentally defying all norms of road etiquette and safety by biking alone down a highly trafficked, extremely windy two-lane road. What did he expect aggressive Southern suburban drivers to do? Not try to pass him for two whole miles of winding road?*

In this internal monologue, I see something else: a belief that my father owed it to me and those he loved to protect himself better. Anyone who's ever been part of a social movement knows that when facing a behemoth rival, you cannot do so alone. You cannot go rogue and decide that you're going to face it on your own. You can't protest police brutality as a single person and not expect to be brutalized by the cops. You must do so with others. Even then, you'll likely face violence, but the likelihood of you being *outright murdered in cold blood* is far less when there are people who support you by your side.

My father knew this. He knew that he shouldn't bike alone, as a lone ranger. He knew that he was safer in a pack. Aggressive drivers will always, always try to pass a single person on a bike. But if there are seven of you, they will be forced to wait and respect your collective right to the roadway.

Why did my father think he could stray from the pack and be okay? Didn't he love me enough to protect me from that? The honest answer is no. I think a small part of him probably enjoyed the risk. The feeling of being a loner, a cowboy. I think he liked the solitude of biking alone every now and then, somehow believing himself to be above the risk, an exception to the harrowing stories about maiming and death. His own impish "fuck you" to drivers who refuse to share the road.

When I see a group of cyclists, all I think is *They better stay in that pack. They better not separate.* My trauma response doesn't hit nearly as hard.

It's only when I see someone foolish enough to bike *alone* that I lose it. In an instant, they become my father, biking alongside me, taunting me, saying, *Look how heroic and bold I am,* moments before hot asphalt makes its way into their skull.

• • •

I would like to think that I am above men. That, as a nonbinary-trans-lady-who-will-never-transition or whatever the fuck I am, I have transcended the awful ways men think and am better than them.

But I am no different. None of us are. At the end of the day, we are all human beings with brains that are susceptible to becoming violent when exposed to enough trauma. It took my father being killed by a reckless driver for me to get it, but I am not above anyone and never will be.

At the end of the day, I am my father's child. I, too, am reckless. I, too, have never grown up. I, too, have stayed in touch with my childlike sense of impishness and joy.

Which, I'm sure, is what my father was *actually* feeling as he biked down that curving two-lane road. I don't think the possibility of being run off the road and ripping his face open was anywhere in his mind.

Instead, I imagine he was communing with his inner child as he zipped on his bike down a beautiful road. In the moments leading up to his skull bashing rock, I imagine he was simply feeling *free.* He was feeling the gorgeous, perfect late-summer wind whipping by his face. He was feeling the boyish thrill of biking *fast,* of *almost* flying. He was looking at the lush, late-summer trees, sun dappling their leaves. He was feeling beautiful and alive and whole. He was rejecting the imperative that being an adult man means always being serious. He was embracing play. Just him and his bike. No longer a middle-aged man. He was a glorious, happy child once more.

It's the same feeling I have when I wear a pretty dress on a perfect spring day, put in my headphones, play my song du jour, and strut down the sidewalk like the supermodel I am. As I stroll and sashay and vogue and *turn*, I am not an adult in their thirties with back problems. I am a child, rummaging once more in the freedom of the dress-up bin. I am not a nonbinary person bravely facing transphobia; I am simply a kid at play. Dancing through the street, I am the star of my own film, *alive*, vivacity jolting through my whole body, lightning and butterflies in my fingertips, rainbows on the soles of my shoes. I am just happy. I am just me. Joy incarnate.

As I flit and flutter down the street, I don't think about the fact that I, too, am taking on absurd risk. I don't think about the fact that any man with enough transphobic hate in his heart could bash my brains out at any moment. I don't sing, "Bye, bye, Miss American Pie." This will not be the day that I die.

Like my father, I am foolishly putting myself in danger by expressing joy in a way that defies the rules of the road. Like my father, I am taunting aggressive drivers, tempting them to make a pass, daring them to punish me for the "reckless" way I wield my individuality.

When I understand myself as my father on a bike, it all snaps into place.

When men pass me on the street, wearing something beautiful and bold, openly defying the dominance of masculinity, many of them must feel the same way I do when I see a biker on a crowded road, openly defying the dominance of cars.

To a man who has watched someone he loves face abuse because they were foolish enough to stand up to a man, who has been traumatized by witnessing violence or loss, I am no different from a cyclist. Replace "father who was run over by a car because he had the audacity to bike" with "little brother who was abused by your father because he had the audacity to express his femininity" and the inner monologue rewrites itself.

Fuck you. I hope you get hurt, too. And believe, me, you will. It may not be today, it may not be tomorrow, but one of these days you will lose the war you are foolishly waging with men. You will lose badly. You will be crushed or maimed or sliced to bits. You will be mangled by fists or guns or knives turned your way. If you're lucky, you'll die then and there. If you're unlucky, you'll survive their attack. Then you and everyone you love will get to enjoy rehabilitating your brutalized body, which will never be the same. You might be paralyzed, or lose a limb, or never be able to talk again from the head trauma. Whatever it is, it won't be pretty. You and everyone you love will regret it for the rest of your life.

And you think that everyone who knows you and loves you will be sympathetic. You think that they'll consider the whole thing as a horrific act of malice by the man who attacked you. You think they'll blame the man who hurt you and left you for dead. But I got bad news for you, you risk-seeking idiot of a nonbinary child-person: they will all secretly blame you. They will hate you for putting them through that. They will hate you for your hubris. At your hospital bed, they will look down at you and think, "If only they hadn't been so fucking stupid. Why did they put themself in harm's way like that? Why didn't they love us enough to keep themself safe? Why did they pursue a gender expression that is tantamount to self-harm? Why in the world did they think they could wage a war with all men and win?" David and Goliath is a myth—a biblical allegory—not actual advice.

Like that, the hatred many men feel for me makes sense. They hate me not because they want me to be hurt, but because my very existence in the world reminds them of how much they *already have been hurt.* They hate me not because they actually want me to be injured, but because, to their trauma-addled minds, I am putting myself and everyone I love at risk, just to wear a stupid dress. Ironically enough, they want to protect me. They want me to be safe. But they have only ever experienced a world where people like me get hurt for not playing by the rules. And they are furious that I could be so foolish as to expose myself, and everyone I love, to that risk.

Which leads their trauma-riddled minds to the same place it led mine.

> You should hurt them. How dare they do this to the people they love? How fucking dare they? How dare they do this to *me*? Beat them like your father beat your little brother when he found him wearing that dress. People who are idiotic enough to defy gender norms in public, to wear lipstick alongside their five-o'clock shadow and walk alone down the street, need to be taught. If you assault this person, you can teach everyone. Maybe if some other kid in the neighborhood had gotten beaten up real bad for being a sissy, your little brother wouldn't've been so fucking stupid. Maybe he could've been spared if someone else had been the example. If someone had done you the courtesy of beating up a different faggot in your neighborhood, maybe that would've been enough of a warning to your little brother. Maybe you wouldn't have had to go through that.

> Which is why you should assault this person right now. You should hurt them so they stop. They are putting themself and everyone else at risk. They are terrifying you and retraumatizing you and now all you can think about is your little brother crying out for you and your mother, begging your father to stop as his fists landed blow after blow.

> "Dad, please. Dad, I won't do it again. Dad, PLEASE," he begged. "DAD, I—"

. . .

It's hard, watching your own words turn against you so quickly. But I'm afraid this is what empathy requires.

It requires finding the common thread between you and the person you've deemed a monster.

It requires identifying the monster inside of your own heart.

We must understand men differently. We must give them every bit as much compassion as we want for ourselves. We must know them to be people like us: People who have been brutalized. People whose souls and minds have also been ripped to shreds by trauma. People whose trauma responses are often so powerful, they too no longer make sense.

People who—like us—are in need of healing, kindness, and, most of all, *help.*

EPILOGUE

Dear Men,

I wanted to end this book with a conversation between us. Just me, you, and the dead tree this is printed on. I'm here to ask one question and make one suggestion. That's it. It shouldn't take long.

My question is this: *Do you feel exhausted?*

I only ask because I was. I was so tired. If I had to identify the one thing most feminists miss when talking about masculinity, it's that being a man isn't a privilege so much as it is strenuous and stressful and takes inordinate energy to maintain. Trying to be "man enough" made me tired in my very bones.

You may not find it as exhausting as *I* did, but surely on some level you can agree: it's a constant performance. Carry yourself correctly. Position your body in the correct way. Push your limits all the time. Always be hustling. Always be proving yourself. Always be taking up as much space as possible. Always be competing. Never stop competing.

For me, manhood was a competition I could never win. For a while, I thought that was just because I am nonbinary and have never been very good at masculinity. But the older I got, the more I realized that it had *nothing to do with me or my gender.*

For everyone, manhood is a competition that can never truly be won. It is a race you must run until the day you die. It is a marathon whose finish line moves forward in perpetuity. We're all just Sisyphus pushing the burden of manhood forever up the mountain. Or, in my case, *Sissyphus*.

No man on earth feels man enough. No man on earth feels he has won. Look at billionaires—the more money they make and the more they "prove themselves" as men, *the more they must prove themselves* and *the harder it becomes to do so.*

I recently watched a documentary series about Tyson Fury, the former heavyweight champion of the world. The documentary was about him attempting to retire and stop fighting. He tried to quit. He'd been the world champion for years and wanted to figure out what else was out there for him. But he couldn't. Six episodes later, he was just announcing another fight. He doesn't need any more money. He's already world champion many times over. The older he becomes, the riskier fighting becomes for his body, but he cannot seem to stop. Fighting to prove himself is all that he knows. Perpetual domination. Perpetual victory. Victory that must happen over and over and over again forever. No victory is enough. It knocks me on the floor, the degree to which manhood is gamified.

And I think that's part of why men become so defensive when critiqued. Because we spend so much cultural energy saying, *Men are bad,* and so little cultural energy asking, *Aren't you tired?*

So here it is. My final suggestion. My last piece of advice.

Stop competing for a while. Stop trying to be man enough. Stop trying to win an unwinnable race. Drop out of the never-ending competition and figure out what it might actually mean to be happy. Tell yourself the truth for once in your life:

You are already enough.

Because here's the secret: you don't even *have to* be a man. And by that I don't mean that you have to be a woman or nonbinary or whatever. You don't have to be anything at all. Contrary to everything you've been told, you don't owe the world a gender. You can simply stop caring what others think and just be *you.* You are in full control of your gender destiny, my dude.

I know it sounds ridiculous. It feels absurd to let go of an identity that was given to you before you were even given your name. But you can. You can just stop caring.

In your own mind and your own heart, you are free. Completely and totally free. No one on earth can stop you.

It doesn't have to be a massive shift, either. In fact, the more casually and informally you can do it, the better.

The answer to the question "Are you a man?" doesn't have to be "I am not a man. I am a person who defies all gender."

The answer can just be an "I dunno" or a simple "Nah" or "Sure, I guess" or an equally lazy "Dude, I'm just me" or even a "Yeah, but not like *that*."

And if people push you to explain yourself, you don't even have to. You don't need a good answer for why you stopped. No feminist manifesto required. You can just tell people the truth: That being a man made you tired. Or that you just wanna do you. Or, even better, that being a man got boring.

Because being a man *is* boring. Being a man isn't a personality. It isn't an occupation. It isn't a real skill. It isn't anything concrete at all. Being a man is just this weird thing we tell ourselves we have to do because we have penises and then spend the rest of our lives never questioning again.

And honestly? I'm just not sure that manhood, in its current iteration, is good for you. I don't think that you're hurting other people simply by being a man—manhood is not inherently harmful—but I worry that you might be hurting yourself a little bit. Or maybe a lot. Is your own masculinity safe *for you*? Were the rules of masculinity that you were taught as a child safe for your exuberant, juvenescent heart? Is your identity as a man *actually* making you safer in the world? When you think about other men sizing you up and judging your masculinity on endless repeat for the rest of your life, do you *still* feel safe?

If you want, you can still think of yourself as a man. I don't mind. Go for it. If it helps you to understand yourself as a man, do it. For real. I'm not being snarky. I get that it can be hard to leave behind the idea altogether, and you are under no obligation to stop. There is nothing inherently wrong with men or being a man. I love men, okay?

But for the love of God, don't make it your whole thing. Find *at least* four or five identities you hold that are more important to you than being a man. Take pride in things that matter more than just some metaphysical sticker slapped on you at birth.

Take pride in being a carpenter. Take pride in being a weight lifter. Take pride in being Mexican or Syrian or Ethiopian or Chinese or Thai or Norwegian or Honduran or Eritrean or Greek. Take pride in being a labor organizer or a member of a union. Take pride in driving trucks. Take pride in knowing a ton about trains—or should I say *locomotives.* Take pride in being a singer or playing guitar or tooting a tuba. Take pride in being a father or an uncle or a grandfather or a foster parent or a cousin or a brother or a cat dad. Take pride in racing cars. Take pride in crocheting cool shit. Take pride in crocheting cool shit *while* you race cars. Take pride in being from Wisconsin, if you want. I don't get it, necessarily, but take pride in being from Kenosha. Take pride in having red hair.

Take pride in anything you want, form any other identities you'd like, but for the sake of your personhood and your own beating heart, find a few things that are more meaningful to you than being a man.

It sounds small, but it's not. The most crushing, exhausting thing about being a man in our contemporary world is being told that *it must be what matters most to you.* Fight back against that edict. Knock your gender down a few notches. Humble that motherfucker. Teach your gender who's boss.

I say that because, even as someone who has sorta made a career out of being a trans/nonbinary gender disaster, I have only found true freedom when *I stopped caring so much about my gender, too.* Each year that "being nonbinary" was the most important thing about me, I was miserable. Each year that something else took the front seat, I was cruising. These days, I try my absolute best not to care about my gender at all. I dream of living in a world where my gender is finally as boring *to others* as it is *to me.*

Men, here is my challenge to you. Love yourself enough to value yourself differently. It isn't my custom, but I'm going to end this book with a simple worksheet. If you care about your own spiritual freedom, about your own power, about your self-actualization, or about your God-given right to set your destiny *for yourself,* follow these instructions:

1. Take the next page, rip it out of the book, and fold it up. Put it in your wallet, pocket, book bag, or fanny pack. Even if you're borrowing this from the library, rip out the page and take it with you. There are five worksheets in each book. I've fought my publisher hard on this. Please don't disrespect me by leaving this book intact. (Though if four have been ripped out already and there's only one left, maybe just copy it into your journal or onto a piece of scrap paper.)

2. Take the page with you to your favorite quiet place—your bedroom, your reading chair, your desk at work, your favorite bench, the garage, the woodshed, the pier, the pond in your neighborhood, your kayak, the top of your favorite mountain, the base of your favorite waterfall, anywhere where *you* most feel like *you*—and fill in four things about yourself that matter more than being a man. Four things you love enough about yourself to value them above your gender. Four things that define you as a person in this world.

After you've done so, I hope you feel it, the psychic shift. I hope that the pressure and exhaustion and strain release in a grand moment. That you realize, perhaps for the first time, that you are so much more than just a man.

That you have always been so much more.

Be safe, dude,
Jacob

what matters

1. _____

2. _____

3. _____

4. _____

5. I'm a man. _____

what matters

1. _____

2. _____

3. _____

4. _____

5. I'm a man. _____

what matters

1. _____

2. _____

3. _____

4. _____

5. I'm a man. _____

what matters

1. _____

2. _____

3. _____

4. _____

5. I'm a man. _____

what matters

1. _____

2. _____

3. _____

4. _____

5. I'm a man. _____

NOTES

Epigraphs

vii **Suppose someone has made you:** Thich Nhat Hanh, *How to Fight* (Parallax, 2017), 58.

vii **There's a happy medium:** Rebecca Solnit, *Men Explain Things to Me* (Haymarket Books, 2014), 5.

vii **He who is truly a man:** Robert Bly, *Iron John: A Book About Men* (Da Capo, 1990), 42.

Introduction: To the Boys in the Back

xix **By the time I:** I also tell this story in my previous book, *Sissy: A Coming-of-Gender Story* (G. P. Putnam's Sons, 2017), 52.

xxiv **political attacks:** Bill Barrow, "Trump and Vance Make Anti-Transgender Attacks Central to Their Campaign's Closing Argument," Associated Press, November 1, 2024, https://apnews.com/article/trump-harris-transgender -politics-61cff97a64fac581ffc5f762be4c57d3.

xxiv **ban our books:** Samantha Laine Perfas, "Who's Getting Hurt Most by Soaring LGBTQ Book Bans? Librarians Say Kids," *Harvard Gazette,* June 28, 2023, https://news.harvard.edu/gazette/story/2023/06/lgbtq-book-challenges-are-on -the-rise-heres-why/.

xxiv **transphobic legislators:** Elana Redfield, Kerith J. Conron, and Christy Mallory, *The Impact of 2024 Anti-Transgender Legislation on Youth* (Williams Institute, UCLA School of Law, April 2024), https://williamsinstitute.law.ucla.edu/wp -content/uploads/2024-Anti-Trans-Legislation-Apr-2024.pdf.

xxv **a few naysayers:** Abby Gardner, "A Complete Breakdown of the J. K. Rowling Transgender-Comments Controversy," *Glamour,* September 3, 2024, https:// www.glamour.com/story/a-complete-breakdown-of-the-jk-rowling-transgender -comments-controversy.

xxvi **there is still a pay gap:** Carolina Aragão, "Gender Pay Gap in U.S. Hasn't Changed Much in Two Decades," Pew Research Center, March 1, 2023, https:// www.pewresearch.org/short-reads/2023/03/01/gender-pay-gap-facts/.

xxvi **discrimination to address:** Gillian K. SteelFisher, Mary G. Findling, Sara N. Bleich, et al., "Gender Discrimination in the United States: Experiences of Women," *Health Services Research* 54, no. S2 (2019): 1442–53, https://doi.org/10 .1111/1475-6773.13217.

xxvi **healthcare inadequacy:** Kweilin Ellingrud, Lucy Pérez, Anouk Petersen, and Valentina Sartori, "Closing the Women's Health Gap: A $1 Trillion Opportunity to Improve Lives and Economies," McKinsey Health Institute, January 17, 2024, https://www.mckinsey.com/mhi/our-insights/closing-the-womens-health-gap-a -1-trillion-dollar-opportunity-to-improve-lives-and-economies.

xxvi **a legacy of sexual violence:** World Health Organization, on behalf of the United Nations Inter-Agency Working Group on Violence Against Women Estimation and Data (VAW-IAWGED), *Violence Against Women Prevalence Estimates, 2018* (World Health Organization, March 9, 2021), https://www.who .int/publications/i/item/9789240022256.

xxvii **beyond or above help:** Samantha Laine Perfas, "Strong, Silent, and Suffering Inside," *Harvard Gazette,* August 8, 2023, https://news.harvard.edu/gazette/ story/2023/08/stigma-mental-health-care-men/.

xxvii **belittled and erased:** Tania Reynolds, "Man Up and Take It: Do We Under-Detect Men's Suffering?," *Queer Majority,* March 18, 2021, https://www.queermajority .com/essays-all/man-up-and-take-it-do-we-under-detect-mens-suffering.

xxviii **global and imperial:** Juanita Elias and Christine Beasley, "Hegemonic Masculinity and Globalization: 'Transnational Business Masculinities' and Beyond," *Globalizations* 6, no. 2 (2009): 281–96, https://doi.org/10.1080/ 14747730902854232.

xxviii **colonizing communities:** Kerry Carrington, Alison McIntosh, and John Scott, "Globalization, Frontier Masculinities and Violence: Booze, Blokes and Brawls," *British Journal of Criminology* 50, no. 3 (2010): 393–413, https://doi.org/10 .1093/bjc/azq003.

xxviii **death, violence, poverty, and despair:** Joshua S. Goldstein, *War and Gender: How Gender Shapes the War System and Vice Versa* (Cambridge University Press, 2001).

xxviii **conscripted from birth:** Terry Miller, "The Culture of Violence in Boys and Men," *Mindfulness Bell* 37 (2004), https://www.parallax.org/mindfulnessbell/ article/the-culture-of-violence-in-boys-and-men/.

xxviii **begin your training:** American Psychological Association, "How to Prevent Harmful Masculinity and Violence," December 6, 2023, https://www.apa.org/ topics/men-boys/harmful-masculinity.

xxviii **punished, beaten, raped, and murdered:** Andrea L. Roberts, Margaret Rosario, Heather L. Corliss, Karestan C. Koenen, and S. Bryn Austin, "Child-hood Gender Nonconformity: A Risk Indicator for Childhood Abuse and Posttraumatic Stress in Youth," *Pediatrics* 129, no. 3 (2012): 410–417, https://doi .org/10.1542/peds.2011-1804.

xxix **a sense of purpose:** Duane France, "The Violence of Action Paradox: Emotional Contradiction of Veterans," *Headspace and Timing: Veteran Mental Health from a Combat Veteran Perspective* (blog), February 19, 2016, https:// veteranmentalhealth.com/the-violence-of-action-paradox-emotional -contradiction-of-veterans/.

xxix **talk to defectors:** Christina Couch, "The Psychological Trauma of Defecting from North Korea," *Nova Next,* February 16, 2017, https://www.pbs.org/wgbh/ nova/article/north-korea-mental-health/.

xxix **what it's really like:** Ashifa Kassam, "Iraq War Resisters Who Fled to Canada ask Justin Trudeau to Allow Them to Stay," *Guardian,* August 2, 2016, https://www.theguardian.com/world/2016/aug/02/iraq-war-resisters-canada-trudeau-us-military.

xxix **escaped the institution altogether:** Dan Park, "The Soldiers Who Resisted the First Gulf War Deserve Recognition," War Resisters, May 15, 2021, https://wagingnonviolence.org/wr/2021/05/the-soldiers-who-resisted-the-first-gulf-war-deserve-recognition/.

xxx **men are not okay:** "The Men—and Boys—Are Not Alright," *The Ezra Klein Show* (podcast); printed in *The New York Times,* March 10, 2023, https://www.nytimes.com/2023/03/10/opinion/ezra-klein-podcast-richard-reeves.html.

xxx **Men are suffering ruthlessly:** Jemima Atar, "Hollow Men: Poisonous Patriarchy and Men's Mental Health," *New Thinking,* November 21, 2022, https://www.newthinking.com/health/hollow-men-poisonous-patriarchy-and-mens-mental-health.

See also: Veronika Ilich, "How Patriarchy Hurts Men Too," Next Gen Men, 2021, https://www.nextgenmen.ca/blog/why-patriarchy-hurts-men-too.

xxx **our common enemy:** Laura Capelle, "With 'I Hate Men,' a French Feminist Touches a Nerve," *New York Times,* January 10, 2021, https://www.nytimes.com/2021/01/10/books/pauline-harmange-i-hate-men.html.

xxx **"The radical feminist labeling of all men as oppressors":** bell hooks, *The Will to Change: Men, Masculinity, and Love* (Atria, 2004).

xxxi **insisting that they are a monster:** Tyler Zimmer, "Men Aren't Monstrous, but Masculinity Can Be," *Slate,* November 29, 2017, https://slate.com/human-interest/2017/11/men-arent-monsters-the-problem-is-toxic-masculinity.html.

xxxii **the suffering of people who were exploited:** Bureau of International Labor Affairs, "Addressing Child Labor and Forced Labor in the Coffee Supply Chain in Honduras," U.S. Department of Labor, https://www.dol.gov/agencies/ilab/addressing-child-labor-and-forced-labor-coffee-supply-chain-honduras.

xxxiii **"intentionally decide to stay in relationship with humanity":** adrienne maree brown, *Loving Corrections* (AK Press, 2024).

xxxiv **In most positions of power:** Emily Peck, "At the CEO Level, Women Finally Outnumber Men Named John," Axios, April 27, 2023, https://www.axios.com/2023/04/27/women-men-ceo-sp500.

Interstice

3 **Men are four times more likely:** Sherry L. Murphy, Kenneth D. Kochanek, Jiaquan Xu, and Elizabeth Arias, "Deaths: Final Data for 2021," *National Vital Statistics Reports* 73, no. 8 (2024): 6, https://www.cdc.gov/nchs/data/nvsr/nvsr73/nvsr73-08.pdf.

Catcalls

5 **gender nonconforming people have been murdered:** Xoai Pham, "The State of Trans Lives in the Birthplace of the American LGBTQ Movement," *Autostraddle,* March 20, 2021, https://www.autostraddle.com/roots-of-anti-trans-violence-ny/.

6   **Nowhere is safe:** "Regional Reports—New York," Transgender Law Center, accessed November 13, 2024, https://transgenderlawcenter.org/regional-reports-new-york/.

See also: James McKinley, "Manslaughter Charges in Beating Death of Transgender Woman in 2013," *New York Times,* March 3, 2015, https://www.nytimes.com/2015/03/04/nyregion/manslaughter-charges-in-beating-death-of-transgender-woman-in-2013.html.

See also: Nina Siegal, "Watershed of Mourning at the Border of Gender," *New York Times,* July 24, 2000, https://www.nytimes.com/2000/07/24/nyregion/watershed-of-mourning-at-the-border-of-gender.html.

See also: Dorian Geiger, " 'This Is a Mystery': Family of Black Trans Woman Whose Body Was Found in Trash in NYC Seek Answers," Oxygen True Crime, June 30, 2021, https://www.yahoo.com/entertainment/mystery-family-black-trans-woman-131900132.html.

7   **even looked like:** For more on this, see my essay "Why I'm Genderqueer, Professional and Unafraid," HuffPost, June 10, 2014, https://www.huffpost.com/entry/genderqueer-professional_b_5476239.

7   **A common trait of PTSD:** "Post-Traumatic Stress Disorder (PTSD): Symptoms and Causes," Mayo Clinic, accessed November 13, 2024, https://www.mayoclinic.org/diseases-conditions/post-traumatic-stress-disorder/symptoms-causes/syc-20355967.

7   **It's an evolutionary response:** Michael Christopher, "A Broader View of Trauma: A Biopsychosocial-Evolutionary View of the Role of the Traumatic Stress Response in the Emergence of Pathology and/or Growth," *Clinical Psychology Review* 24, no. 1 (2004): 75–98, https://doi.org/10.1016/j.cpr.2003.12.003.

10 **don't get me started on the NYPD:** Amanda Arnold, "A Guide to the 'Walking While Trans' Ban," *The Cut,* July 22, 2020, https://www.thecut.com/2020/07/walking-while-trans-law-in-new-york-explained.html.

See also: Katelyn Burns, "Why Police Often Single Out Trans People for Violence," Vox, June 23, 2020, https://www.vox.com/identities/2020/6/23/21295432/police-black-trans-people-violence.

12 **The studies are out there:** Ziyi Cai, Alvin Junus, Qingsong Chang, and Paul S. F. Yip, "The Lethality of Suicide Methods: A Systematic Review and Meta-Analysis," *Journal of Affective Disorders* 300, no. 1 (2022): 121–29, https://doi.org/10.1016/j.jad.2021.12.054.

See also: Jeffrey R. Savarino, Emily Rubin, Peter T. Masiakos, et al., "The Experience of Survivors of Firearm Suicide Attempts: A Retrospective Case Series," *Annals of Surgery Open* 5, no. 2 (2024): e418, https://doi.org/10.1097/as9.0000000000000418.

See also: C. E. Rhyne, D. I. Templer, L. G. Brown, and N. B. Peters, "Dimensions of Suicide: Perceptions of Lethality, Time, and Agony," *Suicide and Life-Threatening Behavior* 25, no. 3 (1995): 373–80, https://doi.org/10.1111/j.1943-278X.1995.tb00959.x.

12 **Pills are ineffective:** Paul S. Nestadt, "Suicide by the Numbers: Myths and Facts," *Psychiatric Times,* June 18, 2020, https://www.psychiatrictimes.com/view/suicide-numbers-myths-and-facts.

13 **In 2015, I was featured:** "True Life: I'm Genderqueer," *True Life,* season 18, episode 16, produced by Amelia D'Entrone, Craig D'Entrone, and Alexis

Charizopoulos, featuring Jacob Tobia and Brennan Beckwith, aired November 17, 2015, on MTV.

15 *Empathy* **is a watered-down buzzword:** John Brandon, "Here's Why 'Kindness' Is a Much Better Buzzword for 2020 Than 'Empathy,'" *Inc.*, December 31, 2019, https://www.inc.com/john-brandon/heres-why-kindness-is-a-much-better -buzzword-for-2020-than-empathy.html.

15 **When a dog aggressively barks:** ASPCA, "Barking," accessed November 13, 2024, https://www.aspca.org/pet-care/dog-care/common-dog-behavior-issues/ barking.

Interstice

21 **Men commit eighty-one percent:** "All Violent Offender Demographics," Crime Data Exporter, Federal Bureau of Investigation, accessed September 5, 2024, https://cde.ucr.cjis.gov/LATEST/webapp/#/pages/explorer/crime/crime -trend.

Don't You Know That You're Toxic?

23 **It's everywhere and ubiquitous:** Jennifer Schuessler, "'Toxic' Is Oxford's Word of the Year. No, We're Not Gaslighting You," *New York Times,* November 14, 2018, https://www.nytimes.com/2018/11/14/arts/toxic-oxford-word-of-the-year -2018.html.

23 **Historically speaking, has it been used:** Daniel Penny, "The Strange History of 'Toxic' Masculinity," *GQ,* August 16, 2024, https://www.gq.com/story/the -strange-history-of-toxic-masculinity.

24 **great strategic blunders:** Michael Salter, "The Problem with a Fight Against Toxic Masculinity," *Atlantic,* February 27, 2019, https://www.theatlantic.com/ health/archive/2019/02/toxic-masculinity-history/583411/.

24 **"Feminism is flawed because":** Roxane Gay, *Bad Feminist* (Harper Perennial, 2014), x.

24 **"We should disavow the failures":** Gay, *Bad Feminist,* xiii.

26 **it would've required rigorous definition:** Maya Salam, "What Is Toxic Masculinity?," *New York Times,* January 22, 2019, https://www.nytimes.com/ 2019/01/22/us/toxic-masculinity.html.

27 **"Toxic Masculinity" has stopped referring to metaphors:** Carol Harrington, "What Is 'Toxic Masculinity' and Why Does It Matter?," *Men and Masculinities* 24, no. 2 (2020): 345–52, https://doi.org/10.1177/1097184X20943254.

27 **men have picked up on this:** Richard Reeves, "Toxic Masculinity Is a Harmful Myth. Society Is in Denial About the Problems of Boys and Men," *Big Think,* October 17, 2022, https://bigthink.com/the-present/toxic-masculinity -myth/.

27 **they've felt it:** Michael Flood, "'Toxic Masculinity': What Does It Mean, Where Did It Come from—and Is the Term Useful or Harmful?," *Salon,* October 8, 2022, https://www.salon.com/2022/10/08/toxic-masculinity-what -does-it-mean-where-did-it-come-from—and-is-the-term-useful-or-harmful _partner/.

27   **They've heard it:** Adi Jaffe, "Men Will Be Men: The Troubling Origin of Toxic Masculinity," *Psychology Today,* January 29, 2020, https://www.psychologytoday .com/us/blog/all-about-addiction/202001/men-will-be-men-the-troubling -origin-of-toxic-masculinity.

27   **"a political stalemate":** Richard V. Reeves, *Of Boys and Men: Why the Modern Male Is Struggling, Why It Matters, and What to Do About It* (Brookings Institution Press, 2022), xiv.

27   **"Both sides have dug into an ideological":** Reeves, *Of Boys and Men,* 30.

27   **That masculinity itself is harmful:** Victor Garcia, " 'Toxic Masculinity' and Heroism Spring from Same Aggressive Impulses," Fox News, May 11, 2019, https://www.foxnews.com/us/dr-drew-masculinity-also-creates-heroes.

28   **most men have shut down:** Ben Shapiro, "The 'Toxic Masculinity' Smear," *National Review,* June 7, 2017, https://www.nationalreview.com/2017/06/ masculinity-not-toxic-stop-blaming-men-everything/.

28   **They've dismissed us:** Robert Booth, "Gen Z Boys and Men More Likely Than Baby Boomers to Believe Feminism Harmful, Says Poll," *Guardian,* February 1, 2024, https://www.theguardian.com/news/2024/feb/01/gen-z-boys-and -men-more-likely-than-baby-boomers-to-believe-feminism-harmful-says -poll.

28   **increasingly acerbic and imprecise:** F. Diane Barth, "Toxic Masculinity Is Terrible Shorthand for a Real Problem Plaguing Men," *Think: Opinions, Analysis, Essays,* January 14, 2019, https://www.nbcnews.com/think/opinion/ toxic-masculinity-terrible-shorthand-real-problem-plaguing-men-ncna957941.

28   *all men* **are toxic:** Simon Fokt, "Redefining Toxic Masculinity," *Man's Compass,* July 2, 2024, https://medium.com/mans-compass/redefining-toxic-masculinity -fe766f2d6b2c.

29   *"Is it okay":* The Quote Circle, "Is it Okay to be a Man? Addressing Men's Mental Health," video featuring Jordan Peterson, TikTok, accessed February 4, 2025, https://www.tiktok.com/@thequotecircle/video/7034999623823510790.

31   **Only women, children, and dogs:** emav.russ, 2021, TikTok comment on Jordan Peterson.

31   **Thank you Jordan:** NB_Toronto_Bari, 2021, TikTok comment on Jordan Peterson.

31   **It's the fact that:** Preston Logan, 2022, TikTok comment on Jordan Peterson.

32   **"Toxic Masculinity" does the opposite:** Richard Gater, "Is It Actually Helpful to Talk About Toxic Masculinity?," *Greater Good Magazine,* October 25, 2023, https://greatergood.berkeley.edu/article/item/is_it_actually_helpful_to_talk _about_toxic_masculinity.

33   *Astrophysics for Babies:* Chris Ferrie and Julia Kregenow, *Astrophysics for Babies* (Sourcebooks Explore, 2018).

36   **"She's still a war criminal":** Nancy Mancias, "War Criminal of the Week: Condoleezza Rice!," *CodePink,* July 26, 2010, https://www.codepink.org/war _criminal_of_the_week_condoleezza_rice.

Interstice

37   **Ninety percent of American veterans:** Nancy A. Glowacki, "2019 Gender and Veteran Demographics," Veterans Employment and Training Service, U.S.

Department of Labor, accessed September 7, 2024, https://www.dol.gov/sites/
dolgov/files/VETS/files/2019-Gender-and-Veteran-Demographics-Transcript
.pdf.

37 **One out of every seven American men:** Glowacki, "2019 Gender and Veteran
Demographics."

37 **7,000 American service members:** Neta C. Crawford and Catherine Lutz,
"Human Cost of Post–9/11 Wars: Direct War Deaths in Major War Zones,"
Watson Institute for International and Public Affairs, Brown University,
accessed September 7, 2024, https://watson.brown.edu/costsofwar/figures/
2019/direct-war-death-toll-2001-801000.

37 **134,000 American veterans died by suicide:** "Data Appendix, 2023 National
Veteran Suicide Prevention Annual Report," U.S. Department of Veterans
Affairs, Office of Mental Health and Suicide Prevention, accessed September 7,
2024, https://www.mentalhealth.va.gov/suicide_prevention/data.asp.

Child Soldiers

39 **the global, systemic violence of the American Military:** "Civilians Killed and
Wounded: Costs of War," Watson Institute for International and Public Affairs,
Brown University, October 2024, https://watson.brown.edu/costsofwar/costs/
human/civilians.

    See also: "Iraq Conflict Has Killed a Million, Says Survey," January 30, 2008,
Reuters, https://www.reuters.com/article/world/middle-east/iraq-conflict-has
-killed-a-million-says-survey-idUSL30488579/.

39 **what that violence does to the young men:** Congressional Research Service,
"American War and Military Operations—Casualties: Lists and Statistics,"
July 29, 2020, https://sgp.fas.org/crs/natsec/RL32492.pdf.

    See also: Department of Veterans Affairs, "America's Wars Factsheet,"
November 2023, https://www.va.gov/opa/publications/factsheets/fs_americas
_wars.pdf.

40 **the story of Sadako Sasaki:** Manhattan Project National Historical Park, "The
Story of Sadako Sasaki," National Park Service, accessed November 13, 2024,
https://www.nps.gov/articles/000/the-story-of-sadako-sasaki.htm.

41 **The Hiroshima Children's Peace Monument:** "Children's Peace Monument,"
Wikipedia, accessed November 13, 2024, https://en.wikipedia.org/wiki/
Children%27s_Peace_Monument.

41 **As Colin Powell was lying:** Jon Schwarz, "Lie After Lie: What Colin Powell
Knew About Iraq 15 Years Ago and What He Told the U.N.," *Intercept*,
February 6, 2018, https://theintercept.com/2018/02/06/lie-after-lie-what
-colin-powell-knew-about-iraq-fifteen-years-ago-and-what-he-told
-the-un/.

41 **fervent nationalism was swelling:** Qiong Li and Marilynn B. Brewer, "What
Does It Mean to Be an American? Patriotism, Nationalism, and American
Identity After 9/11," *Political Psychology* 25, no. 5 (2004): 727–39, https://www
.jstor.org/stable/3792341.

42 **a watch that'd been frozen in time:** Vibeke Venema, "When Time Stood Still:
A Hiroshima Survivor's Story," BBC News, July 24, 2014, https://www.bbc.co
.uk/news/special/2014/newsspec_8079/index.html.

42 **a piece of stone:** "Human Shadow Etched in Stone," Hiroshima Peace Memorial Museum, accessed November 13, 2024, https://hpmmuseum.jp/modules/exhibition/index.php?action=ItemView&item_id=112&lang=eng.

42 **wax figurines:** Paul Walsh, "A-bomb Mannequins Retired After 44 Years of Controversy," *Get Hiroshima*, April 25, 2017, https://gethiroshima.com/news/a-bomb-mannequins-retired-after-44-years-of-controversy/.

43 **a necessary evil:** Ben Norton, "Atomic Bombing of Japan Was Not Necessary to End WWII. US Gov't Documents Admit It," *Geopolitical Economy Report*, August 7, 2023, https://geopoliticaleconomy.com/2023/08/07/atomic-bombing-japan-not-necessary/.
See also: Karl T. Compton, "If the Atomic Bomb Had Not Been Used," *Atlantic*, December 1946, https://www.theatlantic.com/magazine/archive/1946/12/if-the-atomic-bomb-had-not-been-used/376238/.

43 *Oppenheimer* **in adolescent hands:** Kai Bird and Martin J. Sherwin, *American Prometheus: The Triumph and Tragedy of J. Robert Oppenheimer* (Vintage Books, 2005).

43 *But it is necessary,* **the pundits said:** George W. Bush White House Archives, "President Bush Addresses the Nation," March 19, 2003, https://georgewbush-whitehouse.archives.gov/infocus/iraq/news/20030319-17.html.
See also: Carroll Doherty and Jocelyn Kiley, "A Look Back at How Fear and False Beliefs Bolstered U.S. Public Support for War in Iraq," Pew Research Center, March 14, 2023, https://www.pewresearch.org/politics/2023/03/14/a-look-back-at-how-fear-and-false-beliefs-bolstered-u-s-public-support-for-war-in-iraq/.

45 **American Manhood and war:** R. W. Connell, *Masculinities* (University of California Press, 1995), 213.

45 **American Boyhood and basic training:** Susan M. Alexander and Kelsey Collins, "From Patriotic Troops to Branded Boyhood: Hegemonic Boyhood Masculinity as Depicted in *Boy's Life* Magazine, 1911–2012," *Boyhood Studies* 8, no. 1 (2015): 84–109, https://doi.org/10.3167/bhs.2015.080106.
See also: Michael C. Reichert and Joseph Derrick Nelson, "The State of America's Boys: An Urgent Case for a More Connected Boyhood," Global Boyhood Initiative, 2020, https://www.boyhoodinitiative.org/sites/default/files/2023-06/State-of-American-Boys-Report.pdf.

45 **American Masculinity and military violence:** Ann-Dorte Christensen and Morten Kyed, "From Military to Militarizing Masculinities," *Norma* 17, no. 1 (2022): 1–4, https://doi.org/10.1080/18902138.2022.2028428.

45 **the justification in public discourse:** "Religious Beliefs Underpin Opposition to Homosexuality," Pew Research Center, November 18, 2003, https://www.pewresearch.org/politics/2003/11/18/religious-beliefs-underpin-opposition-to-homosexuality/.

46 **The Bible told them so:** David Kirkpatrick, "Rally Against Gay Marriage Draws Thousands to Capital," *New York Times*, October 16, 2004, https://www.nytimes.com/2004/10/16/us/rally-against-gay-marriage-draws-thousands-to-capital.html.

46 **"family values":** Evelyn Nieves, "Family Values Groups Gear Up for Battle over Gay Marriage," *Washington Post*, August 17, 2003, https://www.washingtonpost.com/wp-dyn/articles/A4132-2003Aug16.html.

46 **especially not Leviticus:** Lev. 11:9–12 (New Revised Standard Edition).
See also: Lev. 19:19 (NRSV).

46 **they *themselves* were gay:** Jeanna Bryner, "Homophobes Might Be Hidden Homosexuals," *Scientific American,* April 10, 2012, https://www.scientificamerican.com/article/homophobes-might-be-hidden-homosexuals/.

49 **According to the Hasbro corporation:** Hasbro, "G.I. Joe Classified Series Retro Cardback Duke: Product Description," accessed November 13, 2024, https://www.hasbropulse.com/product/gi-joe-classified-series-retro-cardback-duke/F96765X00.

49 **obsessed with the fact that Barbie:** Leah Kuntz, "Think Pink: Barbie and Unrealistic Body Expectations in 2023," *Psychiatric Times,* July 3, 2023, https://www.psychiatrictimes.com/view/think-pink-barbie-unrealistic-body-expectations-in-2023.

50 **we consider it entertainment:** CBC Radio, "How Hollywood Became the Unofficial Propaganda Arm of the U.S. Military," Canadian Broadcasting Corporation, May 11, 2020, https://www.cbc.ca/radio/ideas/how-hollywood-became-the-unofficial-propaganda-arm-of-the-u-s-military-1.5560575.

50 **an official recruitment ad for the U.S. Army:** U.S. Army, "Be All You Can Be—U.S. Army's New Brand Trailer," YouTube video, accessed March 6, 2023, https://www.youtube.com/watch?v=Lwx-2R9swDg.

51 **a history of *caring* about American women:** Jennifer Greenburg, "Deserted: The U.S. Military's Sexual Assault Crisis as a Cost of War," Watson Institute for International and Public Affairs, Brown University, August 14, 2024, https://watson.brown.edu/costsofwar/files/cow/imce/papers/2023/2024/8.14.24%20Greenburg_Sexual%20Assault%20Crisis_Costs%20of%20War.pdf.

52 **a documentary short:** Petra Epperlein and Michael Tucker, *The Army We Had: Iraq War Veterans, 20 Years Later,* Op-Docs, *New York Times,* accessed March 20, 2023, https://www.youtube.com/watch?v=RIWfH3iEgXU.

55 **I don't know one veteran:** Brian James (@TenTonNuke), 2023, comment on Epperlein and Tucker, *The Army We Had.*

55 **I lost about 20 friends:** Johnny Paratrooper (@johnnyparatrooper1326), 2024, comment on Epperlein and Tucker, *The Army We Had.*

55 **I spent time in Tikrit:** J B, (@JB-bw8nj), 2024, comment on Epperlein and Tucker, *The Army We Had.*

57 **"the problem that has no name":** Betty Friedan, *The Feminine Mystique* (1963; repr., Dell, 1964), 15, 11, 21; emphasis mine.

58 **police training facilities:** Jordan Blair Woods, "Destabilizing Policing's Masculinity Project," *George Washington Law Review* 89, no. 6 (2021): 1527–67, https://www.gwlr.org/wp-content/uploads/2021/12/89-Geo.-Wash.-L.-Rev.-1527.pdf.

59 **We will volunteer for hours outside:** Lauren Rankin, "Keep Listening to My Voice: What It's Like to Be an Abortion Clinic Escort," *Time,* April 5, 2022, https://time.com/6163613/abortion-clinic-escorts.

59 **military recruitment centers or police academies:** Kyoko Thompson, "Police in the U.S. Have a Toxic Masculinity Problem," *Baltimore Sun,* May 14, 2021, https://www.baltimoresun.com/2021/05/14/police-in-the-us-have-a-toxic-masculinity-problem-commentary/.

60 **trillions of dollars go to buy fighter jets:** "The F-35 Will Now Exceed $2 Trillion as the Military Plans to Fly It Less," United States Government Accountability Office, May 16, 2024, https://www.gao.gov/blog/f-35-will-now-exceed-2-trillion-military-plans-fly-it-less.

60   **Americans cannot afford healthcare:** Megan Cerullo, "Working-Age Americans Are Struggling to Pay for Health Care, Even Those with Insurance, Report Finds," CBS News, October 30, 2023, https://www.cbsnews .com/news/health-care-costs-unaffordable-even-for-insured-americans -commonwealth-fund/.

60   **or buy food:** USAFacts Team, "Americans Are Struggling to Afford Enough Food," USAFacts, February 5, 2024, https://usafacts.org/articles/food-insecurity -in-the-us/.

60   **the Department of Defense sways Hollywood:** Alissa Wilkinson, "The Long, Long, Twisty Affair Between the US Military and Hollywood," Vox, May 27, 2022, https://www.vox.com/23141487/top-gun-maverick-us-military -hollywood-oscar-winner-best-sound.

61   **veterans who have fallen prey to this system:** Monica Diaz, "Veteran Homelessness Increased by 7.4% in 2023," *Veteran Affairs News,* December 15, 2023, https://news.va.gov/126913/veteran-homelessness-increased-by-7-4-in -2023/.
       See also: Benjamin J. Darter, Amy J. Armstrong, Katherine Inge, et al., "Current Life Experiences in Veterans with Limb Loss: A Description of Survey Methods and Summary Results," *Journal of Rehabilitation* 88, no. 3 (2022): 20–28, https://pmc.ncbi.nlm.nih.gov/articles/PMC10977926/.

63   **every secretary of defense in American history:** "Secretaries of Defense," Historical Office, Office of the Secretary of Defense, accessed September 7, 2024, https://history.defense.gov/DOD-History/Secretaries-of-Defense/.

Interstice

65   **Men are eleven times more likely:** "National Census of Fatal Occupational Injuries in 2022," U.S. Bureau of Labor Statistics, accessed September 7, 2024.

The Rites of Men

68   **Duke Chapel has a crypt:** Bryan Roth, "Uncovering Duke's Mysteries," *Duke Today,* January 17, 2016, https://today.duke.edu/2016/01/uncovering-duke%E2 %80%99s-mysteries.

68   **funded by tobacco money:** Thomas F. Heston, "Big Tobacco, Cigarettes and the Foundation of Duke University," *Journal of Clinical Medical Research* 4, no. 3 (2023): 1–4, http://dx.doi.org/10.46889/JCMR.2023.4302.

68   **Iraq War profiteer of choice:** Jamie Doward, "Ex-Presidents Club Gets Fat on Conflict," *Guardian,* March 22, 2003, https://www.theguardian.com/business/ 2003/mar/23/iraq.theobserver.

68   **research money from the Department of Defense:** "Department of Defense," Duke University Government Relations, accessed September 7, 2024, https:// governmentrelations.duke.edu/research/department-of-defense/.

68   **frats ruled everything:** DukeObserver, "Reasons Why You May Dislike Duke: A Memoir from an Unhappy Student," College Confidential, March 2017, accessed November 14, 2024, https://talk.collegeconfidential.com/t/reasons -why-you-may-dislike-duke-a-memoir-from-an-unhappy-student/1896033.

68   **ornate hazing rituals:** Duke Magazine Staff, "Hazing Concerns," *Duke Magazine,* June 4, 2012, https://alumni.duke.edu/magazine/articles/hazing -concerns.

69   **It was a biography, in French:** Roger Dorsinville, *Toussaint Louverture; ou, La Vocation de la Liberté* (René Julliard, 1965).

70   **Duke has a longish tradition:** Tim Pyatt, "Shhhh! Secret Societies at Duke," *Duke Magazine,* April 1, 2011, https://alumni.duke.edu/magazine/articles/ shhhh.

70   **secret societies with literal American presidents:** Rose Horowitch, "Skull and Bones and Equity and Inclusion," *Atlantic,* January 11, 2024, https://www .theatlantic.com/ideas/archive/2024/01/yale-skull-and-bones-secret-societies -diversity/677030/.

70   **the Trident Society:** Ashwin Kulshrestha, "Chronquiry: What's Up with All the Weird Guys in Robes? Looking at Duke's Secret Societies," *Chronicle* (Duke University), October 14, 2019, https://www.dukechronicle.com/article/2019/10/ chronquiry-duke-secret-societies-trident-society-old-trinity-club.

70   **the White Duchy:** Jake Klein, "Secret Societies of Duke," *Rival Magazine* 8, no. 1 (2012): 4, https://alyssandrabarnes.wordpress.com/wp-content/uploads/ 2012/02/pregame-fall-2012.pdf.

71   **the administrator responded:** Samantha Lachman, "Trasked with Secrecy," *Chronicle* (Duke University), March 16, 2013, https://www.dukechronicle.com/ article/2013/03/trasked-secrecy.

71   *hit one of the dining hall staff with his car:* Alexandra Samuels, "Duke VP Hits Parking Attendant with Car, Allegedly Calls Her the 'N' Word," *USA Today,* March 1, 2016, https://www.usatoday.com/story/college/2016/03/01/duke-vp -hits-parking-attendant-with-car-allegedly-calls-her-the-n-word/37413575/.

71   **blue-collar workers who make the place run:** Jessica Wood, "Black History at Duke University: African American Employees," Duke University Libraries, accessed November 14, 2024, https://guides.library.duke.edu/c.php?g= 289661&p=1933861.

71   **widespread student protest:** Jamilah King, "Duke Students Protest VP Tallman Trask for Calling a Black Worker a Stupid N*gger," Yahoo! News, April 7, 2016, https://www.yahoo.com/news/duke-students-protest-vp-tallman-200700571.html.

72   **rituals are fundamental:** Rebecca J. Lester, "The Importance of Ritual," *Psychology Today,* May 19, 2020, https://www.psychologytoday.com/us/blog/ anthropology-in-mind/202005/the-importance-of-ritual.
       See also: Joanna Wojtkowiak, "Towards a Psychology of Ritual: A Theoretical Framework of Ritual Transformation in a Globalising World," *Culture & Psychology* 24, no. 4 (2018): 460–76, https://doi.org/10.1177/ 1354067X18763797.

72   **ritual is as old as human civilization:** "Coming-of-Age Rite," *Britannica,* accessed November 14, 2024, https://www.britannica.com/topic/coming-of-age-rite.

73   **rituals for demarcating the end of childhood:** Chip Brown, "The Many Ways Society Makes a Man," *National Geographic,* January 2017, https://www .nationalgeographic.com/magazine/article/how-rites-of-passage-shape -masculinity-gender.
       See also: Kristina Rodulfo, "12 Captivating Coming of Age Ceremonies from Around the World," *Elle,* November 23, 2015, https://www.elle.com/culture/ travel-food/news/g27293/coming-of-age-ceremonies-around-the-world/.

73   **Get circumcised without anesthesia:** Noor Khamis, "Becoming a Man," Reuters: The Wider Image, November 24, 2014, https://widerimage.reuters .com/story/becoming-a-man.

73   **wipe its blood on your face:** Jack Royston, "Prince Harry's Face Was Pressed into Wound of a Stag He Killed in Ritual," *Newsweek*, January 10, 2023, https:// www.newsweek.com/prince-harry-face-was-pressed-wound-stag-killed -blooding-ritual-balmoral-spare-1772461.

73   **a glove filled with bullet ants:** Rachel Nuwer, "When Becoming a Man Means Sticking Your Hand into a Glove of Ants," *Smithsonian Magazine*, October 27, 2014, https://www.smithsonianmag.com/smart-news/brazilian-tribe-becoming -man-requires-sticking-your-hand-glove-full-angry-ants-180953156/.

73   **shift in the mine:** John McDowell, "The Life of a Coal Miner," *World's Work* 4 (1902): 2659–60, https://energyhistory.yale.edu/rev-john-mcdowell-life-of-a -coal-miner-1902/.

74   **presented with a gun by your father:** Levi Gahman, "Gun Rites: Hegemonic Masculinity and Neoliberal Ideology in Rural Kansas," *Gender, Place & Culture* 22, no. 9 (2014): 1203–19. https://doi.org/10.1080/0966369X.2014 .970137.

74   **mostly sexist and shitty:** Nancy Schwartz, "Coming of Age: A Masculine Myth?," *Velvet Light Trap* 6 (1972): 33, https://www.proquest.com/ openview/f91b378ae8984bdd99b987666b7760c6/1?pq-origsite =gscholar&cbl=1816652.

   See also: Cody Delistraty, "The Coming-of-Age Con," *Aeon*, September 8, 2017, https://aeon.co/essays/why-the-coming-of-age-narrative-is-a-conformist -lie.

74   **fallen out of favor in popular media:** Indra Adnan, "A Coming of Age Ceremony for Teens? Like, Whatever," *Guardian*, August 2, 2007, https://www .theguardian.com/commentisfree/2007/aug/03/britishidentity.children.

   See also: Srimati Basu, "Rites of Gun Passage," *Ms.*, May 8, 2013, https:// msmagazine.com/2013/05/08/rites-of-gun-passage/.

   See also: Zoe Pearl, "Shouts and Murmurs: Modern Coming-of-Age Rituals," *New Yorker*, April 13, 2019, https://www.newyorker.com/humor/daily-shouts/ modern-coming-of-age-rituals.

   See also: Melinda Wenner Moyer, "Sexism Starts in Childhood," *Slate*, November 6, 2017, https://slate.com/human-interest/2017/11/how-to-stop -sexism-and-raise-a-son-who-respects-women.html.

   See also: Whoa-Man, "Rituals of Adulthood and Equality?," *Exponent II*, June 23, 2011, https://exponentii.org/blog/rituals-of-adulthood-and-equality/.

   See also: Chandrika Manjunath, "The Unwelcome Custom of Celebrating My Menstrual Experience," *Feminism in India*, January 15, 2018, https:// feminisminindia.com/2018/01/15/unwelcome-custom-menstrual-experience/.

75   **miserable and lost:** Christine Emba, "Men Are Lost. Here's a Map Out of the Wilderness," *Washington Post*, July 10, 2023, https://www.washingtonpost.com/ opinions/2023/07/10/christine-emba-masculinity-new-model/.

   See also: Andrew Yang, "The Data Are Clear: The Boys Are Not All Right," *Washington Post*, February 8, 2022, https://www.washingtonpost.com/opinions/ 2022/02/08/andrew-yang-boys-are-not-all-right/.

75   **young men have turned to the internet:** Steve McCullough, "Online Misogyny: The 'Manosphere'—Extremist Digital Sexism with Dangerous Real-World

Consequences," Canadian Museum for Human Rights, September 12, 2023, https://humanrights.ca/story/online-misogyny-manosphere.

76   **on Wednesdays we wear pink:** *Mean Girls,* directed by Mark Waters (Paramount Pictures, 2004).

80   **psychedelics have been proven:** Michael Pollan, *How to Change Your Mind: What the New Science of Psychedelics Teaches Us About Consciousness, Dying, Addiction, Depression, and Transcendence* (Penguin Books, 2018).

Interstice

83   **In 1990, fifty-five percent of American men:** Daniel A. Cox, "The State of American Friendship: Findings from the May 2021 American Perspectives Survey," American Enterprise Institute, accessed September 7, 2024, https://www.americansurveycenter.org/research/the-state-of-american-friendship-change-challenges-and-loss/.

83   **One-third of men over forty-five:** G. Oscar Anderson, "Loneliness Among Older Adults: A National Survey of Adults 45+," AARP Research, accessed September 7, 2024, https://www.aarp.org/pri/topics/social-leisure/relationships/loneliness_2010/.

83   **Fifteen percent of men:** Cox, "The State of American Friendship."

Big Dick Idiocy

85   **Freud's theory on penis envy:** Sigmund Freud, *Three Essays on the Theory of Sexuality,* trans. James Strachey (Basic Books, 2000).

    See also: Riya Yadav, "Sigmund Freud and Penis Envy—a Failure of Courage?," *Psychologist,* May 8, 2018, https://www.bps.org.uk/psychologist/sigmund-freud-and-penis-envy-failure-courage.

85   **Men like to coast on:** Vicki Larson, "Sorry Guys, Your Penis Is Not as Powerful as You Think," *Medium,* August 9, 2020, https://omgchronicles.medium.com/sorry-guys-your-penis-is-not-as-powerful-as-you-think-5b4b6374365.

86   **Penises and vulvas are equally great:** Tiffany Lo, "Penis vs. Vagina: The Ultimate Debate," BuzzFeed, May 5, 2014, https://www.buzzfeed.com/tlo27/penis-vs-vagina-the-ultimate-debate.

86   *thought* **about our genitalia in depth:** Vanessa, "Is It Weird to Be Trans and Feel Indifferent About My Genitals?," Trans Lifeline, accessed November 19, 2024, https://translifeline.org/is-it-weird-that-i-feel-indifferent-about-my-own-genitals/.

    See also: Sam Dylan Finch, "I Have a Vagina. I'm Not a Woman. And I'm Totally Cool with It," Healthline, July 18, 2019, https://www.healthline.com/health/not-every-transgender-person-wants-bottom-surgery#1.

    See also: Andrea Long Chu, "My New Vagina Won't Make Me Happy," *New York Times,* November 24, 2018, https://www.nytimes.com/2018/11/24/opinion/sunday/vaginoplasty-transgender-medicine.html.

86   **our genitals are an open question:** Ian T. Nolan, Christopher J. Kuhner, and Geolani W. Dy, "Demographic and Temporal Trends in Transgender Identities and Gender Confirming Surgery," *Translational Andrology and Urology* 8, no. 3 (2019): 184–190, https://doi.org/10.21037/tau.2019.04.09.

87   **Team Pussy:** Lane Moore, "9 Ways Vaginas Are Better Than Penises," *Cosmo-politan,* December 10, 2015, https://www.cosmopolitan.com/sex-love/news/a50638/ways-vaginas-are-better-than-penises/.

See also: Amanda Schupak, "15 Vagina Facts That Would Make Penises Jealous," *Self,* January 6, 2016, https://www.self.com/story/15-vagina-facts-that-would-make-penises-jealous.

87   **the underdiscussed corollary is equally true:** Editors of Encyclopaedia Britannica, "Karen Horney: German Psychoanalyst," *Britannica,* accessed November 19, 2024, https://www.britannica.com/biography/Karen-Horney #ref669884.

87   *womb envy:* Emma Bayne, "Womb Envy: The Cause of Misogyny and Even Male Achievement?," *Women's Studies International Forum* 34, no. 2 (2011): 151–60, https://doi.org/10.1016/j.wsif.2011.01.007.

87   **Feminists have worked for generations:** Erika Engelhaupt, "The Surprisingly, Very Brief History of the Vagina," Healthline, August 8, 2019, https://www.healthline.com/health/vagina-history.

See also: Mabel Banfield-Nwachi, "London's Vagina Museum to Reopen After Surpassing Fundraising Goal," *Guardian,* October 9, 2023, https://www.theguardian.com/uk-news/2023/oct/09/londons-vagina-museum-to-reopen -after-surpassing-fundraising-goal.

87   **talking about vaginas in a complex manner in public:** Holly Williams, "How Vaginas Are Finally Losing Their Stigma," BBC, November 14, 2019, https://www.bbc.com/culture/article/20191114-how-vaginas-are-finally-losing-their -stigma.

87   **off-Broadway plays about it:** Eve Ensler, *The Vagina Monologues* (Villard Books, 1998).

88   **we didn't overcorrect:** Lauren Valenti, "Vaginal Health Is Finally at the Forefront," *Vogue,* August 20, 2021, https://www.vogue.com/article/vaginal -health-companies-startups.

See also: Jenn Barthole, "This Startup Is on a Mission to Destigmatize Vaginal Health," *Ebony,* March 18, 2022, https://www.ebony.com/destigmatize -vaginal-health/.

88   *two millennia* **brainwashing:** Elizabeth Hlavinka, "The History of the Word 'Vagina' Illuminates Our Persistent Problem with Biased Reproductive Health," *Salon,* September 17, 2023, https://www.salon.com/2023/09/17/the-history-of -the-word-vagina-illuminates-our-persistent-problem-with-biased -reproductive-health/.

89   **penises are often vilified:** Lisa Wade, "Is the Penis Dangerous?," *Sociological Images,* October 7, 2013, https://thesocietypages.org/socimages/2013/10/07/ safer-sex-psas-conflate-the-penis-with-a-firearm/.

89   **Daggers:** Stan Goff, "The Weaponized Phallus (and Five Easy-to-Remember Steps)," HuffPost, November 21, 2006, https://www.huffpost.com/entry/the -weaponized-phallus-an_b_34616.

89   **Spears:** Aliraza Javaid, "The Penis Is a Weapon of Power: A Feminist and Hate Crime Interpretation of Male Sexual Victimisation," *International Journal for Masculinity Studies* 13, no. 1 (2018): 23–40, https://doi.org/10.1080/18902138 .2017.1319708.

89   **Pikes:** Bill Paxton, "Guns Are an Extension of the Penis," *Vulture,* July 30, 2013, https://www.vulture.com/2013/07/bill-paxton-guns-are-an-extension-of-the -penis.html.

90   **we tell the same story over and over:** Sharful Islam Khan, Nancy Hudson-Rodd, Sherry Saggers, Mahbubul Islam Bhuiyan, et al. "Phallus, Performance and Power: Crisis of Masculinity," *Sexual and Relationship Therapy* 23, no. 1 (2008): 37–49, https://doi.org/10.1080/14681990701790635.

90   **achieving male orgasm:** Verena Klein and Terri D. Conley, "The Role of Gendered Entitlement in Understanding Inequality in the Bedroom," *Social Psychological and Personality Science* 13, no. 6 (2022): 1047–57, https://doi.org/10.1177/19485506211053564.

90   **This oversimplification hurts men:** Suzannah Weiss, "Do I Have a Normal Penis? 8 Myths to Stop Believing About Your Penis," *Teen Vogue,* December 11, 2019, https://www.teenvogue.com/story/myths-to-stop-believing-about-your-penis.

90   **double standards around performance:** Grant Stoddard, "Worried About Getting Unwanted Erections? You're Not Alone," NOCD, September 28, 2023, https://www.treatmyocd.com/what-is-ocd/common-fears/worried-about -getting-unwanted-erections-youre-not-alone.
     See also: Geoffrey Whittaker, "Is It Embarrassing When a Guy Can't Get It Up?," Hims, October 12, 2018, https://www.hims.com/blog/the-right-and -wrong-way-to-react-to-a-failed-erection.

90   **The pressure of having a dick:** Alyssa Rose, "The Biggest Bulges of 2012: Packing a Double Standard," Good Men Project, December 31, 2012, https:// goodmenproject.com/arts/the-biggest-bulges-of-2012-packing-a-double -standard/.
     See also: Thomas R. Brooks and Stephen Reysen, "Personality and Sexual Perceptions of Penises: Digital Impression Formation," *Sexuality and Culture* 27 (2023): 1–18, https://doi.org/10.1007/s12119-022-10000-y.

91   **men develop deep, abiding shame:** Joe Kort, "Unhung Heroes: Overcoming Small-Penis Shame," *Psychology Today,* January 16, 2024, https://www .psychologytoday.com/nz/blog/understanding-the-erotic-code/202401/unhung -heroes-overcoming-small-penis-shame.

91   **breeding ground for misogyny:** F. Oswald, D. Khera, and C. L. Pedersen, "The Association of Genital Appearance Satisfaction, Penis Size Importance, and Penis-Centric Masculinity to Chronically Discriminatory Ideologies Among Heterosexual Men," *Psychology of Men & Masculinities* 22, no. 4 (2021): 704–14, https://doi.org/10.1037/men0000360.

92   **Erections are complex neurological phenomena:** Irwin Goldstein, "The Central Mechanisms of Sexual Function," Boston University School of Medicine: Sexual Medicine, February 7, 2003, https://www.bumc.bu.edu/ sexualmedicine/publications/the-central-mechanisms-of-sexual-function/.

92   **in order to get and stay hard:** K. Everaert, W. de Waard, T. Van Hoof, et al., "Neuroanatomy and Neurophysiology Related to Sexual Dysfunction in Male Neurogenic Patients with Lesions to the Spinal Cord or Peripheral Nerves," *Spinal Cord* 48 (2010): 82–191, https://doi.org/10.1038/sc.2009 .172.

94   **erections can be completely involuntary:** Duygu Balan, "An Erection Is Not Consent," *Psychology Today,* April 15, 2024, https://www.psychologytoday.com/ us/blog/un-numb/202404/an-erection-is-not-consent.

95   **virtually no agency over how my erotic consciousness:** Alexandra Schwartz, "We're Shaped by Our Sexual Desires. Can We Shape Them?," *New Yorker,* September 27, 2021, https://www.newyorker.com/magazine/2021/10/04/were -shaped-by-our-sexual-desires-can-we-shape-them.

95   **If conventional Disney movies first programmed:** Rachel Paige, "A Quick Look at How Disney Perfection Affects Guy's Body Image Too," HelloGiggles, March 10, 2015, https://hellogiggles.com/disney-body-image-men/.

95   **desires were formed before I had any power to choose:** Jennifer S. Mills, Amy Shannon, and Jacqueline Hogue, "Beauty, Body Image, and the Media," in *Perception of Beauty,* ed. Martha Peaslee Levine (InTech, 2017).

    See also: Jeff Hayward, "Who Upholds Beauty Standards: The Media, or Its Audience?," *Medium,* March 30, 2023, https://medium.com/modernidentities/who-upholds-beauty-standards-the-media-or-its-audience-3944b76b2fc3.

96   **The more you think:** Raymond C. Rosen, "Psychogenic Erectile Dysfunction: Classification and Management," *Urologic Clinics of North America* 28, no. 2 (2001): 269–78, https://doi.org/10.1016/S0094-0143(05)70137-3.

97   **label someone's dick "dysfunctional":** Ziyan Sheng, "Psychological Consequences of Erectile Dysfunction," *Trends in Urology and Men's Health* 12, no. 6 (2021): 19–22, https://doi.org/10.1002/tre.827.

98   **the fucked-up discourse on the *size* of them:** Christine Dell'Amore, "Women Prefer Bigger Penises, May Have Shaped Evolution," *National Geographic,* April 9, 2013, https://www.nationalgeographic.com/science/article/130408-penises-science-evolution-genitalia-health-weird.

    See also: Brian Alexander, "Science Proves Women Like Men with Bigger Penises," NBC News, April 16, 2013, https://www.nbcnews.com/health/health-news/science-proves-women-men-bigger-penises-flna1c9266567.

    See also: Stephanie Pappas, "Penis Size Matters in Bed, Study Finds," Live Science, October 8, 2012, https://www.livescience.com/23785-penis-size-matters-orgasms.html.

    See also: Brian S. Mautz, Bob B. M. Wong, Richard A. Peters, and Michael D. Jennions, "Penis Size Interacts with Body Shape and Height to Influence Male Attractiveness," *Proceedings of the National Academy of Sciences* 110, no. 17 (2013): 6925–30, https://doi.org/10.1073/pnas.1219361110.

98   **Big Dick Energy phenomenon:** Emily Reynolds, "Big Dick Energy: Explained," Vice News, June 26, 2018, https://www.vice.com/en/article/big-dick-energy-explained/.

98   **Pete Davidson's dick:** Jazmin Kopotsha, "A History of 'Big Dick Energy': The Term Inspired by Women's Obsession with Pete Davidson," *Grazia,* July 26, 2023, https://graziadaily.co.uk/celebrity/news/big-dick-energy-pete-davidson-ariana-grande-kim-kardashian/.

98   **The term spread like a virus:** Constance Grady and Alex Abad-Santos, "How Big Dick Energy Explains Modern Masculinity," Vox, June 27, 2018, https://www.vox.com/culture/2018/6/27/17506898/big-dick-energy-explained/.

99   **full-blown clinical dysmorphia:** Lucy Johnston, Tracey Lee McLellan, and Audrey McKinlay, "(Perceived) Size Really Does Matter: Male Dissatisfaction with Penis Size," *Psychology of Men & Masculinity* 15, no. 2 (2014): 225, http://dx.doi.org/10.1037/a0033264.

99   **Penile Dysmorphia Disorder:** David Veale, Sarah Miles, and Julie Read, "Sexual Functioning and Behavior of Men with Body Dysmorphic Disorder Concerning Penis Size Compared with Men Anxious About Penis Size and with Controls: A Cohort Study," *Sexual Medicine* 3, no. 3 (2015): 147–55, https://doi.org/10.1002/sm2.63.

    See also: C. Brian Smith, "The Long and Short of Dick Dysmorphia," *MEL*

Magazine, accessed November 19, 2024, https://melmagazine.com/en-us/story/the-long-and-short-of-dick-dysmorphia.

99 **an intense disorder:** Brittany Wong, "Yes, Penis Dysmorphia Is a Real Thing," HuffPost, August 28, 2019, https://www.huffpost.com/entry/penis-dysmorphia-body-image_l_5d642f13e4b01d7b5293bf2c.

99 **end in serious self-harm or suicide:** Katharine A. Phillips, Meredith E. Coles, William Menard, et al., "Suicidal Ideation and Suicide Attempts in Body Dysmorphic Disorder," *Journal of Clinical Psychiatry* 66, no. 6 (2005): 717–25, http://dx.doi.org/10.4088/JCP.v66n0607.

99 **Dysmorphia is serious business:** Michael Stahl, "Why Do So Many Men with Big Penises Think They Have Small Ones?," InsideHook, March 25, 2021, https://www.insidehook.com/sex-and-dating/men-underestimate-penis-size.

99 **they need to be compassionately helped:** David Oliver, "Men Often Struggle with Penis Insecurity. But No One Wants to Talk About It," *USA Today,* August 7, 2023, https://www.usatoday.com/story/life/health-wellness/2023/08/07/penis-men-afraid-talk-average-size/70468460007/.

99 **You cannot change the length of your erect penis:** Ava Kofman, "Inside the Secretive World of Penile Enlargement," ProPublica with *The New Yorker,* June 26, 2023, https://www.propublica.org/article/penis-enlargement-enhancement-procedures-implants.

99 **how people are trying:** Michel Alain Danino, Pierre Trouilloud, Mehdi Benkhadra, Arthur Danino, and Romain Laurent, "Cosmetic Male Genital Surgery: A Narrative Review," *Annals of Translational Medicine* 12, no. 1 (2024), https://doi.org/10.21037/atm-23-351.

See also: Landon Trost, Daniel N. Watter, Serge Carrier, et al., "Cosmetic Penile Enhancement Procedures: A Sexual Medicine Society of North America Position Statement," *Journal of Sexual Medicine* 21 (2024): 573–78, https://doi.org/10.1093/jsxmed/qdae045.

See also: Douglas Greenwood, "Why (and How) Are Men Making Their Dicks Bigger?," *Dazed,* January 28, 2019, https://www.dazeddigital.com/beauty/article/43068/1/why-how-men-making-their-dicks-bigger-penis-enlargement-surgery.

100 **the scams:** Colin Drury, "I Wanted a Truncheon in My Pants: The Rise of the Penis Extension," *Guardian,* September 22, 2018, https://www.theguardian.com/lifeandstyle/2018/sep/22/penis-extension-wanted-truncheon-in-pants-rise.

See also: Olivia Petter, "Man Dies from Penis Enlargement Surgery in Sweden," *Independent,* July 31, 2017, https://www.independent.co.uk/life-style/man-dies-penis-enlargement-surgery-sweden-stockholm-plastic-fat-transfer-a7868741.html.

101 **we mock men we hate:** Roz Warren, "I Love Greta Thunberg—but Why Is It OK for Her to Mock Guys with Small Dicks?," *Broad Street Review,* January 9, 2023, https://www.broadstreetreview.com/essays/i-love-greta-thunberg-buy-why-is-it-ok-for-her-to-mock-guys-with-small-dicks.

103 **As comfortable?:** Regina Nuzzo, "Bigger Not Always Better for Penis Size," *Nature* (2013), https://doi.org/10.1038/nature.2013.12770.

103 **As a glorious, fun, oftentimes *preferable*:** Gloria Brame, "Why Small Is Better: The 5 Inch Advantage for Men," Huff Post, April 25, 2017, https://www.huffpost.com/entry/why-small-is-better-the-5-inch-advantage-for-men_b_58ff9812e4b0938fb73e95f2.

103   **Publicly shaming *or* praising a man:** Sebastian Shehadi, "Penis Size Shaming Is Still Too Normalised. It's Time to Talk About It." *Feminist Perspectives—Disciplined and Resistant Bodies,* September 4, 2023, https://www.kcl.ac.uk/penis-size-shaming-is-still-too-normalised.-its-time-to-talk-about-it.

103   **objectify men's bodies:** Anonymous, "Small Penis: Why Is It Still Considered Okay to Shame Small Penises?," *Cosmopolitan,* June 14, 2021, https://www.cosmopolitan.com/uk/love-sex/sex/a36661872/small-penis/.

103   **we don't treat *their* bodies positively, too:** Robin Tran, "4 Reasons Why Penis Size Shaming Is Anti-Feminist," Everyday Feminism, March 22, 2016, https://everydayfeminism.com/2016/03/penis-size-shaming-harmful/.

103   **we cannot dissect the size, shape, or color:** Kate Lister, "Shaming Men for Their Penis Size Isn't Just Humiliating for Them—It's Bad for Women Too," iNews, September 26, 2023, https://inews.co.uk/opinion/shaming-men-penis-size-humiliating-bad-for-women-too-2642194.

105   **so many trout on the line:** "Penis Anxiety Is Impacting Gay Men's Self-Esteem," LGBT Hero, accessed November 19, 2024, https://www.lgbthero.org.uk/fs160-penis-anxiety-is-impacting-gay-mens-self-esteem.

Interstice

107   **Thirty-nine percent of men:** All three statistics are from Medzino, "Manhood Shame," accessed November 19, 2024, https://www.medzino.com/us/manhood-shame/.

Incelopathy

109   **acerbic and intractable cultural phenomena:** Jia Tolentino, "The Rage of the Incels," *New Yorker,* May 15, 2018, https://www.newyorker.com/culture/cultural-comment/the-rage-of-the-incels.

109   **"involuntary celibate":** Niraj Chokshi, "What Is an Incel? A Term Used by the Toronto Van Attack Suspect, Explained," *New York Times,* April 24, 2018, https://www.nytimes.com/2018/04/24/world/canada/incel-reddit-meaning-rebellion.html.

109   **young, lost, predominantly heterosexual men:** AJ Willingham, "What Does the Term 'Incel' Mean?," CNN, March 16, 2023, https://www.cnn.com/2023/03/16/us/incel-involuntary-celibate-explained-cec/index.html.

109   **They find it so difficult to access sex:** Ross Douthat, "The Redistribution of Sex," *New York Times,* May 2, 2018, https://www.nytimes.com/2018/05/02/opinion/incels-sex-robots-redistribution.html.

109   **forced into celibacy:** Robin Hanson, "Two Types of Envy," *Overcoming Bias* (blog), April 26, 2018, https://www.overcomingbias.com/p/two-types-of-envyhtml.

109   ***right to sex:*** Amia Srinivasan, "Does Anyone Have the Right to Sex?" *London Review of Books* 40, no. 6 (March 22, 2018), https://www.lrb.co.uk/the-paper/v40/n06/amia-srinivasan/does-anyone-have-the-right-to-sex.

109   **filled to the brim with misogyny:** "Misogynist Incels," Southern Poverty Law Center, accessed November 17, 2024, https://www.splcenter.org/fighting-hate/extremist-files/ideology/misogynist-incels.

See also: Michael Halpin, Norann Richard, Kayla Preston, Meghan Gosse, and Finlay Maguire, "Men Who Hate Women: The Misogyny of Involuntarily Celibate Men," *New Media & Society* 27, no. 1 (2023): 424–42, https://doi.org/10.1177/14614448231176777.

See also: Michael Halpin and Finlay Maguire, "Yes, the Incel Community Has a Sexism Problem, but We Can Do Something About It," *The Conversation*, June 11, 2023, https://theconversation.com/yes-the-incel-community-has-a-sexism-problem-but-we-can-do-something-about-it-207206.

109   **It's an internet-born movement:** Shannon Zimmerman, "The Ideology of Incels: Misogyny and Victimhood as Justification for Political Violence," *Terrorism and Political Violence* 36, no. 2 (2022): 166–79, https://doi.org/10.1080/09546553.2022.2129014.

110   **acute body-image issues:** Jamilla Rosdahl, "'Looksmaxxing' Is the Disturbing TikTok Trend Turning Young Men into Incels," *The Conversation*, January 30, 2024, https://theconversation.com/looksmaxxing-is-the-disturbing-tiktok-trend-turning-young-men-into-incels-221724.

110   **inability to socialize well:** Jonathan Griffin, "Incels: Inside a Dark World of Online Hate," BBC, August 13, 2021, https://www.bbc.com/news/blogs-trending-44053828.

110   **is a really great thing to hear:** Radicalisation Awareness Network, "The Incel Phenomenon: Exploring Internal and External Issues Around Involuntary Celibates," European Commission of the European Union, July 28, 2021, https://home-affairs.ec.europa.eu/system/files/2021-08/ran_cn_incel_phenomenon_20210803_en.pdf.

110   **incel ideology promises psychic relief:** Miriam Lindner, "The Sense in Senseless Violence: Male Reproductive Strategy and the Modern Sexual Marketplace as Contributors to Violent Extremism," *Adaptive Human Behavior and Physiology* 9 (2023): 217–51, https://doi.org/10.1007/s40750-023-00219-w.

110   **suffering that is . . . very real:** Brandon Sparks, Alexandra M. Zidenberg, and Mark E. Olver, "Involuntary Celibacy: A Review of Incel Ideology and Experiences with Dating, Rejection, and Associated Mental Health and Emotional Sequelae," *Current Psychiatry Reports* 24 (2022): 731–40, https://doi.org/10.1007/s11920-022-01382-9.

See also: Thomas W. Delaney, Thomas V. Pollet, and Clare Cook, "The Mental Well-Being of Involuntary Celibates," *Personality and Individual Differences* 218 (2024), https://doi.org/10.1016/j.paid.2023.112474.

See also: Catriona Aitken, "Incels Need More Mental Health Help—Swansea University Report," BBC News, January 13, 2024, https://www.bbc.com/news/uk-wales-67770178.

110   **Not being able to find partnership, feel desirable:** Joona Räsänen, "Sexual Loneliness: A Neglected Public Health Problem?," *Bioethics* 37, no. 2 (2023): 101–02, https://doi.org/10.1111/bioe.13134.

110   **People of any gender who feel lonely or sexually isolated:** Paul Gorczynski and Fabio Fasoli, "Loneliness in Sexual Minority and Heterosexual Individuals: A Comparative Meta-Analysis," *Journal of Gay & Lesbian Mental Health* 26, no. 2 (2021): 112–29, doi: 10.1080/19359705.2021.1957742.

110   **people who are suffering:** Raheel Mushtaq, Sheikh Shoib, Tabindah Shah, and Sahil Mushtaq, "Relationship Between Loneliness, Psychiatric Disorders and Physical Health: A Review on the Psychological Aspects of Loneliness," *Journal*

of Clinical and Diagnostic Research 8, no. 9 (2014): WE01–04, doi: 10.7860/
JCDR/2014/10077.4828.

110   **born on platforms like Reddit and 4chan:** Rosalie Mary Gillett and Nicolas
Suzor, "Incels on Reddit: A Study in Social Norms and Decentralized Modera-
tion," *AoIR Selected Papers of Internet Research* (2021), https://doi.org/10.5210/
spir.v2021i0.12171.

113   **testimonials of these broken young men:** "r/IncelExit," Reddit, accessed
November 17, 2024, https://www.reddit.com/r/IncelExit/.
        See also: witchcraft_streams, "There's Nowhere for Incels to Get Help,"
Reddit, 2023, https://www.reddit.com/r/Healthygamergg/comments/175qbm0/
comment/k4lmhdh/.

113   **no cultural representations:** GLAAD, *Where We Are on TV: 2023–2024,*
GLAAD Media Institute, accessed November 17, 2024, https://glaad.org/
whereweareontv23/.

113   **not represented as beings worthy of sexual interest or love:** Traci B. Abbott,
The History of Trans Representation in American Television and Film Genres
(Palgrave Macmillan, 2022).

113   **Things are changing:** GLAAD, *Accelerating Acceptance 2024,* GLAAD Media
Institute, accessed November 17, 2024, https://glaad.org/accelerating
-acceptance-2024/.

117   **dying romantically alone:** Katherine V. Bruss, Puja Seth, and Guixiang Zhao,
"Loneliness, Lack of Social and Emotional Support, and Mental Health
Issues—United States, 2022," *Morbidity and Mortality Weekly Report* 73 (2024):
539–45, http://dx.doi.org/10.15585/mmwr.mm7324a1.
        See also: Mary Kekatos and Abimbola Okulaja, "Bisexual, Transgender
Adults Nearly Twice as Likely to Experience Loneliness: CDC," ABC News,
June 20, 2024, https://abcnews.go.com/Health/bisexual-transgender-adults
-experience-loneliness-cdc/story?id=111270479.
        See also: Hana Mohan, "The Romantic Isolation and Loneliness of
Being Transgender," *Medium,* October 28, 2019, https://medium.com/
@unamashana/the-romantic-isolation-and-loneliness-of-being-transgender
-59bc41ae331e.
        See also: Emily Deaton, "Transgender & Non-Binary Loneliness: How to
Feel Less Alone," The Roots of Loneliness Project, accessed November 17, 2024,
https://www.rootsofloneliness.com/transgender-loneliness.

120   **a very small group of extremely powerful people:** Richard Rushfield, "Gang of
Five: the CEOs Deciding Hollywood's Fate," *Ankler,* January 9, 2024, https://
theankler.com/p/gang-of-five-the-ceos-deciding-hollywoods.
        See also: Georg Szalai, "The Hollywood CEO Mega Pay Chart: Top Execu-
tives' Compensation Revealed," *Hollywood Reporter,* May 7, 2024, https://www
.hollywoodreporter.com/business/business-news/hollywood-ceo-pay-chart
-executive-compensation-2023-1235891408/.
        See also: Winston Cho, "After Trump Win, Hollywood Prepares for
Megamergers—and Volatility," *Hollywood Reporter,* November 8, 2024, https://
www.hollywoodreporter.com/business/business-news/trump-hollywood-deals
-mergers-1236056410/.
        See also: Daniel Bessner, "The Life and Death of Hollywood," *Harper's Maga-
zine,* May 2024, https://harpers.org/archive/2024/05/the-life-and-death-of
-hollywood-daniel-bessner/.

121   **which bodies people understand to be sexy:** Maya Singer, "What's Changing—and What Isn't—About Fashion's Relationship to the Body?," *Vogue,* February 22, 2022, https://www.vogue.com/article/fashion-and-the -body.

    See also: Shriya Raghuram, "The Psychological Effects of Fashion on Body Image and Self-Esteem," *Fashion and Law Journal,* January 27, 2023, https:// fashionlawjournal.com/the-psychological-effects-of-fashion-on-body-image -and-self-esteem/.

    See also: Lucy Maguire, Maliha Shoaib, and Madeleine Schulz, "The *Vogue Business* AW24 Size Inclusivity Report," *Vogue Business,* March 11, 2024, https:// www.voguebusiness.com/story/fashion/the-vogue-business-aw24-size -inclusivity-report.

121   **"I see. You think this has nothing":** *The Devil Wears Prada,* directed by David Frankel (20th Century Fox, 2006).

122   **the face of a new brand of gender-neutral makeup:** Shannon Barbour, "Gender Nonconforming Activist Jacob Tobia Lands Gorgeous New Beauty Campaign," *Cosmopolitan,* March 7, 2018, https://www.cosmopolitan.com/style -beauty/a19129235/jacob-tobia-fluide-makeup-campaign/.

122   **Diet Coke Pride Month campaign:** "The Unapologetic Allure of Author and Activist Jacob Tobia," *Out Magazine,* June 11, 2019, https://www.out.com/ out-exclusives/2019/6/11/unapologetic-allure-author-and-activist-jacob -tobia.

125   **People under the spell of cult ideologies:** Steven A. Hassan, "The Definitive Guide to Helping People Trapped in a Cult," *Psychology Today,* April 13, 2021, https://www.psychologytoday.com/us/blog/freedom-mind/202104/the -definitive-guide-helping-people-trapped-in-cult.

125   ***Ms.* magazine is implicitly praising:** Chuka Emezue, "The Danger of Incels— and How We Shift the Thinking of Men Attracted to These Groups," *Ms.,* April 9, 2023, https://msmagazine.com/2023/04/09/incel-violence-women -misogyny-white-supremacy-online/.

125   **an article for *Wired*:** Andrew Kersley, "How Do You Deradicalise an Incel?," *Wired,* October 13, 2021, https://www.wired.com/story/how-do-you -deradicalise-an-incel/.

125   **meager epistemological handfuls of sand:** Eviane Leidig, "Why Terrorism Studies Miss the Mark When It Comes to Incels," International Center for Counterterrorism, August 31, 2021, https://www.icct.nl/publication/why -terrorism-studies-miss-mark-when-it-comes-incels.

125   **"Beyond Violent Extremism: A 3N Perspective of Inceldom":** Molly Ellen-berg, Anne Speckhard, and Arie W. Kruglanski, "Beyond Violent Extremism: A 3N Perspective of Inceldom," *Psychology of Men & Masculinities* 25, no. 3 (2024): 290–99, https://doi.org/10.1037/men0000439.

126   **"A Qualitative Analysis of the Turning Points":** Léa-May Burns and Marie-Aude Boislard, " 'I'm Better Than This': A Qualitative Analysis of the Turning Points Leading to Exiting Inceldom," *Journal of Sex Research* (2024): 1–17, https://doi.org/10.1080/00224499.2024.2340110.

127   **Take the New America think tank:** Megan Kelly, Alex DiBranco, and Dr. Julia R. DeCook, "Misogynist Incels and Male Supremacism: Recommenda-tions," New America, February 18, 2021, https://www.newamerica.org/political -reform/reports/misogynist-incels-and-male-supremacism/.

127   **an "academic problem" or a "counterterrorism initiative":** Joshua Thorburn, "Exiting the Manosphere. A Gendered Analysis of Radicalization, Diversion and Deradicalization Narratives from *r/IncelExit* and *r/ExRedPill*," *Studies in Conflict & Terrorism* (2023): 1–25, https://doi.org/10.1080/1057610X.2023 .2244192.
      See also: Gavin Hart and Antoinette Raffaela Huber, "Five Things We Need to Learn About Incel Extremism: Issues, Challenges and Avenues for Fresh Research," *Studies in Conflict & Terrorism* (April 2, 2023): 1–17, https://doi.org/ 10.1080/1057610X.2023.2195067.

128   **Isla Vista in 2014:** Harriet Sokmensuer, "Remembering the 6 Student Victims of the 2014 Isla Vista Killings," *People,* June 13, 2023, https://people.com/ crime/5-years-later-remembering-the-6-student-victims-of-the-isla-vista -killings/.

128   **Toronto in 2018:** Osita Nwanevu, "The Toronto Van Killer Posted About Sexual Rejection Before Attack," *Slate,* April 24, 2018, https://slate.com/news-and -politics/2018/04/the-toronto-van-killer-was-an-incel-motivated-by-sexual -rejection.html?.

128   **Texas, in 2023:** Jake Bleiberg and Gene Johnson, "What to Know About the Mass Shooting at a Texas Mall," Associated Press, May 10, 2023, https://apnews .com/article/shooting-outlet-mall-allen-texas -200f1ffadf7daefa42cfbe45510b083f.

128   **my good friend Megan:** Megan Phelps-Roper, *Unfollow: A Memoir of Loving and Leaving the Westboro Baptist Church* (Farrar, Straus and Giroux, 2019).

135   **"It used to be the case":** Amia Srinivasan, "Does Anyone Have the Right to Sex?," *London Review of Books* 40, no. 6 (March 22, 2018), https://www.lrb .co.uk/the-paper/v40/n06/amia-srinivasan/does-anyone-have-the-right-to -sex.

Interstice

137   **Forty-three percent of men:** Katharine A. Phillips and David J. Castle, "Body Dysmorphic Disorder in Men," *British Medical Journal* (2001), https://www.ncbi .nlm.nih.gov/pmc/articles/PMC1121529/.

137   **This number has tripled:** Phillips and Castle, "Body Dysmorphic Disorder in Men."

137   **In just three years:** American Society of Plastic Surgeons, "Male Plastic Surgery Trends," *The 2022 Procedural Statistics Release* (2023): 29, https://www .plasticsurgery.org/documents/news/Statistics/2022/plastic-surgery-statistics -report-2022.pdf.

137   **Forty percent of people with body dysmorphic disorder:** Katharine A. Phillips, "Who Gets BDD?," International OCD Foundation, accessed November 17, 2024, https://bdd.iocdf.org/about-bdd/who-gets/.

137   **Of those, an estimated eighty percent:** Katharine A. Phillips, "Suicidality in Body Dysmorphic Disorder," *Primary Psychiatry* 14, no. 12 (2007): 58–66, https://pmc.ncbi.nlm.nih.gov/articles/PMC2361388/.

137   **Twenty-five percent have attempted it:** Phillips, "Suicidality in Body Dysmorphic Disorder."

Get Fucked

139 **You know the book:** Dr. Seuss, *Green Eggs and Ham* (Random House Children's Books, 1960).

140 **reasons why every man on the planet should explore his butt:** Sabrina Felson, "Prostate Orgasm: What It Is," WebMD, December 3, 2022, https://www.webmd.com/sex/prostate-orgasm-what-it-is.

140 **hardwired for anal pleasure:** Adrienne Santos-Longhurst, "Everything You Need to Know About the Male G-Spot," Healthline, January 30, 2024, https://www.healthline.com/health/healthy-sex/male-g-spot.

140 **A gift from God herself:** Melanie Curry, "Here's Exactly How to Have a Prostate Orgasm, According to Sex Experts," *Men's Health,* June 8, 2021, https://www.menshealth.com/sex-women/a36650744/how-to-have-prostate-orgasm/.

140 **doctors and cancer have given a bad name:** Mindy Waizer, "Addressing Fear and Dread of Prostate Cancer Screening," *Oncology Nursing News,* September 28, 2018, https://www.oncnursingnews.com/view/addressing-fear-and-dread-of-prostate-cancer-screening.

140 **the scariest thing they can imagine:** Ramin Zahed, "Don't Be Afraid of the Prostate Exam," Keck Medicine of USC, September 13, 2017, https://www.keckmedicine.org/blog/dont-be-afraid-of-the-prostate-exam/.

140 **every man in America is petrified:** Laura J. James, Germaine Wong, Jonathan C. Craig, et al., "Men's Perspectives of Prostate Cancer Screening: A Systematic Review of Qualitative Studies," *PLoS ONE* 12, no. 11 (2017): e0188258, https://doi.org/10.1371/journal.pone.0188258.

141 *the literal muscle of your cock:* A. Shafik, "Physioanatomic Entirety of External Anal Sphincter with Bulbocavernosus Muscle," *Archives of Andrology* 42, no. 1 (1999): 45–54, https://doi.org/10.1080/014850199263048.

141 **physiologically attached to your anal sphincter:** A. Shafik and O. El-Sibai, "The Anocavernosal Erectile Dysfunction Syndrome II: Anal Fissure and Erectile Dysfunction," *International Journal of Impotence Research* 12 (2000): 279–83, https://doi.org/10.1038/sj.ijir.3900623.

141 **Your dick muscle continues:** Briony Adams, "The Penis," Teach Me Anatomy, August 9, 2024, https://teachmeanatomy.info/pelvis/the-male-reproductive-system/penis/.

141 **Better pack an oxygen tank:** Zachary Zane and Dr. Chauntelle Tibbals, "Here's What Analingus Feels Like, According to 10 People Who've Tried It," *Men's Health,* August 2, 2021, https://www.menshealth.com/sex-women/a19530788/butt-motorboating-explained/.

142 **you did not truly know the fullness of human experience:** Taffy Brodesser-Akner, "Tom Ford on Sex, Death, and Penetration," *GQ,* December 5, 2016, https://www.gq.com/story/tom-ford-interview-nocturnal-animals-moty.

142 **there is not so much separating you and women:** Joe Von Malachowski, "Every Man Should Be Penetrated at Least Once in His Life," *Unicorn Magazine,* no. 005, https://unicornzine.com/issue-005/every-man-should-be-penetrated-at-least-once-in-his-life/.

142 **you will never again correlate being penetrated with:** Zachary Zane, "The Sex Act I Believe Every Man Should Experience," *Bustle,* February 25, 2016, https://www.bustle.com/articles/137828-why-i-believe-every-man-should-experience-being-penetrated.

142 **where your empathy first began to die:** Cory Ohlendorf, "Do Men Have an Empathy Problem?," *Valet Magazine,* June 11, 2020, https://www.valetmag .com/living/features/2020/do-men-have-an-empathy-problem-061120 .php.

See also: Samantha Rodman Whiten, "Sexual Empathic Ruptures," *Dr. Psych Mom,* September 15, 2023, https://www.drpsychmom.com/sexual-empathic -ruptures/.

142 **knowing *next to nothing* about what she's going through:** Allison Carter, Jessie V. Ford, Maya Luetke, et al., "Fulfilling His Needs, Not Mine: Reasons for Not Talking About Painful Sex and Associations with Lack of Pleasure in a Nationally Representative Sample of Women in the United States," *Journal of Sexual Medicine* 16, no. 12 (2019): 1953–65, https://doi.org/10.1016/j.jsxm.2019 .08.016.

142 **the cognitive dissonance is foundational:** Debby Herbenick, Vanessa Schick, Stephanie A. Sanders, et al., "Pain Experienced During Vaginal and Anal Intercourse with Other-Sex Partners: Findings from a Nationally Representative Probability Study in the United States," *Journal of Sexual Medicine* 12, no. 4 (2015): 1040–51, https://doi.org/10.1111/jsm.12841.

146 **not *so* dissonant, you know:** Mark Gaspar, Shayna Skakoon-Sparling, Barry D. Adam, David J. Brennan, et al., "You're Gay, It's Just What Happens: Sexual Minority Men Recounting Experiences of Unwanted Sex in the Era of MeToo," *Journal of Sex Research* 58, no. 9 (2021): 1205–14, https://doi.org/10.1080/ 00224499.2021.1962236.

148 **fullness in the way queer people have sex:** Terry Evans, "I've Never Ever Felt Like That in My Life Before . . . Never Ever Felt That Intense: Penetration of the Male Body as Transformative Experience," *Transformations Journal of Media, Culture, and Technology* 11 (2005), http://www.transformationsjournal.org/wp -content/uploads/2017/01/Evans_Transformations11.pdf.

148 **Queer sex is necessarily more empathetic:** Mark J. T. Sergeant, Thomas E. Dickins, Mark N. O. Davies, and Mark D. Griffiths, "Aggression, Empathy and Sexual Orientation in Males," *Personality and Individual Differences* 40, no. 3 (2006): 475–86, https://doi.org/10.1016/j.paid.2005.07.002.

149 **learn to have sex in a dissociative way:** Sara I. McClelland, "Intimate Justice: Sexual Satisfaction in Young Adults" (PhD diss., City University of New York, 2009), ProQuest (3365820).

See also: Coraline Pettine, "Male Pleasure Prioritized over Female Discomfort, Pain," *Loquitur,* May 3, 2018, https://theloquitur.com/male-pleasure -prioritized-over-female-discomfort-pain/.

149 **eroticize the pain:** Diana T. Sanchez, Janell C. Fetterolf, and Laurie A. Rudman, "Eroticizing Inequality in the United States: The Consequences and Determinants of Traditional Gender Role Adherence in Intimate Relationships," *Journal of Sex Research* 49, no. 2–3 (2012): 168–83, https://doi.org/10.1080/00224499 .2011.653699.

See also: Marjorie Jolles, "Pleasure, Pain, and the Feminist Politics of Rough Sex," in *Gender, Sex, and Politics: In the Streets and Between the Sheets in the 21st Century,* ed. Shira Tarrant (Routledge, 2015).

See also: Margaret Jackson, "Facts of Life, or the Eroticization of Women's Oppression? Sexology and the Social Construction of Heterosexuality," in *The Cultural Construction of Sexuality,* ed. Pat Caplan (Routledge, 1987).

149   **whether it feels good for them or not:** Willibrord Weijmar Schultz, Rosemary Basson, Yitzchak Binik, et al., "Women's Sexual Pain and Its Management," *Journal of Sexual Medicine* 2, no. 3 (2005): 301–16, https://doi.org/10.1111/j .1743-6109.2005.20347.x.

149   **Many people settle for this type of painful sex:** Lili Loofbourow, "The Female Price of Male Pleasure," *The Week,* January 25, 2018, https://theweek.com/ articles/749978/female-price-male-pleasure.

149   **try to eroticize abuse or trick ourselves:** Jenny Bivona and Joseph Critelli, "The Nature of Women's Rape Fantasies: An Analysis of Prevalence, Frequency, and Contents," *Journal of Sexual Research* 46, no. 1 (2009): 33–45, https://doi .org/10.1080/00224490802624406.

        See also: Justin Lehmiller, *Tell Me What You Want: The Science of Sexual Desire and How It Can Help You Improve Your Sex Life* (Hachette Books, 2018).

149   **a kinky motherfucker who enjoys pain in an erotic way:** Cara R. Dunkley, Craig D. Henshaw, Saira K. Henshaw, and Lori A. Brotto, "Physical Pain as Pleasure: A Theoretical Perspective," *Journal of Sex Research* 57, no. 4 (2020): 421–37, https://doi.org/10.1080/00224499.2019.1605328.

149   **men's aversion to *being penetrated*:** Dianne Elise, "Unlawful Entry: Male Fears of Psychic Penetration," *Psychoanalytic Dialogues* 11, no. 4 (2001): 499–531, https://doi.org/10.1080/10481881109348624.

149   **you should *never* be penetrated:** Jonathan Kemp, *The Penetrated Male* (Punctum Books, 2013).

149   **being penetrated makes you weak:** Jonas Ekblom, "Power, Penises and Penetration—Is Sex Really All About It?," *Europe & Me,* July 1, 2018, http:// europeandme.eu/power-penises-and-penetration-is-sex-really-all-about-it/.

150   *A man is someone who penetrates:* Chase Amante, "Men Are Penetrators. Women Are Receivers," Girls Chase, accessed November 18, 2024, https://www .girlschase.com/content/men-are-penetrators-women-are-receivers. (This article is *atrocious.*)

        See also: Stefanos Sifandos, "The Penetrative Man," *Medium,* May 28, 2019, https://stefanossifandos.medium.com/the-penetrative-man-a4b9ac3fb35a.

150   *A woman is someone who is penetrated:* Colleen Gallagher, "The Power of a Man's Penetration," ColleenGallagher.co, accessed November 18, 2024, https:// colleengallagher.co/blog/the-power-of-a-mans-penetration.

150   **is solely for women to endure:** Charlie Glickman and Aislinn Emirzian, *Ultimate Guide to Prostate Pleasure: Erotic Exploration for Men and Their Partners* (Cleis, 2013), chapter 13, "Real Men Don't."

150   **This ideology hurts male survivors of sexual assault:** Patrizia Riccardi, letter to the editor, "Male Rape: The Silent Victim and the Gender of the Listener," *Primary Care Companion to the Journal of Clinical Psychiatry* 12, no. 6 (2010), https://doi.org/10.4088/PCC.10l00993whi.

150   **male survivors of sexual assault are erased:** Susan Svrluga, Steve Hendrix, Nick Anderson, and Emma Brown, "Male Survivors of Sex Assaults Often Fear They Won't Be Taken Seriously," *Washington Post,* June 12, 2015, https://www .washingtonpost.com/local/education/male-victims-often-fear-they-wont-be -taken-seriously/2015/06/12/e780794a-f8fe-11e4-9030-b4732caefe81_story .html.

150   **Not all assault involves penetration:** RaeAnn E. Anderson, Erica L. Goodman, and Sidney S. Thimm, "The Assessment of Forced Penetration: A Necessary and

Further Step Toward Understanding Men's Sexual Victimization and Women's Perpetration," *Journal of Contemporary Criminal Justice* 36, no. 4 (2020): 480–98, https://doi.org/10.1177/1043986220936108.

See also: Siobhan Weare, "From Coercion to Physical Force: Aggressive Strategies Used by Women Against Men in Forced-to-Penetrate Cases in the UK," *Archives of Sexual Behavior* 47 (2018): 2191–2205, https://doi.org/10.1007/s10508-018-1232-5.

150   **feeling shame that they *allowed it to happen*:** Andi Rierden, "How Shame and Fear Take a Toll on Men Who Are Raped," *New York Times,* July 4, 1993, https://www.nytimes.com/1993/07/04/nyregion/how-shame-and-fear-take-a-toll-on-men-who-are-raped.html.

150   **The sociological data and qualitative studies:** John C. Thomas and Jonathan Kopel, "Male Victims of Sexual Assault: A Review of the Literature," *Behavioral Sciences* 13, no. 4 (2023): 304, https://doi.org/10.3390/bs13040304.

See also: Lara Stemple and Ilan H. Meyer, "The Sexual Victimization of Men in America: New Data Challenge Old Assumptions," *American Journal of Public Health* 104, no. 6 (2014): e19–e26, https://doi.org/10.2105/AJPH.2014.301946.

150   **feel they should've been able to stop it:** "Sexual Assault of Men and Boys," Rape, Abuse & Incest National Network (RAINN), accessed November 18, 2024, https://rainn.org/articles/sexual-assault-men-and-boys.

150   **test of their strength or masculinity:** "Masculinity, Self-Esteem, and Identity," 1in6, accessed November 18, 2024, https://1in6.org/topics/masculinity-self-esteem-and-identity/.

150   **prevalent among adult male survivors, too:** Luis Caballero, Roman Konopa, and Parker Whittenburg, "Man Up: How the Stigma of Masculinity Can Hurt Male Survivors," *RISE Blog,* Risk Intervention & Safety Education, Texas Tech University, April 14, 2022, https://www.depts.ttu.edu/rise/Blog/manup.php.

151   **we've barely begun to do:** "Where We Stand: Male Victims," National Alliance to End Sexual Violence, accessed November 18, 2024, https://endsexualviolence.org/where_we_stand/male-victims/.

151   ***celebrate penetration itself:*** Charlie Brinkhurst-Cuff, "Should Every Man Be Penetrated at Least Once in His Life?," *Vice,* December 8, 2016, https://www.vice.com/sv/article/should-every-man-be-penetrated-at-least-once-in-his-life/.

152   **It must be a sexual activity available to all:** Kate Lister, "Why All Straight Men Should Try Pegging Once," iNews, March 26, 2024, https://inews.co.uk/opinion/straight-men-try-pegging-once-2973640?.

Interstice

157   **Sixty-three percent of young adult men are currently single:** Risa Gelles-Watnick, "For Valentine's Day, 5 Facts About Single Americans," Pew Research Center, February 8, 2023, https://www.pewresearch.org/fact-tank/2023/02/08/for-valentines-day-5-facts-about-single-americans/.

157   **Fifty-two percent of young men:** Daniel A. Cox, "The State of American Friendship: Change, Challenges, and Loss—Findings from the May 2021 American Perspectives Survey," Survey Center on American Life, June 8, 2021, https://www.americansurveycenter.org/research/the-state-of-american-friendship-change-challenges-and-loss/.

157 **One in three young men:** Peter Ueda, Catherine H. Mercer, Cyrus Ghaznavi, and Debby Herbenick, "Trends in Frequency of Sexual Activity and Number of Sexual Partners Among Adults Aged 18 to 44 Years in the US, 2000–2018," *JAMA Network Open* (2020), https://doi.org/10.1001/jamanetworkopen.2020 .3833.

   See also: Indiana University Newsroom, "Nearly 1 in 3 Young Men in the US Report Having No Sex, Study Finds," news release, June 15, 2020, https://news .iu.edu/live/news/26924-nearly-1-in-3-young-men-in-the-us-report-having-no.

It's Been a Privilege

161 **at best, ineffective:** Parul Sehgal, "How 'Privilege' Became a Provocation," *New York Times Magazine,* July 14, 2015, https://www.nytimes.com/2015/07/19/ magazine/how-privilege-became-a-provocation.html.

161 **(biologically essentialist):** Mere Abrams, "Gender Essentialism Is Flawed— Here's Why," Healthline, January 27, 2020, https://www.healthline.com/health/ gender-essentialism.

   See also: Sarah Swea, "Let's Talk About Bioessentialism and Transphobia," *Women's Republic,* accessed November 15, 2024, https://www.womensrepublic .net/lets-talk-about-bioessentialism-and-transphobia/.

162 **how it feels to men:** Claudia Rankine, "I Wanted to Know What White Men Thought About Their Privilege. So I Asked." *New York Times Magazine,* July 17, 2019, https://www.nytimes.com/2019/07/17/magazine/white-men-privilege .html.

163 **men shut down and walk away:** Tal Fortgang, "Why I'll Never Apologize for My White Male Privilege," *Time,* May 2, 2014, https://time.com/85933/why-ill -never-apologize-for-my-white-male-privilege/.

   See also: Teresa Hopke, "White Men Are Feeling Left Out of Diversity, Equity, & Inclusion. Why Should We Care and What Should We Do?," *Forbes,* May 30, 2022, https://www.forbes.com/sites/teresahopke/2022/03/30/white -men-are-feeling-left-out-of-dei-diversity-equity--inclusion-why-should-we -care-and-what-should-we-do/.

   See also: Todd Pettigrew, "I'm Tired of Hearing How 'Privileged' I Am," *Maclean's,* March 27, 2013, https://macleans.ca/education/uniandcollege/im -tired-of-hearing-how-privileged-i-am/.

   See also: Allie Grasgreen, "Majority Disaffection," *Inside Higher Ed,* March 21, 2013, https://www.insidehighered.com/news/2013/03/22/white-men -alienated-higher-ed-workplace-survey-suggests.

166 **Men are mostly just cursed:** Jamie R. Abrams, "Debunking the Myth of Universal Male Privilege," *University of Michigan Journal of Law Reform* 49, no. 2 (2016): 303–34, https://doi.org/10.36646/mjlr.49.2.debunking.

169 **men are more likely to have their medical concerns:** Harvard Health Publishing, "Women and Pain: Disparities in Experience and Treatment," *Harvard Health Blog,* October 9, 2017, https://www.health.harvard.edu/blog/ women-and-pain-disparities-in-experience-and-treatment-2017100912562.

169 **still disproportionately men themselves:** Association of American Medical Colleges, "2022 Physician Specialty Data Report: Executive Summary," January 2023, https://www.aamc.org/media/63371/download?attachment.

See also: Emma Charlton, "7 out of 10 Global Health Leaders are Men: Study," World Economic Forum, April 16, 2020, https://www.weforum.org/stories/2020/04/global-health-leadership-gender-equality-report/.

169   **more likely to be paid a living wage:** International Labour Office, "Global Wage Report 2018/19: What Lies Behind Gender Pay Gaps," International Labour Organization, https://www.ilo.org/sites/default/files/wcmsp5/groups/public/%40dgreports/%40dcomm/%40publ/documents/publication/wcms_650553.pdf.

169   **access to adequate medical care:** "Uneven Access to Health Services Drives Life Expectancy Gaps," World Health Organization, April 4, 2019, https://www.who.int/news/item/04-04-2019-uneven-access-to-health-services-drives-life-expectancy-gaps-who.

See also: "Billions Left Behind on the Path to Universal Health Coverage," World Health Organization, September 18, 2023, https://www.who.int/news/item/18-09-2023-billions-left-behind-on-the-path-to-universal-health-coverage.

169   **or a living wage:** "Only 4% of Companies Commit to Living Wages, Missing a Key Opportunity to Reduce Inequalities," World Benchmarking Alliance, accessed November 15, 2024, https://www.worldbenchmarkingalliance.org/publication/social/findings/only-4-of-companies-commit-to-living-wages-missing-a-key-opportunity-to-reduce-inequalities/.

172   **when you add an intersectional analysis:** T. Hasan Johnson, "Challenging the Myth of Black Male Privilege," *Spectrum: A Journal on Black Men* 6, no. 2 (2018): 21–42, https://doi.org/10.2979/spectrum.6.2.02.

See also: Zakary A. Clements, Brittany N. Derr, and Sharon S. Rostosky, "Male Privilege Doesn't Lift the Social Status of All Men in the Same Way: Trans Masculine Individuals' Lived Experiences of Male Privilege in the United States," *Psychology of Men & Masculinities* 23, no. 1 (2022): 123–32, https://doi.org/10.1037/men0000371.

See also: Bedford Palmer II, "Men's Intersectional Relationship to Male Privilege," *Psychology Today,* January 1, 2018, https://www.psychologytoday.com/us/blog/who-we-ought-to-be/201801/mens-intersectional-relationship-to-male-privilege.

See also: Bethany M. Coston and Michael Kimmel, "Seeing Privilege Where It Isn't: Marginalized Masculinities and the Intersectionality of Privilege," *Journal of Social Issues* 68, no. 1 (2012): 97–111, https://doi.org/10.1111/j.1540-4560.2011.01738.x.

Interstice

173   **Only twenty-one percent of men:** Daniel A. Cox, "The State of American Friendship: Change, Challenges, and Loss—Findings from the May 2021 American Perspectives Survey," Survey Center on American Life, June 8, 2021, https://www.americansurveycenter.org/research/the-state-of-american-friendship-change-challenges-and-loss/.

173   **Only twenty-five percent of men:** Cox, "The State of American Friendship."

Teeth

175 **Emmy Award–winning Amazon series** *Transparent:* "Transparent: Awards and Nominations," Television Academy, accessed November 15, 2024, https://www.emmys.com/shows/transparent.

175 *Transparent* **was historic:** Katey Rich, "*Transparent*'s Emmy Wins Make Two Kinds of History," *Vanity Fair,* September 20, 2015, https://www.vanityfair.com/hollywood/2015/09/transparent-emmy-win.

175 *behind* **the scenes:** Stacey Wilson Hunt, "TV Is Breaking into Us: *Transparent*'s On- and Offscreen Transgender Talent on the Future of Gender," *Vulture,* September 2019, https://www.vulture.com/2016/09/transparent-roundtable-transgender-actors-writers-producers.html.

175 **climb the ladder** *at all:* Kyle Paoletta, "Why It's Harder Than Ever to Make It in Hollywood," *New Republic,* July 16, 2020, https://newrepublic.com/article/158491/its-harder-ever-make-hollywood.

175 **care about us:** Mey Rude, "My Day on the Set of 'Transparent,' Where Trans Voices Actually Get Heard," *Autostraddle,* December 13, 2015, https://www.autostraddle.com/transparent-wants-to-give-trans-people-power-over-their-own-stories-and-in-the-industry-320237/.

176 *Transparent* **pilot:** "Pilot," *Transparent,* season 1, episode 1, directed by Joey Soloway, aired August 27, 2014, Amazon Studios.

177 **failed to be an "ideal woman":** Riley Silverman, "Maura Pfefferman Is Allowed to Be a Flawed, Often Unlikeable Character on 'Transparent'—and That's Important," Decider, June 8, 2017, https://decider.com/2017/06/08/maura-pfefferman-transparent-jeffrey-tambor-top-50-lgbtq-tv-characters/.

177 **Harvey Weinstein's serial abuse:** Jodi Kantor and Megan Twohey, "Harvey Weinstein Paid Off Sexual Harassment Accusers for Decades," *New York Times,* October 5, 2017, https://www.nytimes.com/2017/10/05/us/harvey-weinstein-harassment-allegations.html.
    See also: Ronan Farrow, "Harvey Weinstein's Accusers Tell Their Stories," *New Yorker,* October 10, 2017, https://www.newyorker.com/news/news-desk/from-aggressive-overtures-to-sexual-assault-harvey-weinsteins-accusers-tell-their-stories.

177 **#MeToo movement beginning:** Abby Ohlheiser, "The Woman Behind 'Me Too' Knew the Power of the Phrase When She Created It—10 Years Ago," *Washington Post,* October 19, 2017, https://www.washingtonpost.com/news/the-intersect/wp/2017/10/19/the-woman-behind-me-too-knew-the-power-of-the-phrase-when-she-created-it-10-years-ago/.
    See also: Christie D'Zurilla, "In Saying #MeToo, Alyssa Milano Pushes Awareness Campaign About Sexual Assault and Harassment," *Los Angeles Times,* October 16, 2017, https://www.latimes.com/entertainment/la-et-entertainment-news-updates-october-2017-htmlstory.html#in-saying-metoo-alyssa-milano-pushes-awareness-campaign-about-sexual-assault-and-harassment.

177 **harassment at the hands of Jeffrey Tambor:** Seth Abramovitch, "'Transparent' Star Alleges Jeffrey Tambor Sexually Harassed Her, 'Got Physical,'" *Hollywood Reporter,* November 16, 2017, https://www.hollywoodreporter.com/news/general-news/transparent-star-alleges-jeffrey-tambor-sexually-harassed-her-got-physical-1059306/.

177   **denied the allegations:** Laura Bradley, "Jeffrey Tambor Apparently Isn't Quitting Transparent After All," *Vanity Fair,* December 6, 2017, https://www .vanityfair.com/hollywood/2017/12/jeffrey-tambor-not-quitting-transparent -sexual-harassment-allegations-amazon.

177   **paused their work:** Maggie Astor, "Jeffrey Tambor Leaves 'Transparent' After Sexual Misconduct Allegations," *New York Times,* November 19, 2017, https:// www.nytimes.com/2017/11/19/arts/television/jeffrey-tambor-transparent.html.
      See also: Stephen Silver, "Transparent Season 5 May Not Include Jeffrey Tambor," *ScreenRant,* November 17, 2017, https://screenrant.com/transparent -season-5-may-not-include-jeffrey-tambor/.

177   **Jeffrey had been fired:** Colin Dwyer, "Jeffrey Tambor Officially Exits 'Transparent' Following Claims of Misconduct," NPR, February 15, 2018, https://www .npr.org/sections/thetwo-way/2018/02/15/586180438/jeffrey-tambor-officially -exits-transparent-following-claims-of-misconduct.

177   **show would no longer be returning:** Jude Dry, "'Transparent' Season 5: Amazon Unsure About Show's Future After Jeffrey Tambor's Exit," Decider, June 12, 2018, https://decider.com/2018/06/12/transparent-season-five-future-jeffrey-tambor/.
      See also: Dino-Ray Ramos and Dominic Patten, "Transparent to End Fifth and Final Season with Feature-Length Musical Episode," Deadline, October 14, 2018, https://deadline.com/2018/10/transparent-musical-season-5-jill-soloway -faith-soloway-jeffrey-tambor-hakina-nayfack-1202482552/.

177   **Jeffrey had killed Maura:** Matt Zoller Seitz, "The Cultural Vandalism of Jeffrey Tambor," *Vulture,* May 24, 2018, https://www.vulture.com/2018/05/the-cultural -vandalism-of-jeffrey-tambor.html.

178   **the setback was particularly painful:** Christi Carras, "*Transparent*'s Trace Lysette on Accusing Jeffrey Tambor of Sexual Harassment: 'It Was Hell,'" *Variety,* August 7, 2018, https://variety.com/2018/tv/news/transparent-trace -lysette-jeffrey-tambor-sexual-harassment-1202898144/.

178   **sold my first book:** Isabella Biedenharn, "Gender Nonconforming Writer Jacob Tobia Announces Memoir, *Sissy,*" *Entertainment Weekly,* June 23, 2017, https:// ew.com/books/2017/06/23/jacob-tobia-announces-memoir-sissy/.

178   **one of Jeffrey's accusers, Van Barnes:** Van Barnes, interview by Megyn Kelly, *Megyn Kelly Today,* NBC, March 7, 2018; emphasis mine.

179   **sporting black at the Oscars:** Naomi Gordon, "MeToo Founder Says It Doesn't Matter Whether Stars Wear Black to the Oscars: Tarana Burke Says the Movement Isn't a 'Gimmick,'" *Harper's Bazaar,* March 2, 2018, https://www.harpersbazaar .com/uk/culture/culture-news/a19051498/metoo-founder-stars-black-oscars/.

180   **sloppy:** Jill Filipovic, "The Poorly Reported Aziz Ansari Exposé Was a Missed Opportunity," *Guardian,* January 16, 2018, https://www.theguardian.com/ commentisfree/2018/jan/16/aziz-ansari-story-missed-opportunity.

180   **inconsistent:** Bret Stephens, "When #MeToo Goes Too Far," *New York Times,* December 20, 2017, https://www.nytimes.com/2017/12/20/opinion/metoo -damon-too-far.html.

180   **uncaring:** Allison Raskin, "Don't Let Female Creators Be Collateral Damage When Male Abusers Go Down," Splinter, November 13, 2017, https://www.splinter.com/ don-t-let-female-creators-be-collateral-damage-when-mal-1820393875.

180   **punitive in the extreme:** Jeff Green, "#MeToo Has Implicated 414 High-Profile Executives and Employees in 18 Months," *Time,* June 25, 2018, https://time .com/5321130/414-executives-metoo/.

180   **little consideration given to the process:** Karlyn Borysenko, "The Dark Side of #MeToo: What Happens When Men Are Falsely Accused," *Forbes*, February 12, 2020, https://www.forbes.com/sites/karlynborysenko/2020/02/12/the-dark-side -of-metoo-what-happens-when-men-are-falsely-accused/.

180   **complex ramifications:** Evgenia Peretz, "Collateral Damage," *Vanity Fair*, October 2018, https://archive.vanityfair.com/article/2018/10/collateral -damage.

180   **bystanders:** Emily J. Brooks, "Ashleigh Raper on MeToo: We Were Collateral Damage," Future Women, https://www.futurewomen.com/leadership/ashleigh -raper-on-metoo-we-were-collateral-damage/.

180   **innocent people:** Sopan Deb, "When #MeToo Infamy Taints Your Famous Benefactor," *New York Times*, April 2, 2018, https://www.nytimes.com/2018/04/ 02/arts/metoo-celebrities-charities.html.

      See also: Yohana Desta, "Tig Notaro Distances Herself from Louis C.K., Says He Should 'Handle' Sexual Misconduct Rumors," *Vanity Fair*, August 23, 2017, https://www.vanityfair.com/hollywood/2017/08/tig-notaro-louis-ck-one -mississippi.

181   **our turn to hunt:** Claire Berlinski, "The Warlock Hunt," *American Interest*, December 6, 2017, https://www.the-american-interest.com/2017/12/06/the -warlock-hunt/.

181   **find them and punish them:** Madison Pauly, "A Radical New Plan for MeToo Turns Away from 'Law and Order' Feminism," *Mother Jones*, October 26, 2020, https://www.motherjones.com/politics/2020/10/survivors-agenda-me-too -racial-justice/.

182   **find healing through punishment:** Aya Gruber, "#MeToo and Mass Incarcera- tion," *Ohio State Journal of Criminal Law* 17 (2020): 275, https://scholar.law .colorado.edu/faculty-articles/1291.

182   **ruining men and incarcerating them:** Ben Leit, "Harvey Weinstein Is Going to Prison. That Is Not Good Enough," *Spectator*, March 6, 2020, https://spec .hamilton.edu/harvey-weinstein-is-going-to-prison-that-is-not-good-enough -9064e458cdfd.

182   **Harvey Weinstein's teeth are rotting:** Marjorie Hernandez and Priscilla DeGregory, "Harvey Weinstein Begs Judge to Stop Prison Dentist from Pulling His Rotten Teeth," *New York Post*, September 14, 2022, https://nypost.com/ 2022/09/14/harvey-weinstein-begs-judge-to-stop-prison-dentist-from-pulling -his-rotten-teeth/.

      See also: Rachael Bunyan, "This Situation Is an Emergency: Harvey Weinstein Begs Judge to Let Him Out of Prison to See Private Dentist," *Daily Mail*, September 15, 2022, https://www.dailymail.co.uk/news/article-11214691/ Harvey-Weinstein-begs-judge-let-prison-private-dentist.html.

      See also: Victoria Bekiempis, "Harvey Weinstein Has Lost 4 Teeth in Prison," *Vulture*, April 12, 2021, https://www.vulture.com/2021/04/harvey-weinstein -now-almost-technically-blind-losing-teeth.html.

183   **trivialized his request:** Megan Carpentier, "Harvey Weinstein Asks L.A. Judge for Permission to Have Private Dental Work Done on Rotting Teeth," Oxygen True Crime, September 15, 2022, https://www.oxygen.com/crime-news/harvey -weinstein-asks-judge-private-dental-work-done.

      See also: Nancy Dillon, "Nice Try: Harvey Weinstein Loses Bid to Delay Trial over 'She Said' Movie Release, Asks for New Teeth," *Rolling Stone*,

August 29, 2022, https://www.rollingstone.com/tv-movies/tv-movie-news/harvey-weinstein-she-said-movie-new-teeth-1234583891/.

183 *America's two million prisoners:* Maggie Harrison Dupré, "Harvey Weinstein's Rotting Teeth Reveal a Lot About Prison Healthcare," *Neoscope,* September 16, 2022, https://futurism.com/neoscope/harvey-weinstein-prison-healthcare.

184 **Under the Geneva Convention:** United Nations Office of the High Commissioner for Human Rights, "Geneva Convention Relative to the Treatment of Prisoners of War," accessed November 16, 2024, https://www.ohchr.org/en/instruments-mechanisms/instruments/geneva-convention-relative-treatment-prisoners-war.

184 **cruel and unusual punishment:** Bryan A. Stevenson and John F. Stinneford, "The Eighth Amendment: Common Interpretation," National Constitution Center, accessed November 16, 2024, https://constitutioncenter.org/the-constitution/amendments/amendment-viii/clauses/103.

184 **Harvey Weinstein is being tortured:** Winston Cho, "Harvey Weinstein's Lawyer Asks Judge to Improve Holding Cell Conditions as Jury Selection Gets Underway," *Hollywood Reporter,* October 11, 2022, https://www.hollywoodreporter.com/news/general-news/harvey-weinsteins-lawyer-asks-judge-to-improve-holding-cell-conditions-as-jury-selection-gets-underway-1235239459/.

185 **American prisoners are suffering from neglect:** "Prison Health Care Crisis Mounts as Incarcerated Population Ages," Equal Justice Initiative, May 14, 2014, https://eji.org/news/prison-health-care-crisis-mounts-as-incarcerated-population-ages/.

185 **American prisoners are enduring abuse:** Shon Hopwood, "How Atrocious Prisons Conditions Make Us All Less Safe," Brennan Center for Justice, August 9, 2021, https://www.brennancenter.org/our-work/analysis-opinion/how-atrocious-prisons-conditions-make-us-all-less-safe.

185 **American prisoners have been condemned:** Sam Levin, "Hundreds of Deaths in US Prisons Linked to Policy Violations and Failures," *Guardian,* February 15, 2024, https://www.theguardian.com/us-news/2024/feb/15/prison-death-causes-preventable-justice-department.

185 **American prisons are factories of cruelty:** "Solitary Confinement and Prison Guard Abuse," Fair Fight Initiative, accessed November 16, 2024, https://www.fairfightinitiative.org/solitary-confinement-and-prison-guard-abuse/.

185 **rehabilitation remains a pipe dream:** Tenzing Lahdon, "From the Desk of BJA," *Justice Matters Newsletter,* Bureau of Justice Assistance, United States Department of Justice, November 27, 2023, https://bja.ojp.gov/news/justice-matters/desk-bja-november-2023.

185 **cheered for Harvey Weinstein to rot in prison:** Claire Berlinski, "The Warlock Hunt."

186 **we cheered for prisons themselves:** Philippa Greer, "Dismantling Prisons: Abolitionist Feminism, Women, Incarceration and #MeToo," *Engenderings* (blog), February 15, 2021, London School of Economics, https://blogs.lse.ac.uk/gender/2021/02/15/dismantling-prisons-abolitionist-feminism-women-incarceration-and-metoo/.

186 **we were participating in a lie:** Victoria Law, "How Can We Reconcile Prison Abolition with #MeToo?" *Filter* magazine, September 25, 2018, https://filtermag.org/how-can-we-reconcile-prison-abolition-with-metoo/.

186 **conditions . . . tantamount to slavery:** Kica Matos and Jamila Hodge, "The Chains of Slavery Still Exist in Mass Incarceration," Vera Institute, June 17, 2021, https://www.vera.org/news/the-chains-of-slavery-still-exist-in-mass-incarceration.
See also: American Civil Liberties Union, *Captive Labor: Exploitation of Incarcerated Workers* (American Civil Liberties Union and the University of Chicago Law School Global Human Rights Clinic, June 15, 2022), https://www.aclu.org/publications/captive-labor-exploitation-incarcerated-workers.

186 **without the means to properly defend themselves:** "U.S. Fails to Provide Adequate Legal Services for Poor People," Open Society Foundations, March 12, 2003, https://www.opensocietyfoundations.org/newsroom/paper-us-fails-provide-adequate-legal-services-poor-people.
See also: Nazish Dholakia, "How the United States Punishes People for Being Poor," Vera Institute, September 21, 2023, https://www.vera.org/news/how-the-united-states-punishes-people-for-being-poor.

186 **University of Southern California law professor:** Aya Gruber, "Reckoning with Carceral Feminism in the Fight to End Mass Incarceration," *Emancipator*, June 27, 2023, https://theemancipator.org/2023/06/27/topics/legal-system/reckoning-with-carceral-feminism-fight-end-mass-incarceration/.

187 **no feminist way to send someone to jail:** Alex Press, "#MeToo Must Avoid Carceral Feminism," Vox, February 1, 2018, https://www.vox.com/the-big-idea/2018/2/1/16952744/me-too-larry-nassar-judge-aquilina-feminism.

187 **no version of transformative feminism that includes prison sentences:** Lara Bazelon and Aya Gruber, "#MeToo Doesn't Always Have to Mean Prison," *New York Times*, March 2, 2020, https://www.nytimes.com/2020/03/02/opinion/metoo-doesnt-always-have-to-mean-prison.html.

187 **Restorative justice:** "Community Accountability: How Do We Address Violence Within Our Communities?," INCITE! National, accessed November 15, 2024, https://incite-national.org/community-accountability/.

187 **calling for a fundamental rebuilding of how we understand justice:** Sara Davidson, "My Ex Was Just #MeTooed. He Had It Coming. But It's Complicated," *Los Angeles Times*, January 21, 2018, https://www.latimes.com/opinion/op-ed/la-oe-davidson-me-too-ex-20180121-story.html.

187 **funds to file more court cases:** Rebecca Keegan, "#MeToo, Five Years Later: Why Time's Up Imploded," *Hollywood Reporter*, October 3, 2022.
See also: Amy Mackelden, "The TIME'S UP Legal Defense Fund Has Reached Its $15 Million Fundraising Goal," *Elle*, January 7, 2018, https://www.elle.com/culture/celebrities/a14769712/times-up-legal-defense-fund-reached-their-15-million-goal/.
See also: Elizabeth Blair, "Here's How the Time's Up Legal Defense Fund Actually Works," National Public Radio, March 11, 2018, https://www.npr.org/2018/03/11/592307856/heres-how-the-time-s-up-legal-defense-fund-actually-works.

187 **we're mostly lying to them:** Jodie Murphy-Oikonen, Lori Chambers, Ainsley Miller, and Karen McQueen, "Sexual Assault Case Attrition: The Voices of Survivors," *Sage Open* 12, no. 4 (2022), https://doi.org/10.1177/21582440221144612.

187 *if the case even goes to trial at all:* "What to Expect from the Criminal Justice System," Rape, Abuse & Incest National Network (RAINN), accessed November 16, 2024, https://rainn.org/articles/what-expect-criminal-justice-system.

188   **sending their perpetrator to prison will be justice served:** "Finding Justice for Victims in the #MeToo Era," Open Society Foundations, accessed November 16, 2024, https://www.opensocietyfoundations.org/voices/finding-justice-for -victims-in-the-metoo-era.

188   **most perpetrators are found not guilty:** Katharine Webster, "Why Do So Few Rape Cases End in Arrest?," University of Massachusetts Lowell, April 17, 2019, https://www.uml.edu/news/stories/2019/sexual_assault_research.aspx.

188   **if charges are pressed in the first place:** "The Criminal Justice System: Statistics," Rape, Abuse & Incest National Network (RAINN), accessed November 16, 2024, https://rainn.org/statistics/criminal-justice-system.

188   **testify and rip open their wounds afresh:** Daniel Arkin and Diana Dasrath, "Harvey Weinstein Found Guilty of Rape, Sexual Assault in Los Angeles Trial," NBC News, December 19, 2022, https://www.nbcnews.com/news/us-news/ jurors-harvey-weinstein-rape-sexual-assault-trial-reach-verdict-rcna59273.

188   **reengineering and reimagining the justice process itself:** The Survivors' Agenda Team, *Survivors' Agenda,* accessed November 16, 2024, https:// survivorsagenda.org/agenda/.

188   **Harvey was found guilty not just in New York:** "Harvey Weinstein Found Guilty of Sexual Assault, Rape," Al Jazeera, February 24, 2020, https://www .aljazeera.com/news/2020/2/24/harvey-weinstein-found-guilty-of-sexual -assault-rape.

188   **but in Los Angeles:** Arkin and Dasrath, "Harvey Weinstein Found Guilty of Rape, Sexual Assault."

189   **him getting what he deserved:** Jen Chaney, "23 Years Is Exactly What Harvey Weinstein Deserves," *Vulture,* March 11, 2020, https://www.vulture.com/2020/ 03/harvey-weinstein-and-his-23-year-sentence.html.
        See also: Sophie Long and Madeleine Halpert, "Weinstein Begs for Mercy as He Is Sentenced for Another Rape," BBC, February 23, 2023, https://www.bbc .com/news/world-us-canada-64736678.
        See also: Robby Soave, "Harvey Weinstein's Sexual Assault Conviction Is a Well-Deserved Win for #MeToo," *Reason Magazine,* February 24, 2020, https:// reason.com/2020/02/24/harvey-weinstein-conviction-sexual-assault-me-too/.

189   **what we want for ourselves:** Lux Alptraum, "We're Good at Punishing #MeToo Men. Can We Ever Forgive Them?," *New York Times,* June 10, 2024, https://www .nytimes.com/2024/06/10/opinion/metoo-spurlock-second-chance.html.

190   **what we want most of all:** Lupita Nyong'o, "Speaking Out About Harvey Weinstein," *New York Times,* October 19, 2017, https://www.nytimes.com/2017/ 10/19/opinion/lupita-nyongo-harvey-weinstein.html.
        See also: Salma Hayek, "Harvey Weinstein Is My Monster Too," *New York Times,* December 12, 2017, https://www.nytimes.com/interactive/2017/12/13/ opinion/contributors/salma-hayek-harvey-weinstein.html.

190   **prevention of further harm:** Tovia Smith, "Is Redemption Possible in the Aftermath of #MeToo?," National Public Radio, October 5, 2019, https://www .npr.org/2019/10/05/766843292/is-redemption-possible-in-the-aftermath-of -metoo.

190   **transformation of either our perpetrators or the world that created them:** Masha Gessen, "One Year of #MeToo: Punishing Individual Abusers Is Not the Same as Justice," *New Yorker,* October 10, 2018, https://www.newyorker.com/ news/our-columnists/one-year-of-metoo-punishing-individual-abusers-is-not -the-same-as-justice.

190   **receive worse than nothing:** Rowena Chiu, "Harvey Weinstein Told Me He Liked Chinese Girls—Why It Took Me More Than 20 Years to Tell My #MeToo Story," *New York Times,* October 5, 2019, https://www.nytimes.com/2019/10/05/opinion/sunday/harvey-weinstein-rowena-chiu.html.

Interstice

193   **Ninety-three percent of inmates in federal prison:** "Inmate Gender," Inmate Statistics, Federal Bureau of Prisons, accessed September 5, 2024, https://www.bop.gov/about/statistics/statistics_inmate_gender.jsp.

193   **In America, one in every 112 men:** Author's calculation. Based on: E. Ann Carson, "Prisoners in 2022—Statistical Tables," U.S. Department of Justice Office of Justice Programs, Bureau of Justice Statistics, November 2023, p. 5, https://bjs.ojp.gov/document/p22st.pdf, and "Annual Estimates of the Resident Population for Selected Age Groups by Sex for the United States: April 1, 2020 to July 1, 2023," United States Census Bureau, https://www2.census.gov/programs-surveys/popest/tables/2020-2023/national/asrh/nc-est2023-agesex.xlsx.

The Bunker

195   **The metaphor of "The Closet":** Eve Kosofsky Sedgwick, *Epistemology of the Closet* (University of California Press, 1990), 67–69.
          See also: Olivia B. Waxman, "The History Behind Why We Say a Person 'Came Out of the Closet,'" *Time,* October 11, 2017, https://time.com/4975404/national-coming-out-day-closet-metaphor-history/.

197   **old Nova Scotian bunkers:** Mark Collin Reid, "The Path Less Travelled: A Historic Adventure Lies Just Off the Beaten Trail to Peggy's Cove, Nova Scotia," Canada's History, November 14, 2019, https://www.canadashistory.ca/explore/travel/the-path-less-travelled.

198   **You keep a rifle:** Nick Buttrick, "Americans Own Guns to Protect Themselves from Psychological as Well as Physical Threats," *The Conversation,* October 31, 2024, https://theconversation.com/americans-own-guns-to-protect-themselves-from-psychological-as-well-as-physical-threats-239363.

198   **All strangers are a threat:** David Brooks, "The Siege Mentality Problem," *New York Times,* November 13, 2017, https://www.nytimes.com/2017/11/13/opinion/roy-moore-conservative-evangelicals.html.
          See also: WebMD Editorial Contributors, "What Is Siege Mentality?," WebMD, July 25, 2024, https://www.webmd.com/mental-health/what-is-siege-mentality.

Interstice

209   **Men are seven times more likely than women to use a firearm:** Sherry L. Murphy, Kenneth D. Kochanek, Jiaquan Xu, and Elizabeth Arias, "Deaths: Final Data for 2021," *National Vital Statistics Reports* 73, no. 8 (2024): 63, https://www.cdc.gov/nchs/data/nvsr/nvsr73/nvsr73-08.pdf.

Monster Talk

212   **the most sensitive nerve in the human body:** Gabriel Weston, "Mapping the Body: Trigeminal Nerve," *Guardian,* October 17, 2011, https://www.theguardian .com/lifeandstyle/2011/oct/17/mapping-the-body-trigeminal-nerve.

213   **trauma does not always operate with either logic or rationality:** Jim Hopper, "Neurobiology of Trauma," Assault Survivors Advocacy Program, University of Northern Colorado, June 10, 2022, https://www.unco.edu/assault-survivors -advocacy-program/learn_more/neurobiology_of_trauma.aspx.

213   **Trauma feels like a blender:** Kimberly Holland, "Amygdala Hijack: When Emotion Takes Over," Healthline, March 26, 2023, https://www.healthline.com/ health/stress/amygdala-hijack.

213   **Trauma can rewire your brain:** Xi Zhu, Benjamin Suarez-Jimenez, Amit Lazarov, et al., "Sequential Fear Generalization and Network Connectivity in Trauma Exposed Humans with and Without Psychopathology," *Communications Biology* 5 (2022): 1275, https://doi.org/10.1038/s42003-022-04228-5.

  See also: Dawn McClelland and Chris Gilyard, "Calming Trauma—the Brain and the Lymbic System," Phoenix Society for Burn Survivors, August 27, 2019, https://www.phoenix-society.org/resources/calming-trauma.

213   **"lose the war you are foolishly waging with cars":** Pam Fischer and Richard Retting, "A Right to the Road: Understanding & Addressing Bicyclist Safety," Governors Highway Safety Association, 2017, https://www.ghsa.org/sites/ default/files/2017-09/2017BicyclistSafetyReport-FINAL.pdf.

216   **there is a logic of some kind:** Jason A. Haap, "The Private Logic Behind a Trauma-Informed Mindset," Association for Supervision and Curriculum Development, April 9, 2020, https://ascd.org/el/articles/the-private-logic -behind-a-trauma-informed-mindset.

217   **shouldn't bike alone, as a lone ranger:** National Highway Traffic Safety Administration, "Countermeasures That Work: Bicycle Safety," U.S. Department of Transportation, accessed November 14, 2024, https://www.nhtsa.gov/book/ countermeasures-that-work/bicycle-safety.

218   **harrowing stories about maiming and death:** Aaron Gulley, "Is Road Riding Worth the Risk?," *Outside Magazine,* December 7, 2017, https://www .outsideonline.com/outdoor-gear/bikes-and-biking/road-riding-worth-risk/.

219   **taking on absurd risk:** Daniel Trotta, "'Walking While Trans' Can Be a Death Sentence in the U.S.," Reuters, October 20, 2016, https://www.reuters.com/ article/world/us/walking-while-trans-can-be-a-death-sentence-in-the-us -idUSKCN12K0CS/.

Epilogue: Dear Men

223   **constant performance:** Vanessa Mangru-Kumar, "Half of Men Feel Pressured to Act Manly," SWNS Digital, March 4, 2024, https://swnsdigital.com/us/2024/ 03/half-of-men-feel-pressured-to-act-manly/.

223   **Push your limits:** Adam Stanaland and Sarah Gaither, "'Be a Man': The Role of Social Pressure in Eliciting Men's Aggressive Cognition," *Personality and Social Psychology Bulletin* 47, no. 11 (2021): 1596–1611, https://doi.org/10.1177/ 0146167220984298.

223 **a competition that can never truly be won:** Joseph Regina and Tammy D. Allen, "Masculinity Contest Culture: Harmful for Whom? An Examination of Emotional Exhaustion," *Journal of Occupational Health Psychology* 28, no. 2 (2023): 117–28, https://doi.org/10.1037/ocp0000344.

223 **race you must run:** Jennifer L. Berdahl, Marianne Cooper, Peter Glick, Robert W. Livingston, and Joan C. Williams, "Work as a Masculinity Contest," *Journal of Social Issues* 74, no. 3 (2018): 422–48, https://doi.org/10.1111/josi.12289.

223 **It is a marathon:** Nicolas Choquette-Levy, "Masculinity and the Double-Edged Sword of Competition," Men's Allied Voices for a Respectful & Inclusive Community (MAVRIC) Project, Princeton University, February 19, 2020, https://mavricproject.princeton.edu/2020/02/masculinity-and-the-double-edged-sword-of-competition-by-nicolas-choquette-levy/.

224 **Look at billionaires:** Joe Pinsker, "The Reason Many Ultrarich People Aren't Satisfied with Their Wealth," *Atlantic,* December 4, 2018, https://www.theatlantic.com/family/archive/2018/12/rich-people-happy-money/577231/.

224 **a documentary series:** *At Home with the Furys,* season 1, directed by Tina Flintoff, Nick Hornby, and Josh Jacobs, featuring Tyson Fury, aired August 16, 2023, in broadcast syndication, Netflix Studios.

224 **the never-ending competition:** Travis W. Schermer and Cornelius N. Holmes, "Will to Masculinity: An Existential Examination of Men's Issues," *Journal of Humanistic Counseling* 57, no. 3 (2018): 191–207, https://doi.org/10.1002/johc.12082.

ABOUT THE AUTHOR

JACOB TOBIA is a writer, producer, performer, and the bestselling author of *Sissy*. Their work and words have appeared in *The New York Times*, the *Los Angeles Times*, *The Guardian*, *Time*, *PAPER*, and on *The Daily Show with Trevor Noah*, among others. *Before They Were Men* is their second book.

ABOUT THE TYPE

This book was set in Minion, a 1990 Adobe Originals typeface by Robert Slimbach. Minion is inspired by classical, old-style type-faces of the late Renaissance, a period of elegant and beautiful type designs. Created primarily for text setting, Minion combines the aesthetic and functional qualities that make text type highly read-able with the versatility of digital technology.